IMAGES
of America

BENTON PARK WEST

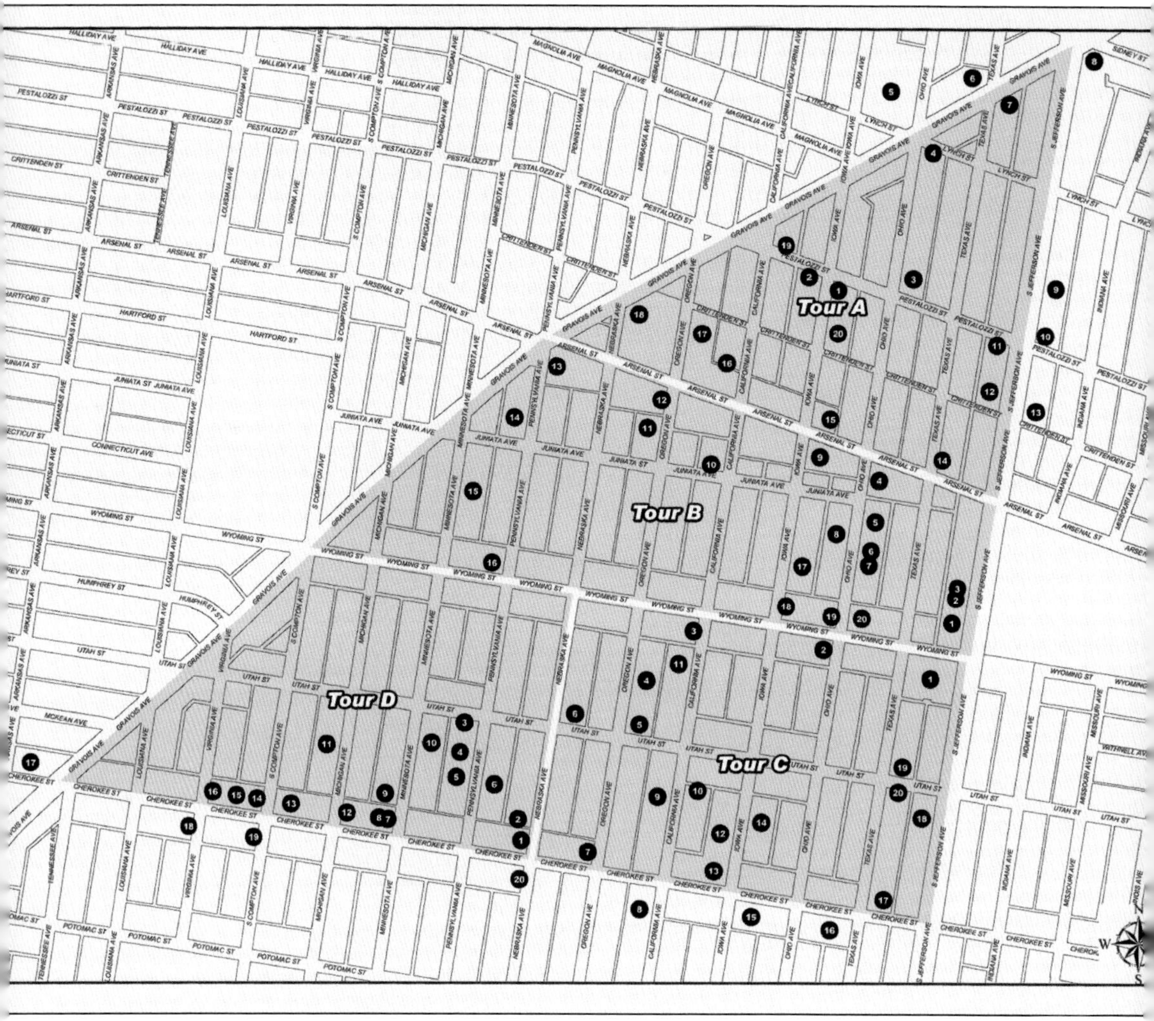

MAP OF BENTON PARK WEST.

IMAGES
of America

BENTON PARK WEST

Edna Campos Gravenhorst

ARCADIA
PUBLISHING

ISBN 978-0-7385-3431-2

Published by Arcadia Publishing
Charleston, South Carolina

Printed in the United States of America

Library of Congress Catalog Card Number: 2005924877

For all general information, please contact Arcadia Publishing:
Telephone 843-853-2070
Fax 843-853-0044
E-mail sales@arcadiapublishing.com

Visit us on the Internet at www.arcadiapublishing.com

Contents

Acknowledgments	6
Introduction	7
1. Tour A	9
2. Tour B	37
3. Tour C	69
4. Tour D	101
Selected Bibliography	125
Photograph Credits	127
A Word from the Author	128

ACKNOWLEDGMENTS

I would like to say thank you to the following people and institutions who, with their help and support, made this book possible: William Bailey, Benton Park West Neighborhood Association, Fran Bunse, Denise Carter, City of St. Louis Planning and Urban Design Agency, Community Development Administration of the City of St. Louis, Sheila Davis, Donna Dorsey, Cheryl Fillion, John Ginsburg, Carol Hawkins, Incarnate Word Foundation of Missouri, Marlene and Bruce Levine, Tony Meyers, Missouri Historical Society, Ken Ortmann, Craig Schmid, SSDN, St. Louis City Hall employees (especially Nick Ballta), Stephanie Dufner Szczerbinski, Joan Thomas, JoAnn Vatcha, Michael Wasileski, and Elizabeth Beachy, my editor at Arcadia Publishing, for her patience and support.

A special thank you to Walter Morris and in memory of Pat Dunaway, who encouraged me to write the book when it was just an idea in my head. The final thank you goes to my husband, Ted, who had the patience to support me from the beginning to the end of this book and was the person who introduced me to Benton Park West.

INTRODUCTION

By the mid-1860s, Benton Park West was already a community that could provide for the basic needs of its residents. There were carpenters, builders, stone masons, dairymen, gardeners, market owners, grocers, saddle and harness makers, a blacksmith, a midwife, and two saloons to serve this area of about 50 city blocks. The homes shown in the book span from the 1860s to the 1930s, with most of them built in the 1880s and 1890s. The book is divided into four walking tours–A, B, C and D–with 20 locations featuring photographs, maps, and images of documents. The text consists of early, and some current, history of each location. The images used are from the Missouri Historical Society, St. Louis City Hall, Ron Untener, neighborhood families, business owners, and the author.

The walk tour begins at the corner of Iowa and Pestalozzi, where the house dates back to the 1860s. Gottlieb Eyermann, a German immigrant who came to St. Louis in the 1850s, left us his footprint. The concrete slab to the side of the house reads, "Gottlieb Eyermann 1865." Benton Park West was considered a working-class neighborhood and a German community. While most of the residents were working class, many owned their own businesses. There were also some very prominent residents. The 1939 photograph of the Ferdinand Herold home, built in 1888, shows a stately three-story mansion with intricate brickwork and handsome architectural character. The head of a Cherokee Indian chief in a terra cotta piece on the arch at the front entrance commands your attention. The photograph captures the artist's details. The gentleman who built this house owned the Cherokee Brewery on Cherokee Street, which is also featured in this book, and a steamboat named *Cherokee*. When he died at the age of 82, the list of honorary pallbearers in his obituary was a list of "who's who" of St. Louis businessmen and brewery owners.

A very important detail which most people do not know is that Dr. William G. Swekosky, a well-known St. Louis historian and photographer, had his dentist office in Benton Park West. The old Federer Building, which housed a store front on the first floor and offices upstairs, is no longer there. Dr. Swekosky's photograph collection and numerous articles about him regarding the preservation of St. Louis history provide valuable information to students, researchers, and writers.

The area includes a planing mill established in 1893, a hat shop that has been at the same location and owned by the same family since 1915, a tent and awning business started in 1911, and several other businesses. There were a number of Union Civil War veterans living in the neighborhood in 1890, including Richard Merkel, the gentleman who purchased the author's house in 1886. Visitors will want to return to Benton Park West to take in the beauty and the history of these historic homes that sit across the street from Benton Park, which was a cemetery until 1866.

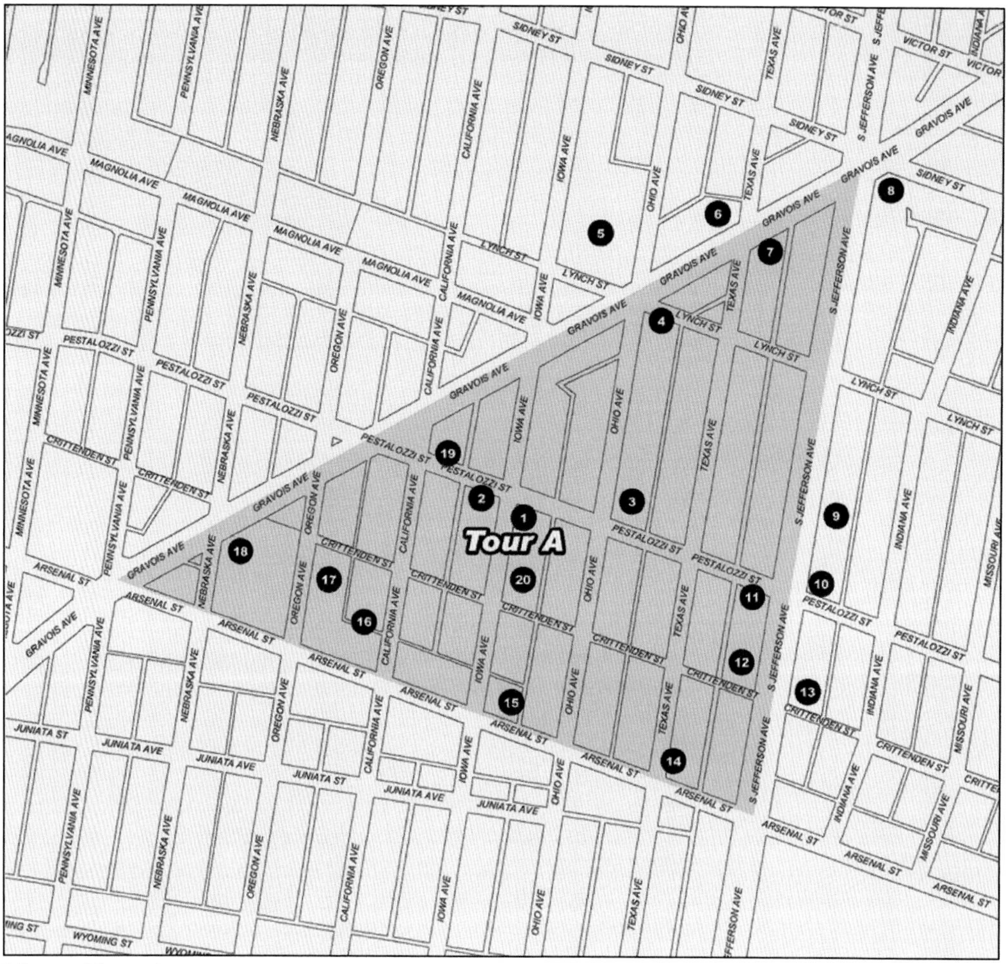
Tour A
1
2
3
4
5
6
7
8
9
10
11
12
13
14
15
16
17
18
19
20
SIDNEY ST
VICTOR ST
MAGNOLIA AVE
LYNCH ST
PESTALOZZI ST
CRITTENDEN ST
ARSENAL ST
JUNIATA AVE
JUNIATA ST
WYOMING ST
GRAVOIS AVE
MINNESOTA AVE
PENNSYLVANIA AVE
NEBRASKA AVE
OREGON AVE
CALIFORNIA AVE
IOWA AVE
OHIO AVE
TEXAS AVE
S JEFFERSON AVE
INDIANA AVE
MISSOURI AVE

Map of Tour A.

One

Tour A

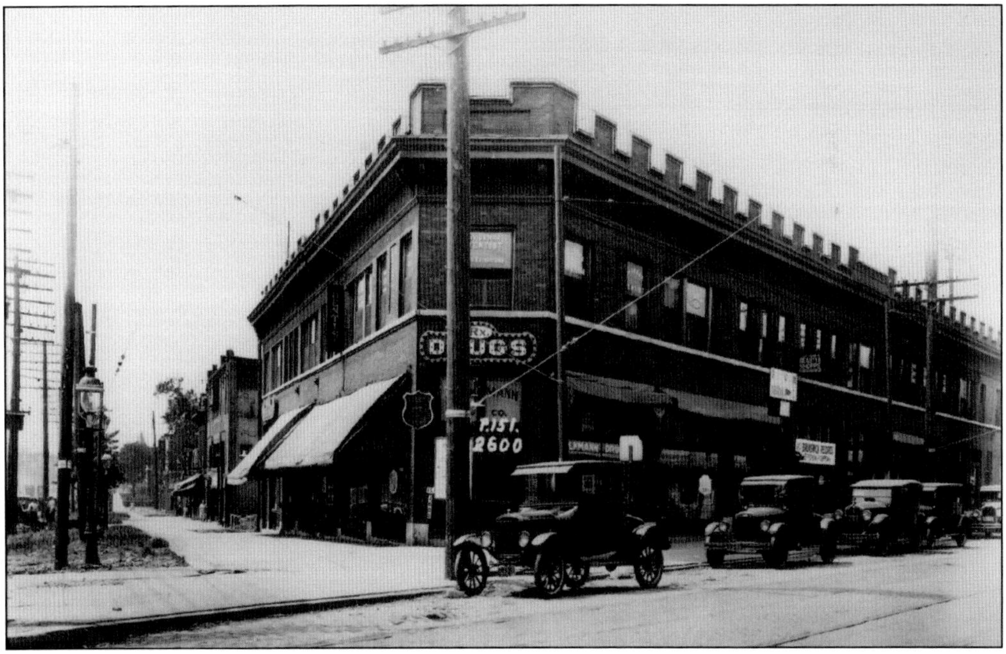

SOUTHWEST CORNER OF JEFFERSON AND GRAVOIS AVENUES. This location was home to William G. Swekosky's dental office. The photograph provides an idea of how the corner looked in the 1920s, but today the building is gone and there is a Lee's Famous Recipe Chicken Restaurant where the Federer building once stood. When the building was torn down in the 1980s, a very important part of St. Louis history was lost. In the 1960s, Dr. William G. Swekosky had his office at 2621 South Jefferson. He was a dentist who made his mark by recording St. Louis history through photographs. A significant portion of his collection is at the Missouri Historical Society here in St. Louis. As a kid, he explored the mansions of Lafayette Square. When he grew up, he went to work as a real estate title examiner, a job in which he traced owners through property titles and became interested in their histories. His father was not pleased with his choice of career and offered to pay for his education in dentistry. Dr. Swekosky died at the age of 69. His former home is located at 2221 Jules in the neighboring McKinley Heights Neighborhood.

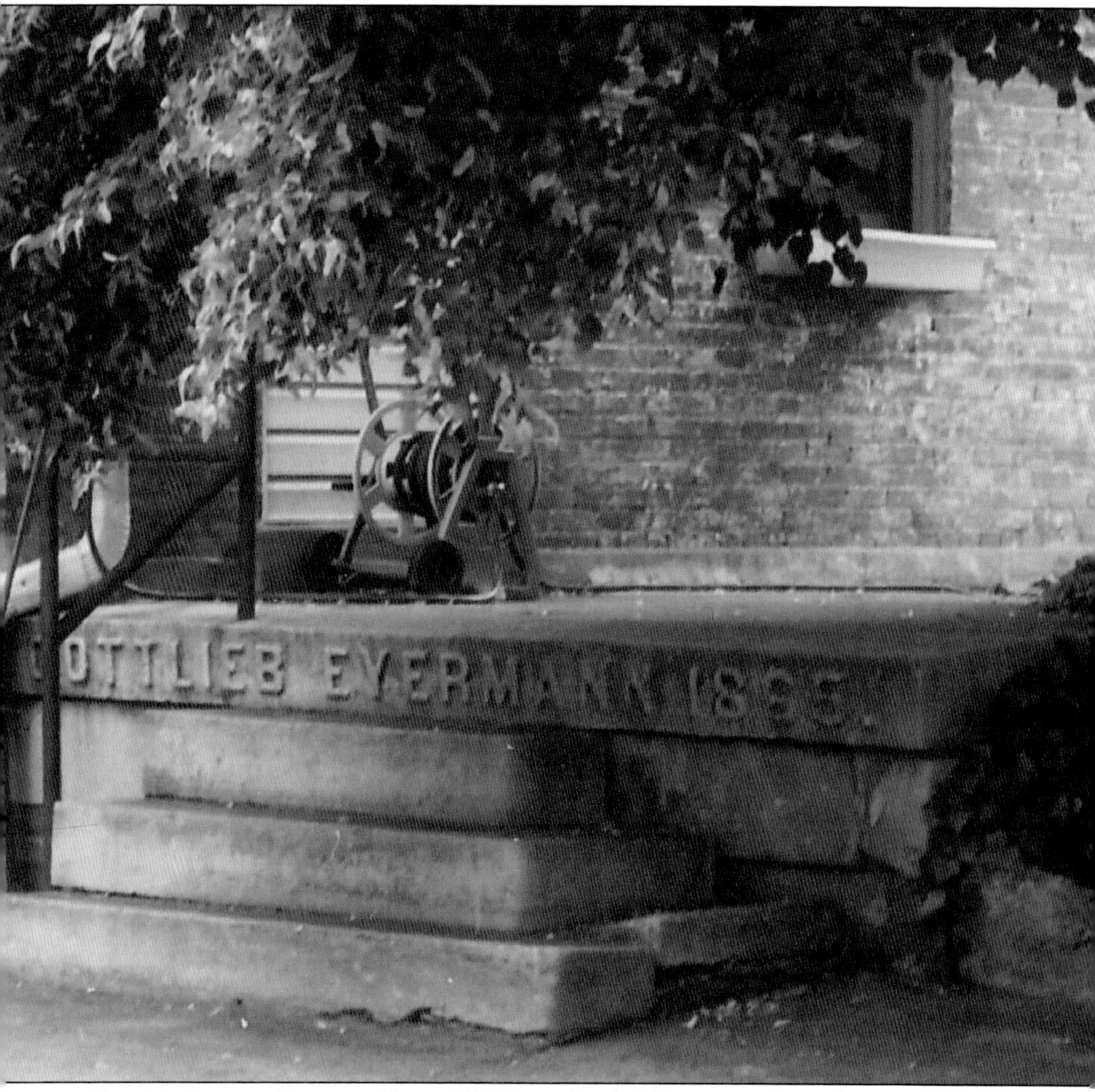

Site A1: Gottlieb Eyermann Home, 2906 Iowa. Gottlieb Eyermman Sr. was born in Germany and immigrated to the United States in the mid-1850s. He came directly to St. Louis and went to work as a bricklayer. In 1865, he established G. Eyermann & Brothers Quarry and began to build this house. In 1870s city directories, he was listed as a stone mason. In 1877, he was listed as the owner of the Gravois Brick Company at Arsenal and the southwest corner of Jefferson. Mr. Eyermann died in 1888. At the time of his death, he owned property throughout the city and lots in Benton Park West on Iowa, Ohio, and California. His children would later build their homes on these streets. After Mr. Eyermann's death, Gottlieb Jr. and George took charge of the family business, which would later consist of quarries on Grand and Virginia Avenue. The Eyermann home stayed in the family for more than 75 years, until 1942. The family is credited with being pioneers of south St. Louis.

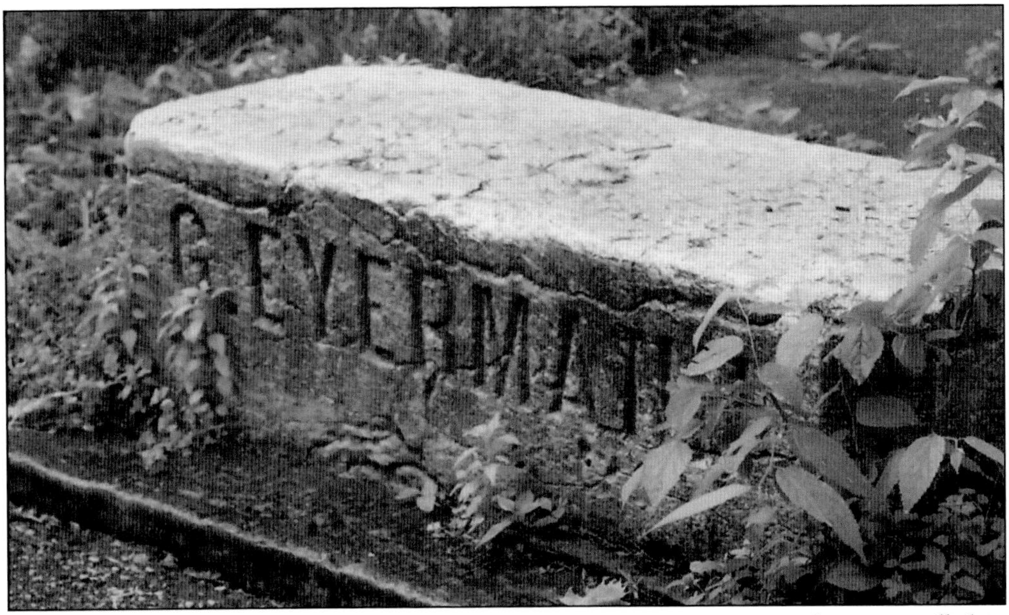

CARRIAGE STONE. There are very few carriage stones, or carriage stoops as they were called in the 1800s, in Benton Park West. This is one of the few left, and it is a treasure since the stones were usually engraved with initials only. Owners would set their stones in front or to the side of their houses to assist folks getting in and out of horse-drawn carriages. They were also used for mounting or dismounting horses.

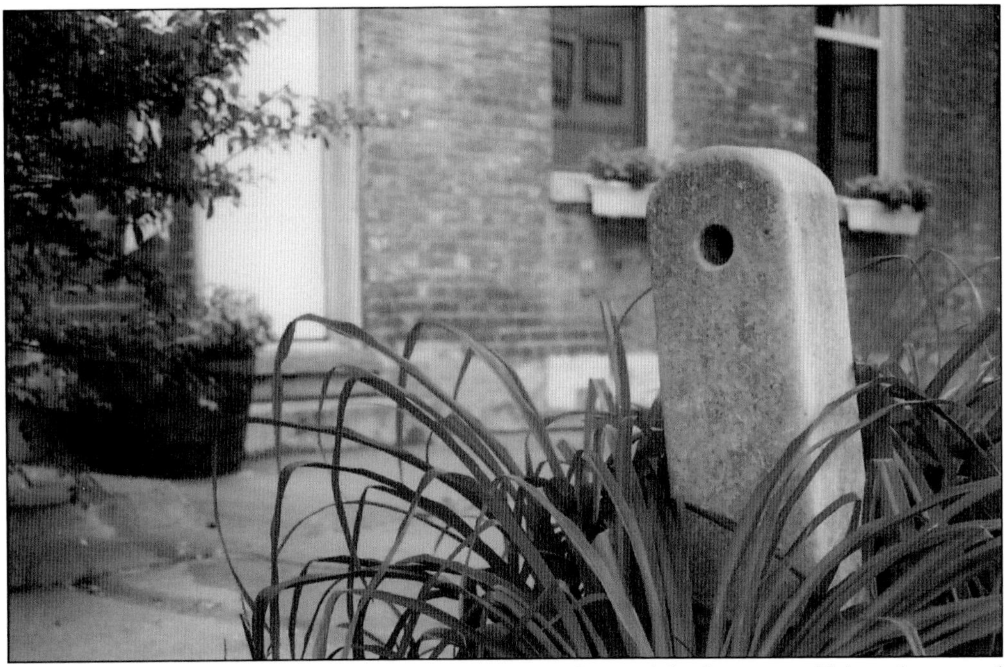

HITCHING POST. This stone with a hole through it in front of the house would have been used for tying up horses. The combination of the carriage stone, hitching post, foundation with the imprint of 1865, and the horse stables in the back of the property marks this address as the most unique location in the neighborhood.

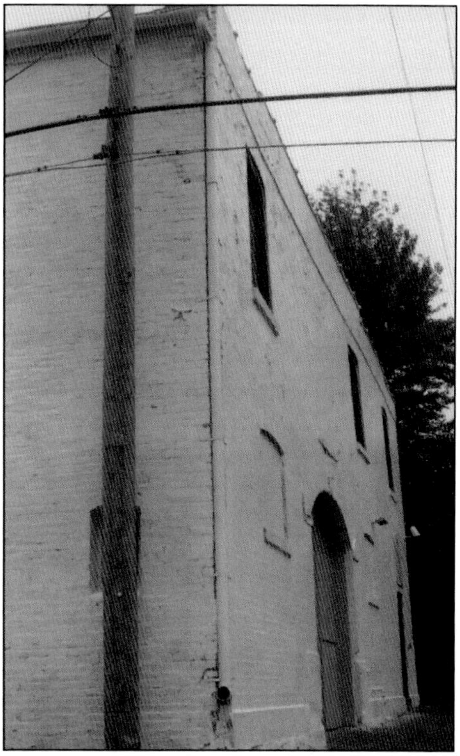

Eyermann Horse Stables. The stables show up in the St. Louis 1883 Hopkins Atlas, but since no building permits were found, the exact year of their construction is unknown. They have served as residences and business offices throughout the years. In the past, they have been home to a landscape gardener, an engineering welding company, and a graphic art and printers supply company.

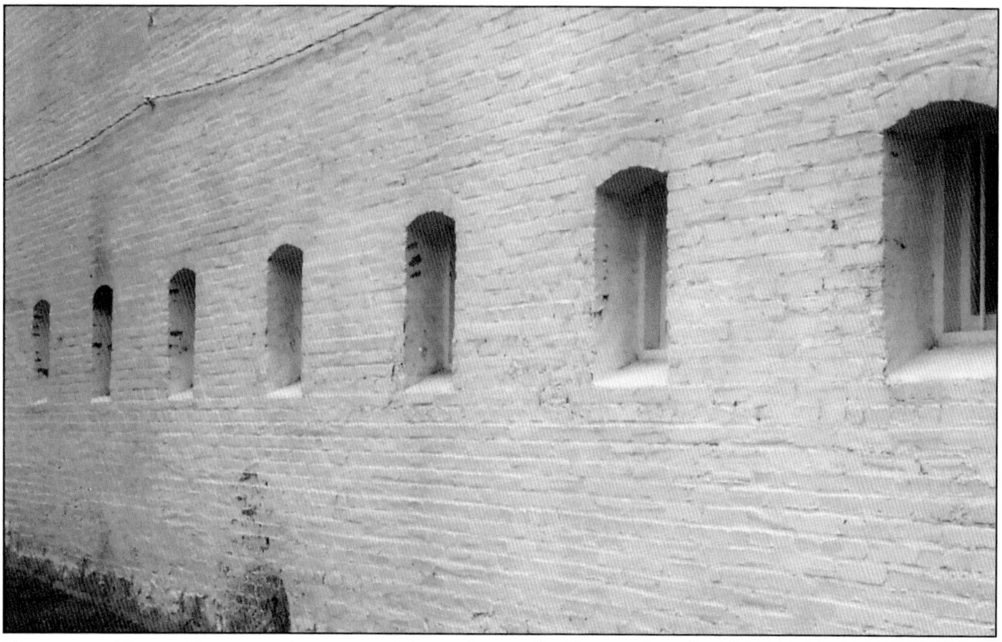

Eyermann Horse Stables, Alley-side View. Since the Eyermann family owned several quarries, they would have housed teams of horses in their stables, which is apparent from the row of windows facing the alley. In 2000, the old stables were bought by the South Side Day Nursery; today they serve as offices for this nonprofit organization, whose roots can be traced back to 1886. SSDN has been in Benton Park West since 1953.

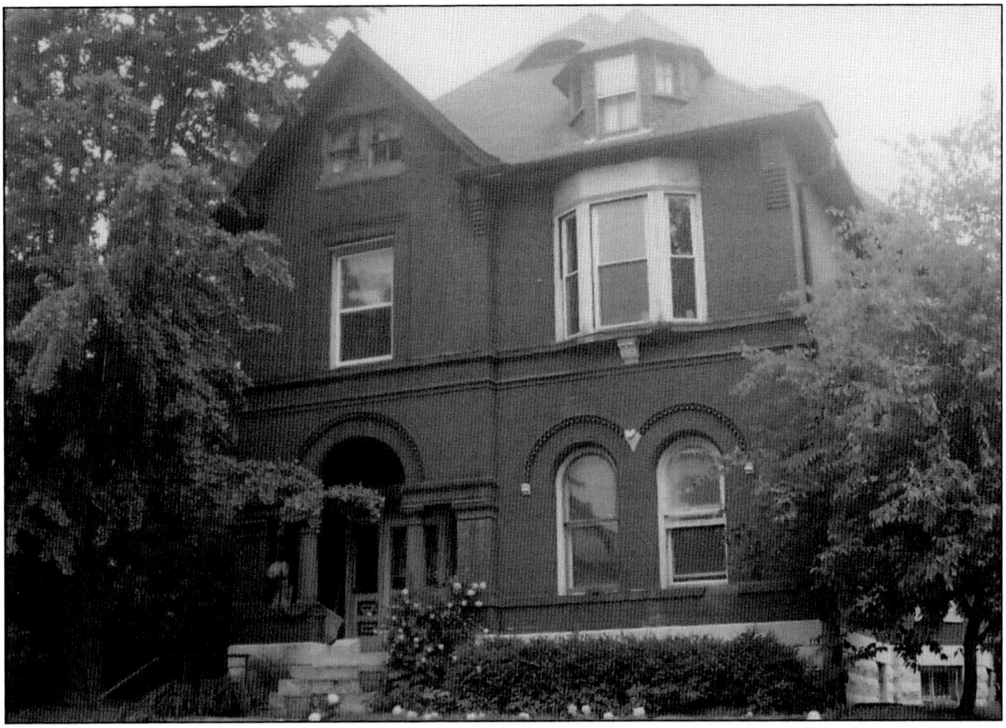

SITE A2: GEORGE EYERMANN HOUSE, 2901 IOWA. The eldest son of Gottlieb Eyermann, Gottlieb Jr. stayed in the family home after his father passed away. His brother George built his house across the street in 1894 for $6,000. Later George was the secretary of the Eyermann Construction Company, while Gottlieb Jr. was the president. George and Gottlieb Eyermann were well-respected businessmen in the city, especially in south St. Louis. Gottlieb Jr. was also president of Chippewa Bank for many years.

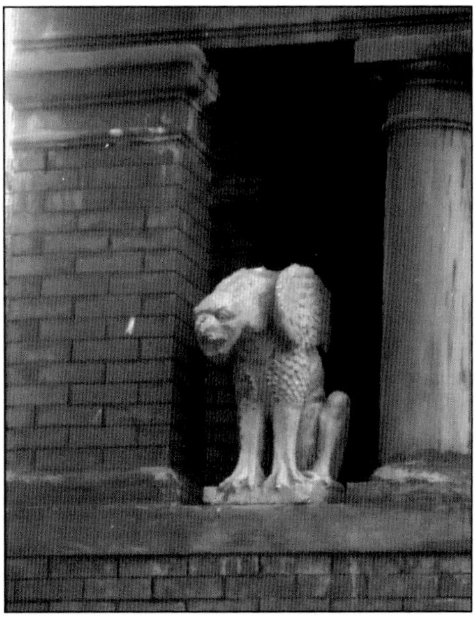

FIFTY YEARS OF EYERMANNS. The eagle guarded the entrance to the George Eyermann family home from 1895 to the mid-1940s. Mrs. Kate Eyermann was the last resident listed. By 1946, Harry Ahrens was the new resident, and the following year, Mrs. Dorothy Larkins was at this address. The eagle still sits at the entrance greeting visitors to this historic neighborhood jewel.

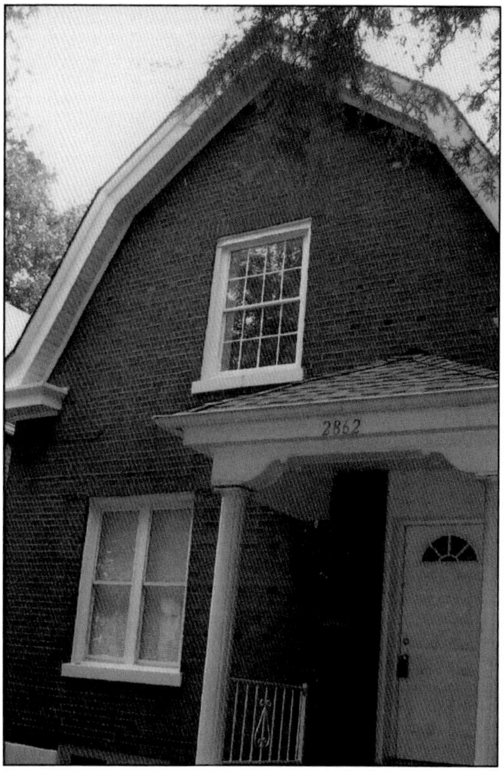

SITE A3: GAMBREL-ROOFED HOUSE, 2862 OHIO. Six houses were built in a row in 1910 by Leisner Realty and Building Company for a total of $15,000. Edwin Leisner was the president and August C. Leisner was the secretary; their business was located in the Pierce Building on Fourth Street. The houses at the addresses of 2862, 2856, and 2850 all have gambrel roofs; there are only a few houses in the neighborhood with this type of roof.

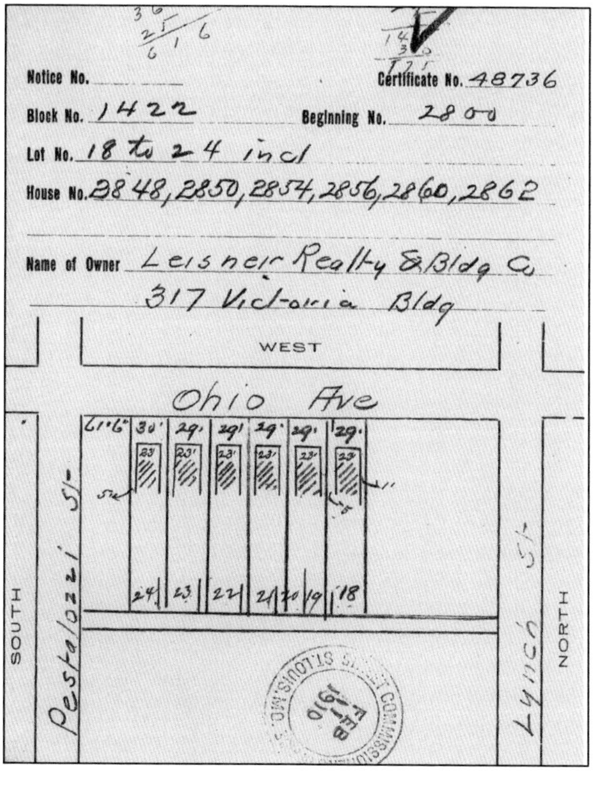

Notice No.

Certificate No. 48736

Block No. 1422 Beginning No. 2800

Lot No. 18 to 24 incl

House No. 2848, 2850, 2854, 2856, 2860, 2862

Name of Owner Leisner Realty & Bldg Co
317 Victoria Bldg

WEST

Ohio Ave

SOUTH Pestalozzi St

Lynch St NORTH

LEISNER HOUSE RESIDENTS. In 1911, railroad switchman Bert Wilcox a lived at 2850, and Marcus M. Gerstner, a baker, lived at 2860. In 1918, switchman Albert L. Wilcox was listed at 2850, and Anthony J. Brom, a shoe worker, lived at 2854. A brewer named Michael Bickel lived at 2856. James R. Herman, a music teacher; and waiter Louis Marsaille and his wife, a saleswoman at Famous & Barr, lived in 2862.

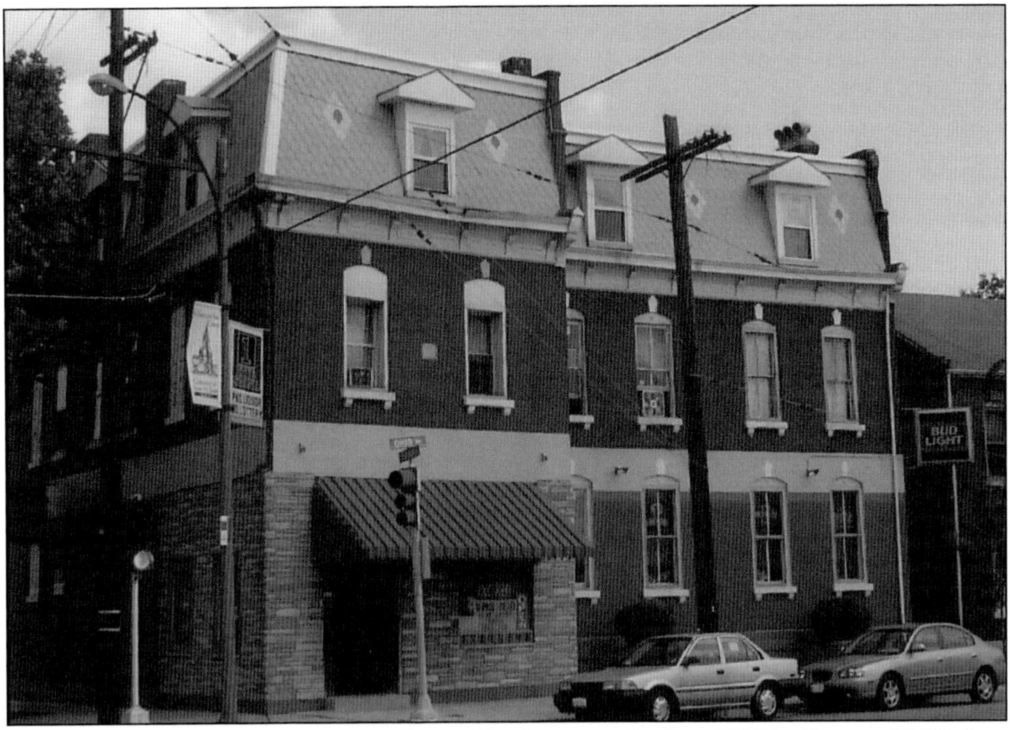

Site A4: H. H. Wolken House, 2800 Ohio. This house was built in 1880 by Herman H. Wolken at a cost of $2,000. The inscription in the front limestone inset reads "H. W. 1880." Mr. Wolken was a dairyman who came to St. Louis from Germany during the Civil War. He was 20 years old when he arrived and went to work immediately in a dairy. In 1867, Herman went into business for himself.

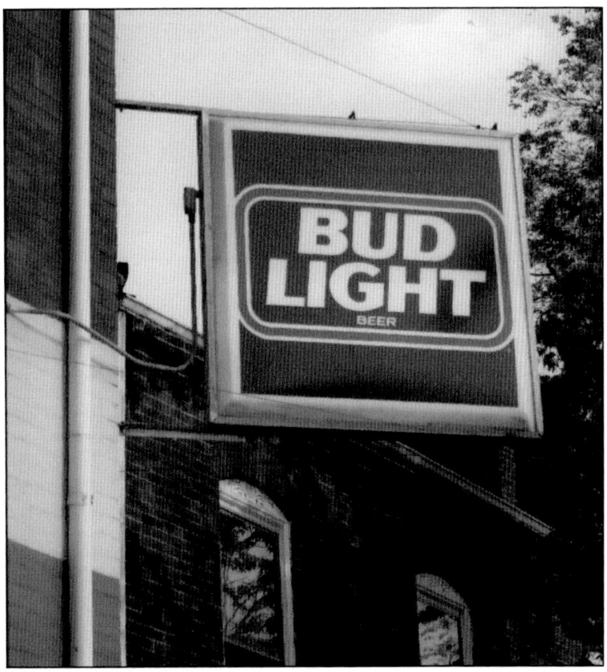

Neighborhood Tavern. Before this location opened up as a bar in the mid-1930s, it was a grocery store from the mid-1920s to the early 1930s. In 1933, the city directory listed this address as South Side Heating & Sheet Metal Company. By 1935, it was listed as a place for liquors; it is still a neighborhood bar today. The current owners of the One Night Stand are Roger and Katherine Huddleston.

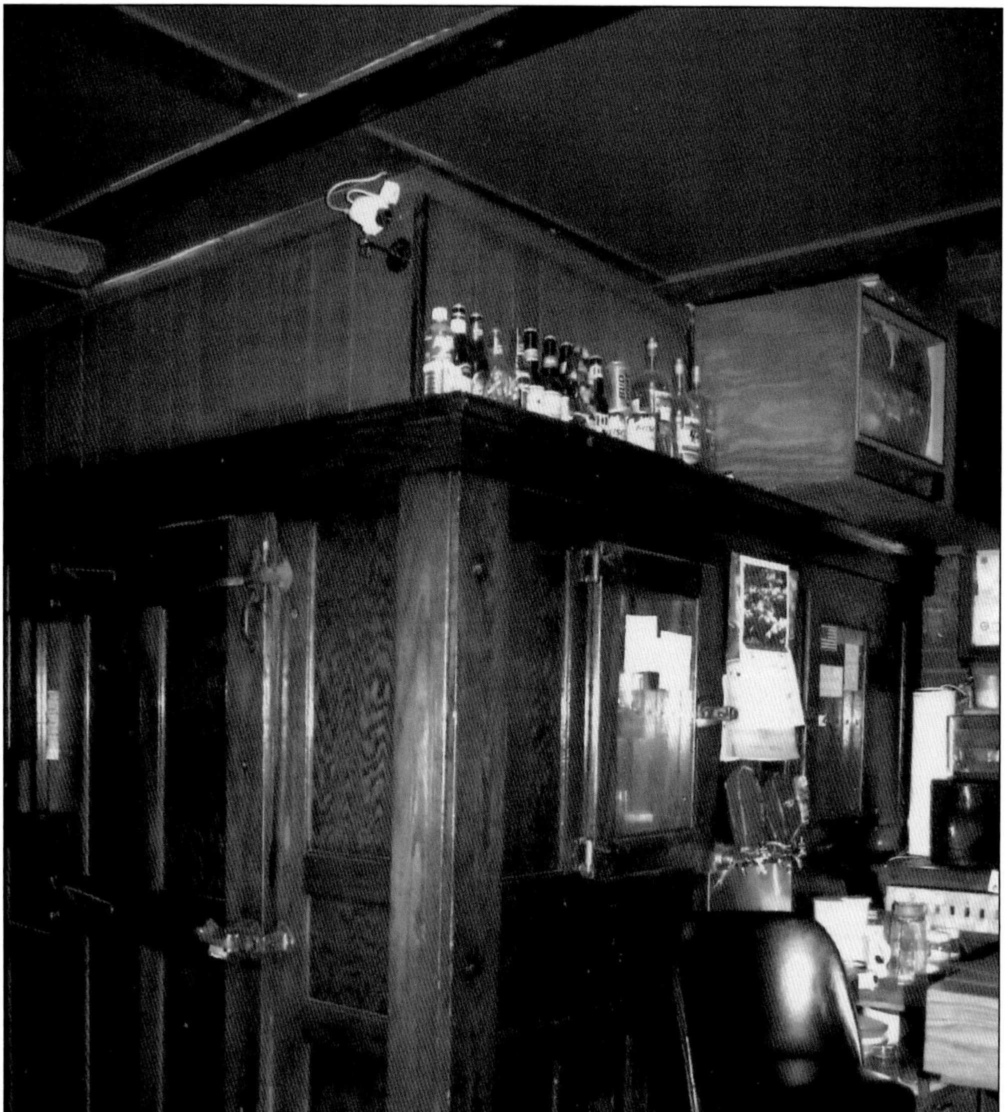

OLD-FASHIONED, WALK-IN ICE BOX. Go inside and take a look at the original bar and walk-in ice box. From 1935 to the early 1950s, this location sold liquors. In 1935, one of the companies that dealt in ice equipment was the Merchants Ice & Coal Company on North Fourth Street. Their advertisement in the city directory read, "Modern Ice Refrigerators and other ice equipment, 38 years of service." The wholesale liquor distributors listed were Herbert & Schuler Company, The Hilfer Louis Company, McKesson-Merrell Drug Company, and the Mercantile Sales Company. Hiram-Walker Incorporated and the Import Distributing Company were listed as liquor distributors. The same year there were 123 retail beer dealers listed, and the main distributors were Anheuser-Busch, Blue Ridge Bottling Company, Central Distributing Company, Griesedieck Western Brewing, Highland Distributing Company, and Louis Schnellmann. In 1955, the bar finally had a gained a name—Ohio Tavern. It would remain under the same name until the early 1960s. From the mid-1960s through the early 1980s, it was known as the Picture Bar Tavern. In the mid-1980s, the name was changed to Pope's Picture Bar, as it would be known until it became the One Night Stand in the late 1990s.

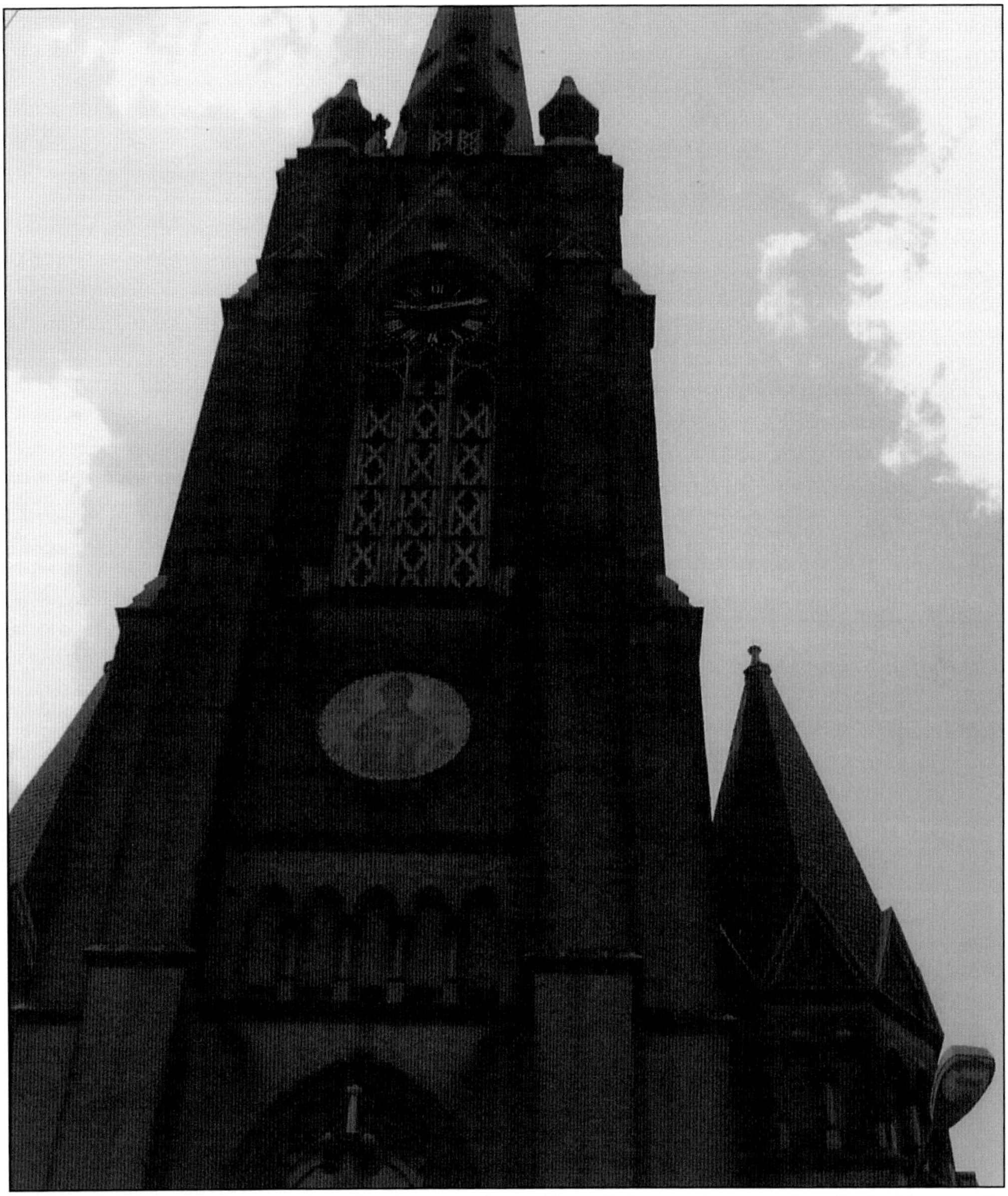

Site A5: St. Francis de Sales Church, 2653 Ohio. Founded as a German church, St. Frances de Sales is known as "the cathedral of South St. Louis." Today it is still serves an immigrant population—the growing Hispanic community. On Sundays, two masses are offered in Spanish. The old church was built in 1867 at this location, but by 1895, the congregation had outgrown the church and plans were made to dismantle it to make room for the new one. The old church was destroyed in the 1896 tornado, saving the congregation the trouble of tearing it down. In 1907, construction began for the new church, while the congregation met in the school hall. When the basement was complete, they held services there until the full building was finished in 1908. The original architect was Engelbert Seibertz of Berlin, and in 1906 the plans were modified by Victor J. Klutho of St. Louis. The steeple is 300 feet high. The Wegener Brothers who laid the brick were from the neighborhood, operating their business from 3137 Nebraska. The church was placed on the National Historic Register on November 2, 1978.

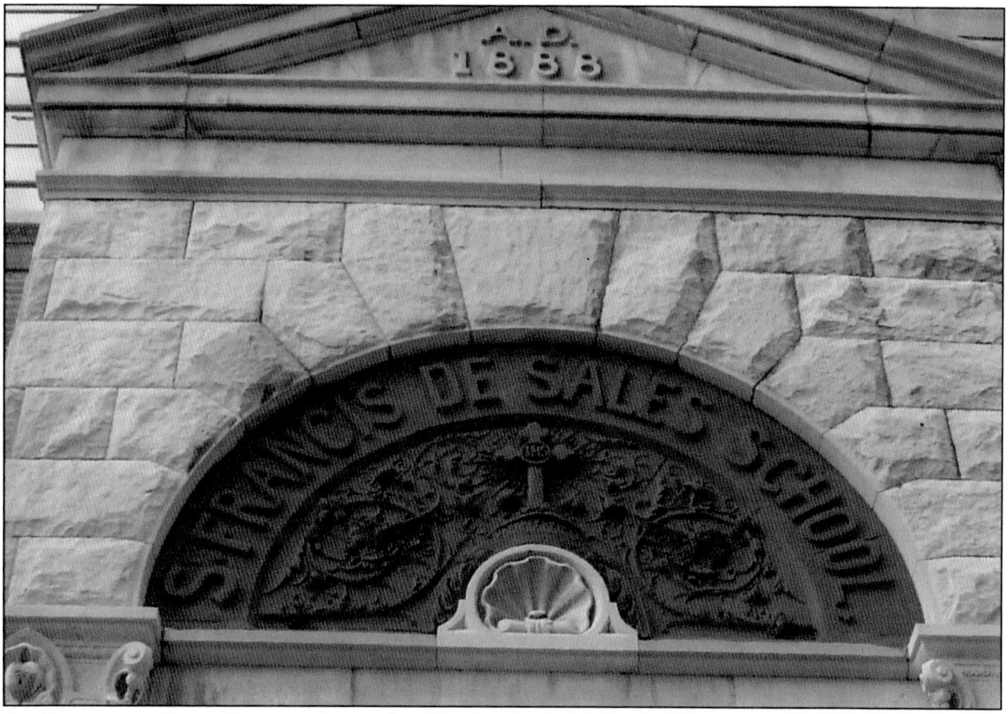

St. Francis de Sales School. A parish school was established in 1869, and this school building was built by father John Peter Lotz. In the early 1900s, mass was said in German and classes were also taught in German. The parish even published half of its literature in German until 1930. There are two former school buildings on the property of St. Frances de Sales. Today they house a day care center and a place for social service programs.

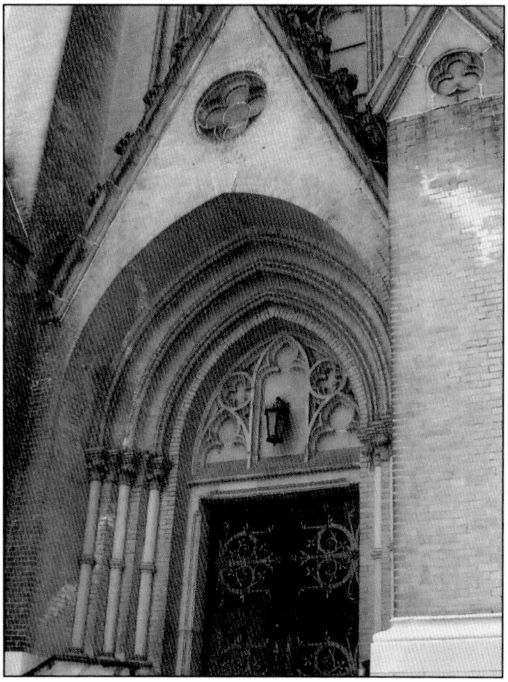

Through the Doors of St. Francis de Sales. The frescos inside the church were painted by Fridolin Fuchs, and the large paintings in the transept were drawn by a Benedictine monk. The stained-glass windows were done by Emil Frei of St. Louis. The Freis first arrived in the United States in San Francisco; homesick and on their way back to Germany, they stopped in St. Louis to visit friends. Embraced by the South St. Louis German community, they decided to remain in the United States.

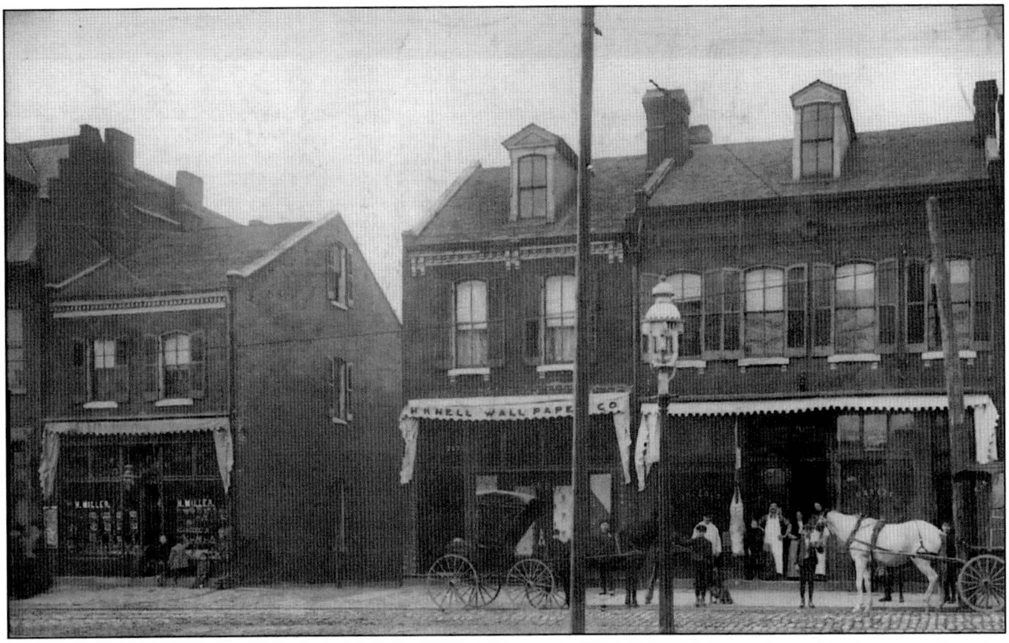

SITE A6: THE OLD GROEBL MARKET AT 2635 GRAVOIS This photograph was taken in 1908. Oscar Groebl was a butcher and his brother Richard of R. Groebl and Company was a dyer next door. Richard was born in Germany in 1878. He came to America with his parents when he was around 13 and came to St. Louis in 1891. For a time he lived in San Francisco and New York, returning to St. Louis in 1897.

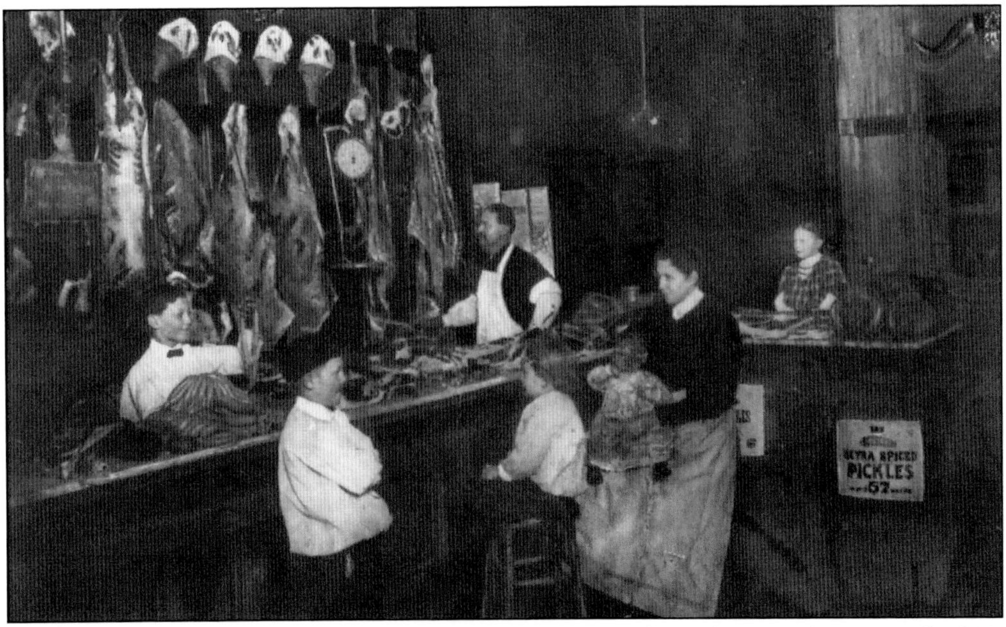

INSIDE THE BUTCHER SHOP. This photograph of the Groebl family was taken around 1913. According to O. John Groebl, Oscar met Anna, a maid in Compton Heights, when he went to the back door to deliver a meat order. Anna and Oscar married in 1896 at St. Francis de Sales Church the day before the cyclone destroyed the church.

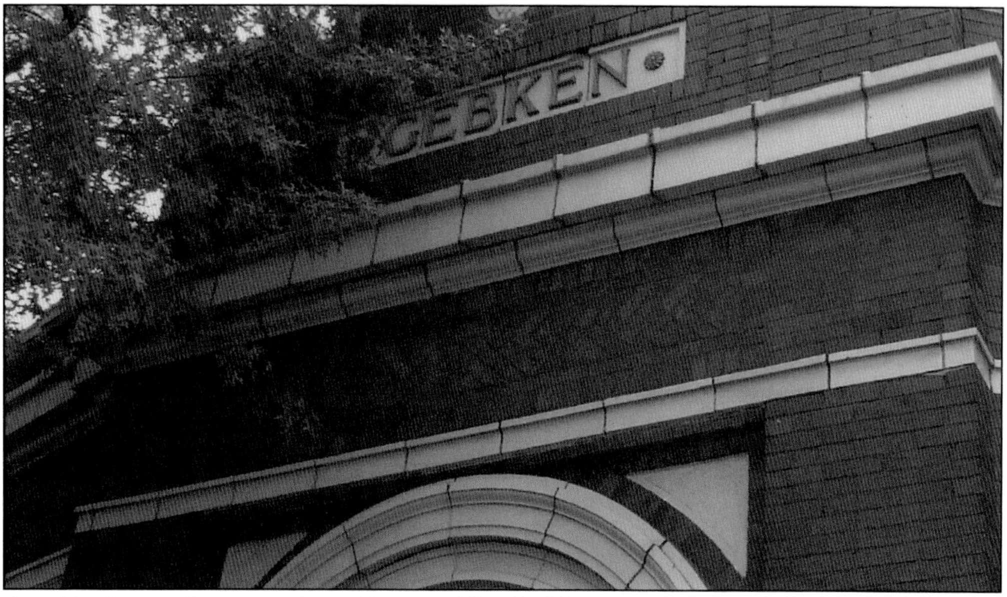

Site A7: Gebken Building, 2630 Gravois. This building was constructed for John H. Gebken, president of a livery and undertaking business. This location and 2842 Meramec Street were funeral parlors. Mr. Gebken was born in St. Louis in 1861 and was educated in parochial schools. He married Dora Heutrich in 1887, and they had ten children. He was a member of several parish societies, including the Catholic Knights of Columbus.

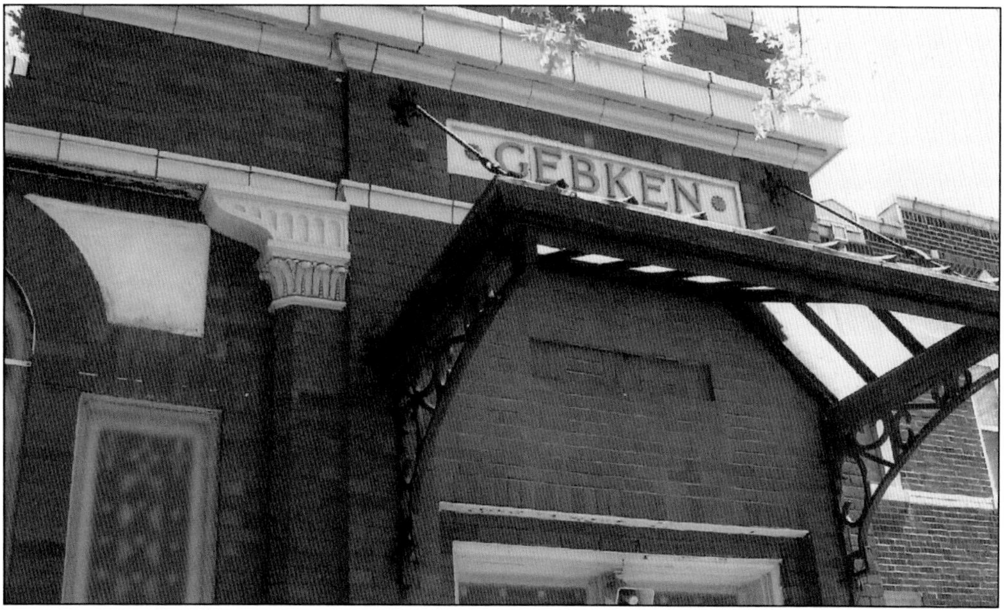

Southeast Corner of Gravois and Texas. The early addresses for this property were 2624–2628 and 2700–2008 Texas. The former funeral home was built in 1924 at the cost of $20,000 for J. H. Gebken. The architect was Kloster & Company. From 1921 to 1923, this corner was used as an amusement park. There were permits issued for tents, Ferris wheels, and merry-go-rounds. The largest event was held in 1923 by the Businessmen of Jefferson and Gravois Areas, who set up 20 canvas tents and a carnival.

SITE A8: BANK OF AMERICA, 2604 SOUTH JEFFERSON. The Jefferson-Gravois Bank was built in 1924. Before its construction, the Witte Clothing Company was located at this corner. In 1902, H. T. Witte was president, Theodore East Witte was vice-president, and Alexander A. Witte was the secretary. Customers found gentleman's clothing, furnishings, hats, trunks, and valises at the Witte store. The last permit for the store was issued to H. T. Witte to alter the brick shop.

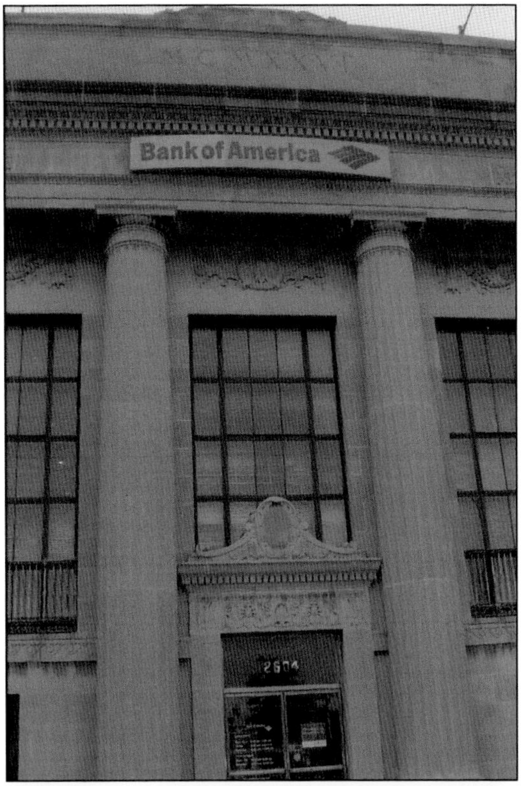

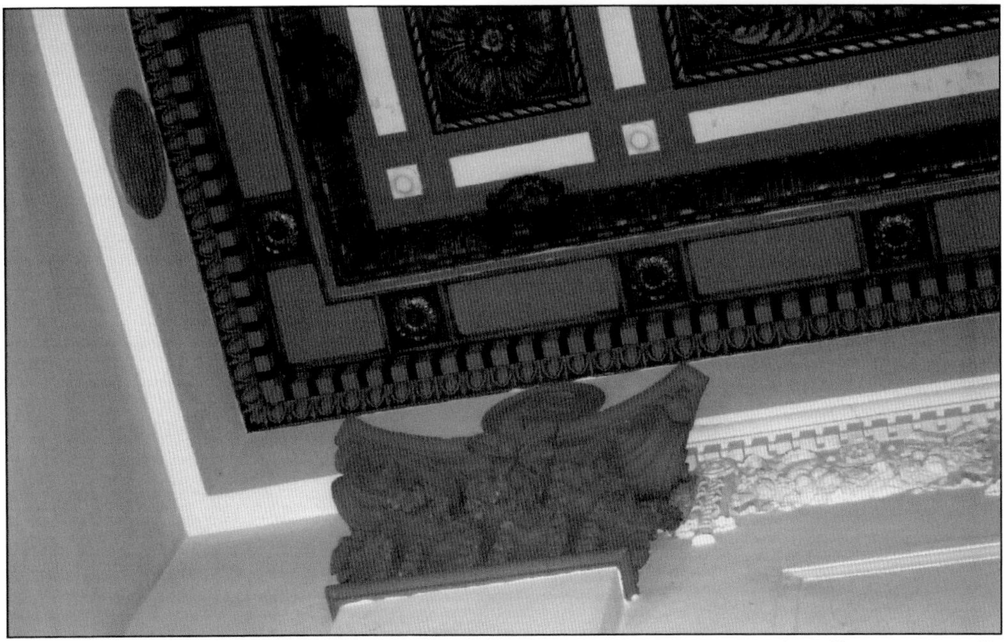

BANK INTERIOR. Though an elegant building today, 2600 to 2608 South Jefferson originally consisted of everyday shops, offices, and a house. The earliest permit found for the area was issued in 1877 to J. F. Riessen for a one-story frame stable. In 1880, a permit was issued to J. Burke for a two-story brick dwelling, which cost $500 to build.

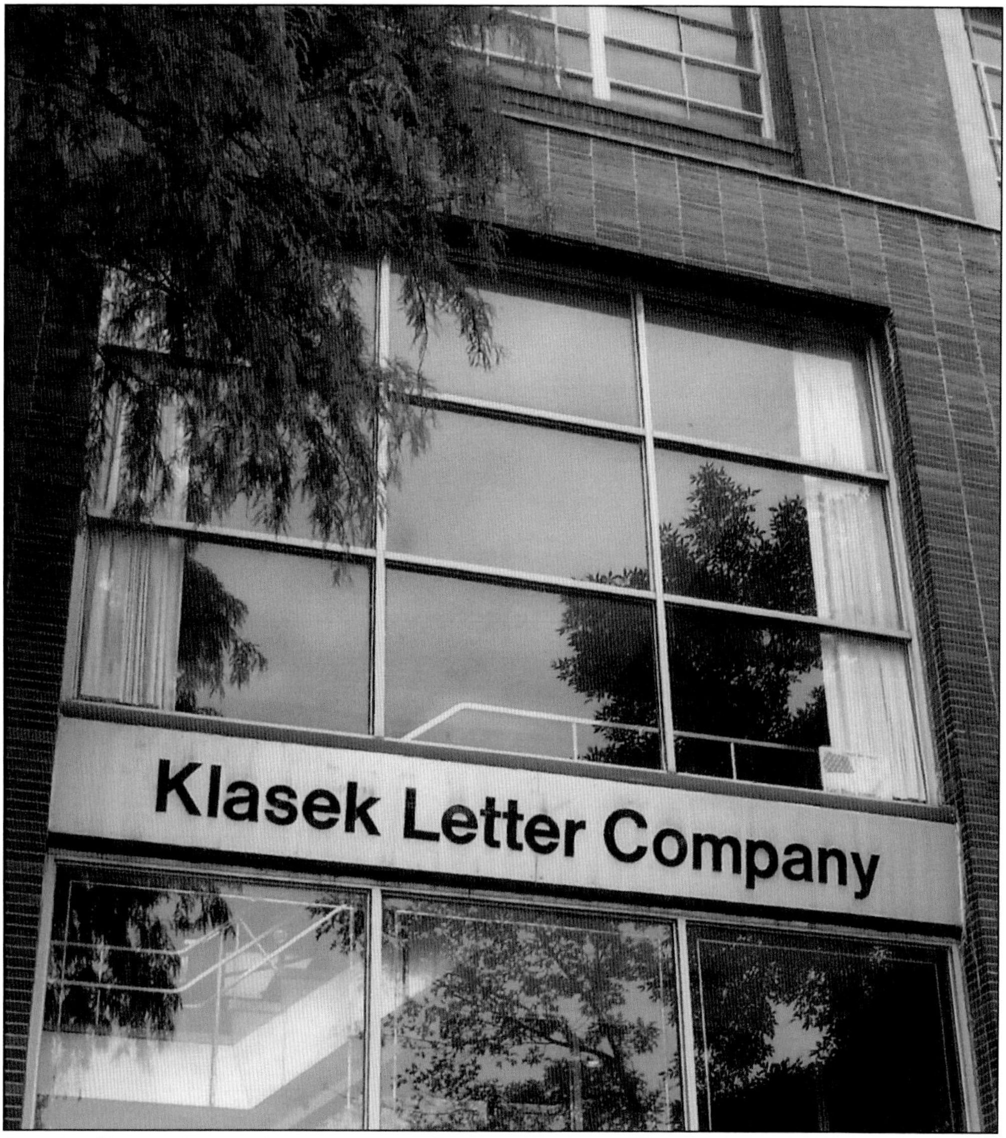

SITE A9: KLASEK LETTER COMPANY, 2850 SOUTH JEFFERSON. The company started out as a letter shop in 1917. It was founded by Charles West Klasek Sr., whose son, Charles Jr., took over the company in 1947. Charles G. Klasek, the current CEO, assumed his position in 1984. The company provides direct mail services. In the 1940s, printing was added to the letter shop services along with addressing systems, and in the 1980s, they added laser printing to their services. Klasek Letter Company acquired the Cliff Kelly Company and Automated Services in the 1990s, increasing its mailing capacity, web printing, and laser printing production. Before the company moved to the area, it was located in several different buildings around the city. In 1918, it was located in the Railway Exchange Building at 611 Olive. In 1925, the company was on the third floor of the Tower Building at 614 Olive. By 1935, it was in the Granite Building at 406 Market, relocating to 3432 Lindell in 1955 and to 3115 Locust in 1965. Klasek moved to 901 South Grand in 1990, and in the late 1990s, expanded to include locations at 2628 South Big Bend and 2850 South Jefferson. Today, the company has this location and the one at 901 South Grand.

SITE A10: CORNER STOREFRONT AT 2870 SOUTH JEFFERSON. The building permit for this storefront was issued in 1890 to Herman Heithaus, a lithographer who resided as 2835 Indiana. The permit also included addresses 2866 and 2868. In 1902, Louis Kaub opened up a saloon at this corner. Born in St. Louis in 1875, Mr. Kaub trained to be a watchmaker after completing his education. In 1898, he opened up his first saloon at a different location, following his army enlistment.

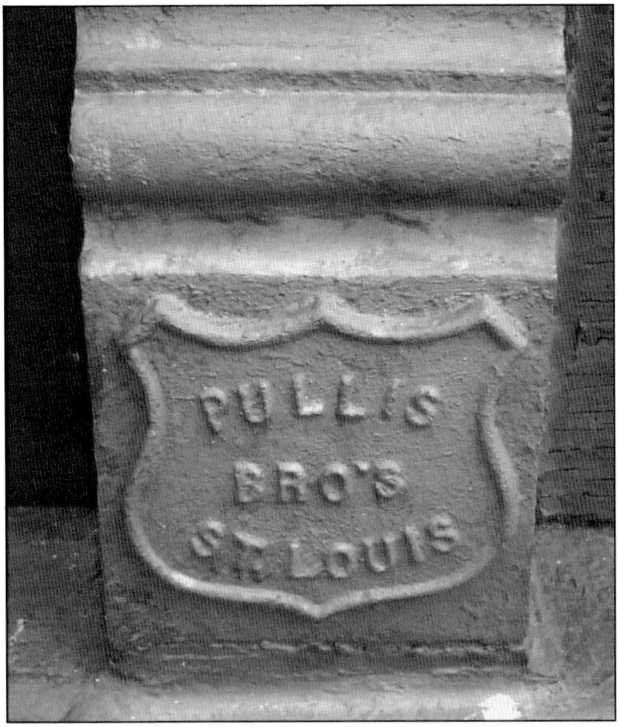

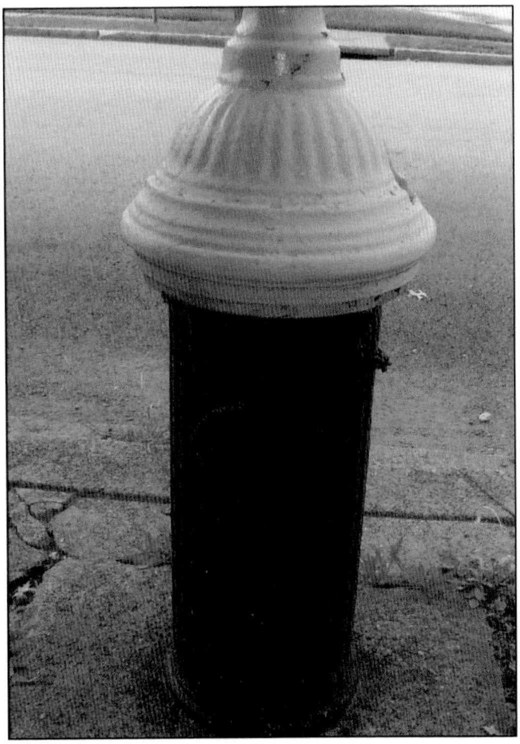

PULLIS BROTHERS STOREFRONT AND FRITZ FIRE HYDRANT. The Pullis family was listed in the city directories as being in the iron business from 1842 to 1898. Thomas R. and John Pullis were the original owners. Thomas R. Jr. became a partner after John retired. When Thomas R. Sr. died, Thomas Jr. and his brothers conducted business under the Pullis Brothers Company. The fire hydrant was manufactured by George J. Fritz, who had established his business in 1874.

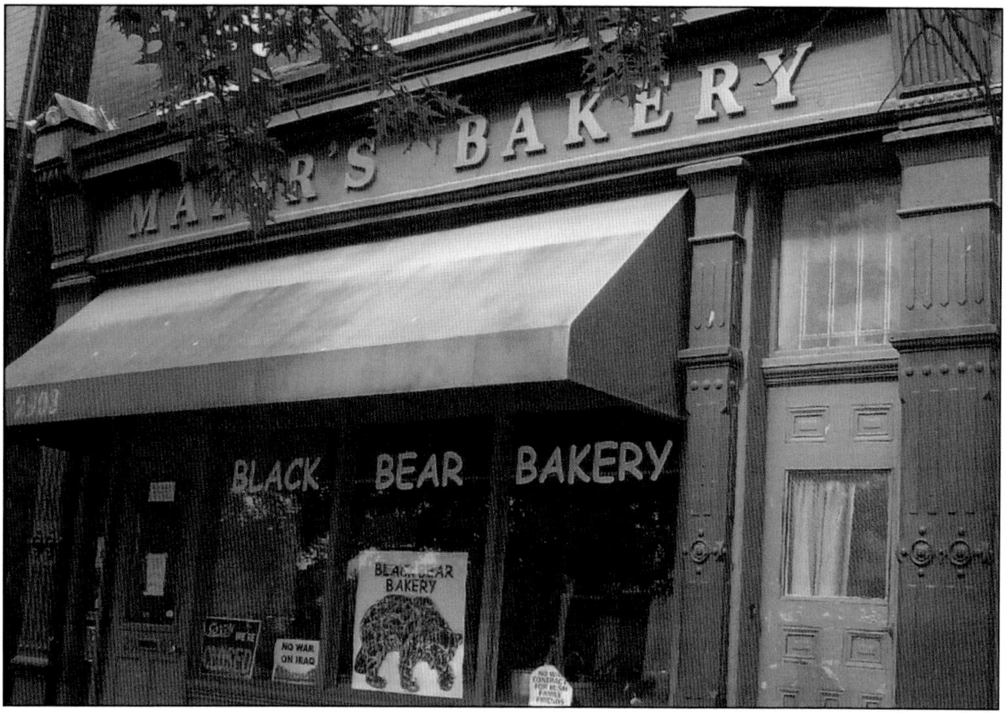

Site A11: Baker Building, 2901–2903 South Jefferson. This location has a long history as a bakery, but originally was built as store space and apartments. The August Heil Plumbing business was at this location. By 1911, a building permit was issued to Louis Malsch and F. J. Leibinger & Son for a one-story, brick bake shop at 2903 South Jefferson. The cost of construction was $2,000.

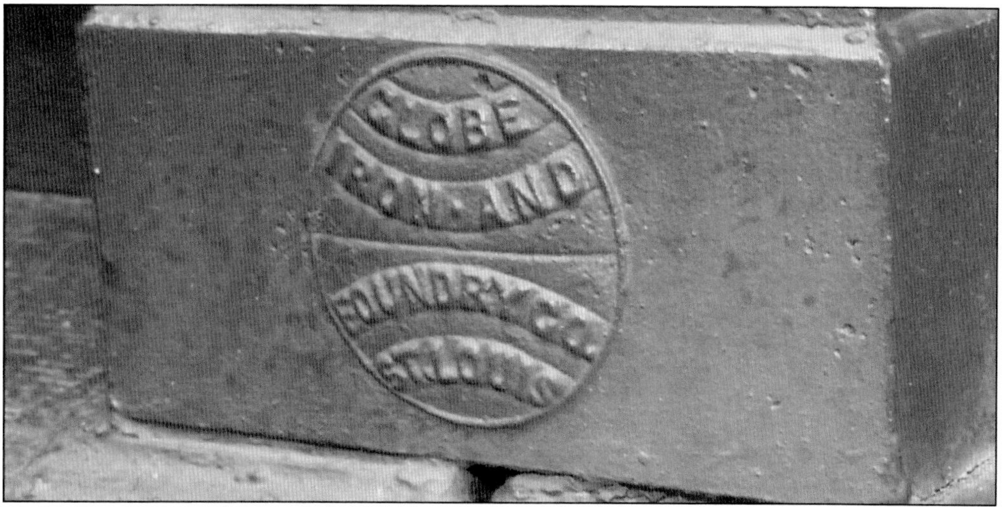

Globe Iron and Foundry Company. This iron storefront was made by Globe Iron and Foundry, located at 911 Victor and owned by Emil Zeis, who lived at 2339 South Twelfth. Globe is listed in the city directories from 1891 to 1903. The company also manufactured iron fences. Look closely at the bottom of the fence posts you come across and you will find the Globe imprint on some of them.

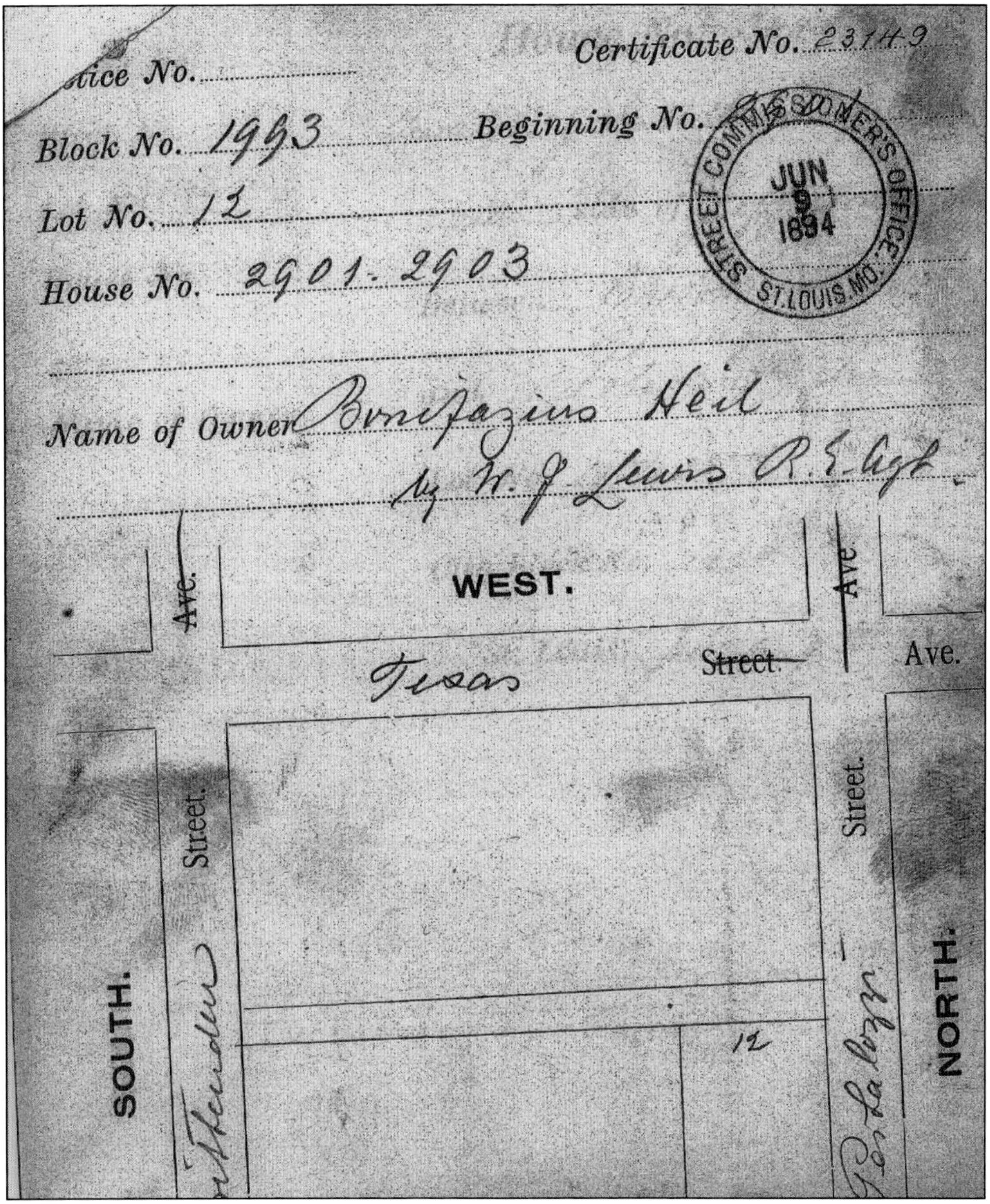

Building Permit for 2901–2903 South Jefferson. A building permit was issued to Bonifazius Heil in 1894 for two adjacent three-story buildings, costing $9,000, and a stable and shop for $700. Mr. Heil was born in St. Louis in 1859. After completing his education, he sold newspapers and worked in a factory. In 1877, he became a plumber's apprentice, and in 1882, he went into business for himself. The bakery business was started in 1911 by the Malschs. By 1930, the bakery was owned by Charles West Koch, and Walter L. Barthel had a restaurant next door. In 1940, the restaurant had been replaced by Doran Liquors. In 1952, the liquor store was owned by Maurice Doughery and the bakery by John Roth. By 1960, the bakery was listed as Mayer's Pastries. John Mayer immigrated to the United States in 1947 from Vienna and was 16 when he started baking. He worked in different bakeries, including one at this location. In 1959, he bought the bakery and ran it until 1994. Today it is home to the Black Bear Bakery.

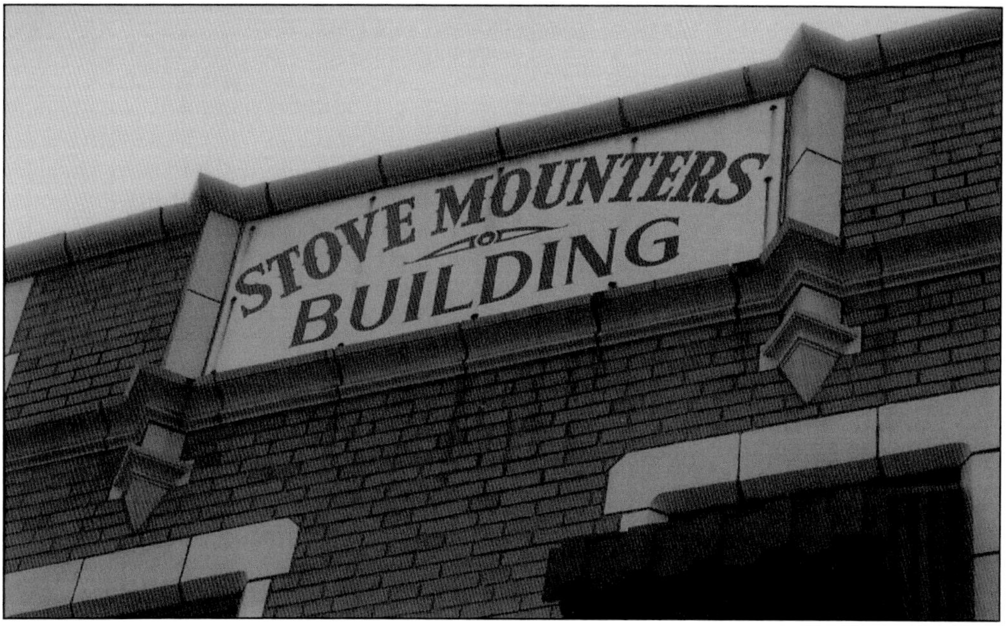

SITE A12: STOVE MOUNTERS BUILDING, 2929 SOUTH JEFFERSON. Local No. 2 International Union of Operating Engineers currently owns this building, but one of its early occupants was William Wingbermuehle Undertaking. William Wingbermuehle married Anna Gebken, the daughter of his former employer, J. H. Gebken. Later the building became Witt Brothers Livery & Undertaking. The Witt Brothers had established their business in 1866. Their first location was at 809–811 Hickory Street. It became the Stove Mounters Building in the early 1960s.

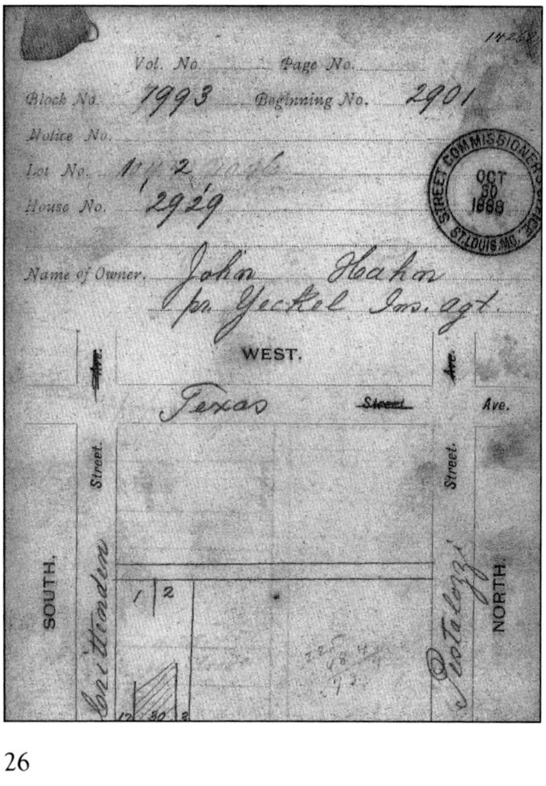
Vol. No. Page No.
Block No. 1993 Beginning No. 2901
Notice No.
Lot No.
House No. 2929
STREET COMMISSIONER'S OFFICE OCT 30 1888 ST. LOUIS MO.
Name of Owner. John Hahn
pr. Yeckel Ins. agt.
WEST.
Texas Ave.
Street.
Street.
SOUTH.
Crittenden
NORTH.
Pestalozzi

BUILDING PERMIT FOR 2929 SOUTH JEFFERSON. In 1888, this building permit was issued to John Hahn, an insurance agent for Yeckel Insurance Company. The building was a funeral home up to the late 1950s and then housed several local unions. In the 1963 city directory, the following groups were listed: Stove Furnace & Allied Appliance Workers International Union, Biscuit & Cracker Workers Union, United Shoe Workers of America, and the current residents, International Union of Operating Engineers.

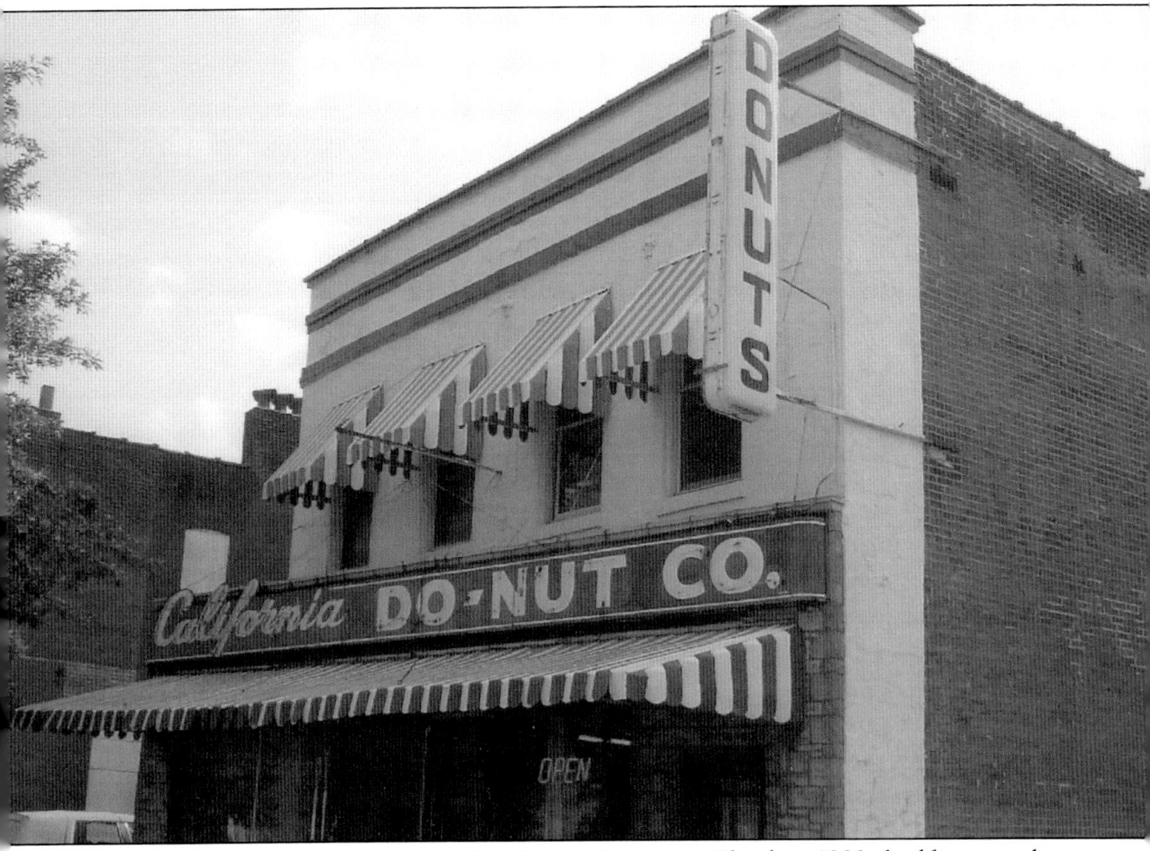

SITE A13: CALIFORNIA DONUTS, 2924–2926 SOUTH JEFFERSON. This late 1800s building was the location for Louis A. W. Reis Horse-Shoeing in the early 1900s. Mr. Reis was born in Illinois in 1879. When he was around 13, he moved to St. Louis with his parents. His first job in the city was in the brewing industry. In 1898, he began working in and learning the horse shoe business. By 1905, he was ready to set up his own business at 2113 Pestalozzi. He spent two years there before moving his business to South Jefferson. Louis Reis was still there in 1915, when there was a building permit issued for an alteration of the building costing $1,400 and another one issued for a heating boiler at a cost of $250. The architect for both projects was F. Rund. In 1925, this address was listed as Groll Sheet Metal Works. In 1930, 2924 South Jefferson was listed as Groll Brothers Hardware and 2926 was listed as Anthony J. Groll, tinner. The donut business was begun in the 1940s by Harry Granger. Along the way, A. G. Carnahan bought the business, which was later bought by one of his former employees, Willie Mae Green. This donut shop was another south St. Louis landmark. Regulars came from all over the city and included employees from businesses in the neighborhood, such as the Gravois Planing Mill and the Jefferson Tent & Awning Company.

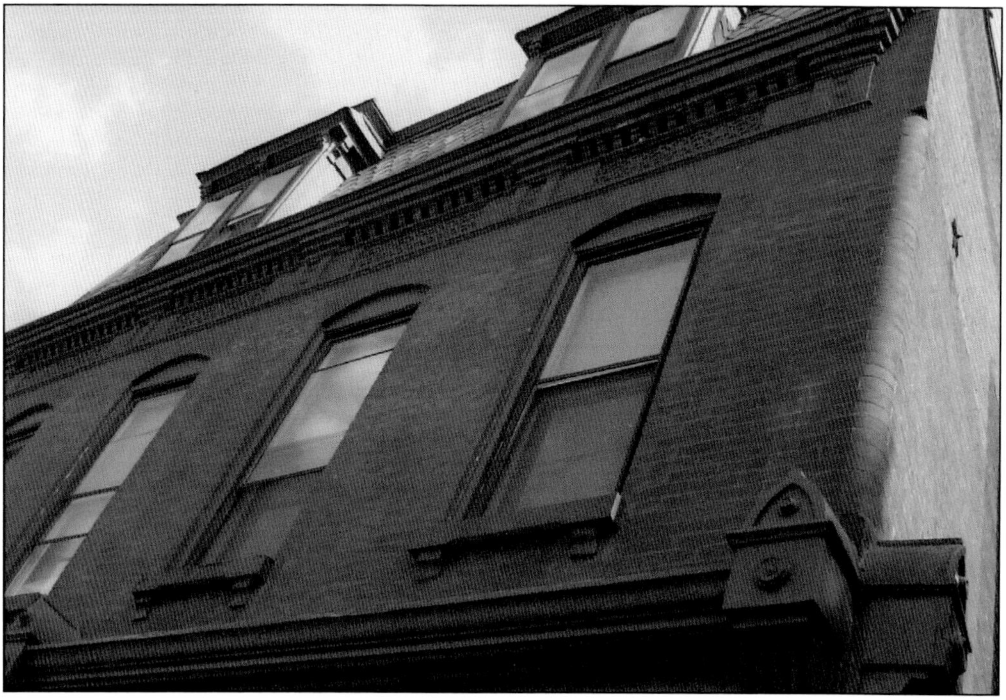

SITE A14: STOREFRONT, 2623 ARSENAL. Charles A. Wagner had this building constructed in 1888 for $4,500, and sold shoes here. In 1890, a census was taken of Union Civil War Veterans. Mr. Wagner, along with Karl Frederick Ditz, was listed at this address. Mr. Ditz served with the Ohio Cavalry in 1861. His disability was a broken arm. The remarks' column reads, "Joined Army in Cincinnati with his father, to play the flute."

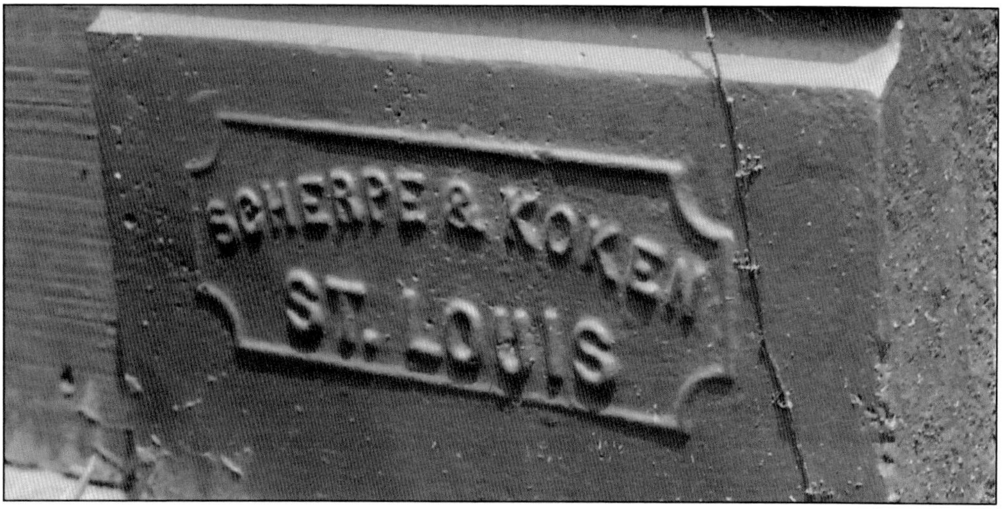

STOREFRONT BY SCHERPE & KOKEN ARCHITECTURAL IRON WORKS AND FOUNDRY. John F. Scherpe and William T. Koken started this business in 1880. At one time, they employed 150 men. They manufactured iron work for building store fronts, jails, vaults, railings, and shutters. Besides Missouri, their iron works can be found in Texas, Arkansas, Kentucky, Illinois, Iowa, Nebraska, Kansas, Colorado, and other states. They also published a catalog with illustrations, which they mailed out to architects and builders.

SITE A15: REINHARDT HOUSE, 2719 ARSENAL. John W. Reinhardt built this house in 1890. The permit was issued to him and to the Argurieo Insurance Agency. Mr. Reinhardt was a stone mason and Adam T. Argurieo, his insurance agent, resided at 2206 Wyoming and had his office at 415 Locust. By 1893, Louis Zeiler, who dealt in cigars, resided at this address. In 2001, the house was bought and is being restored by Todd and Cassandra Schmeckpeper.

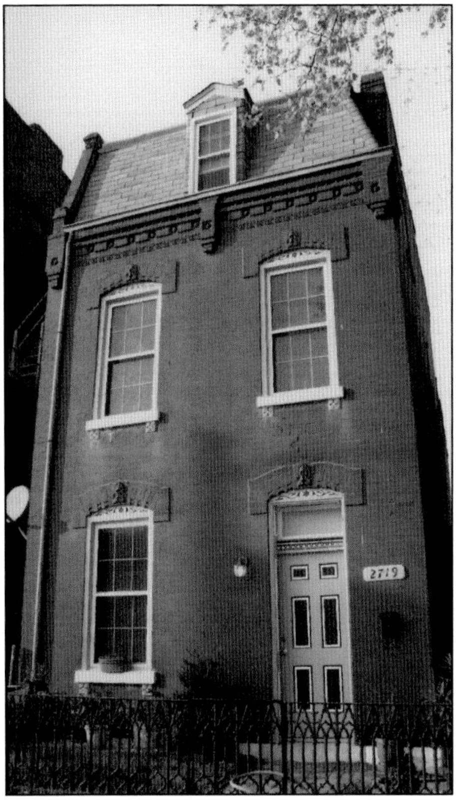

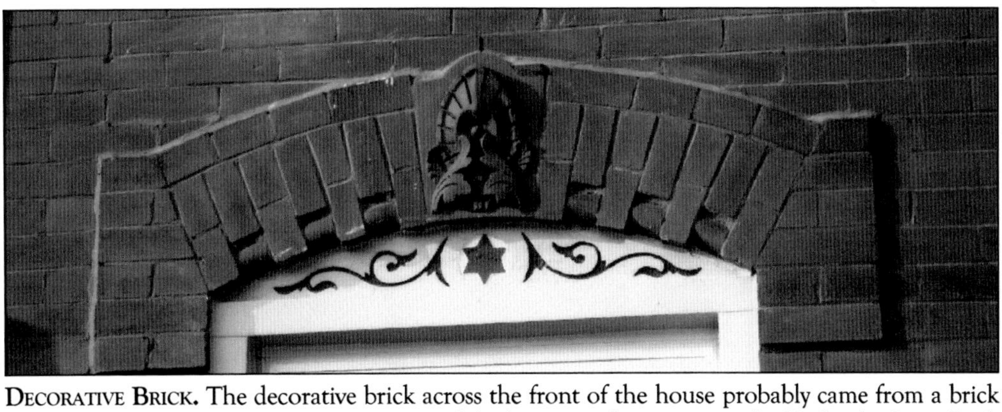

DECORATIVE BRICK. The decorative brick across the front of the house probably came from a brick manufacturer right here in St. Louis. One of the largest at this time was the Hydraulic Press Brick Company founded by Edward C. Sterling in 1868. They owned several brickyards. Yard No. 5 was located at what is now 1616 South Kingshighway, currently Henry Plumbing Supply Company. In the 1890s, Hydraulic Press Brick had 200 standard brick designs in their catalogs.

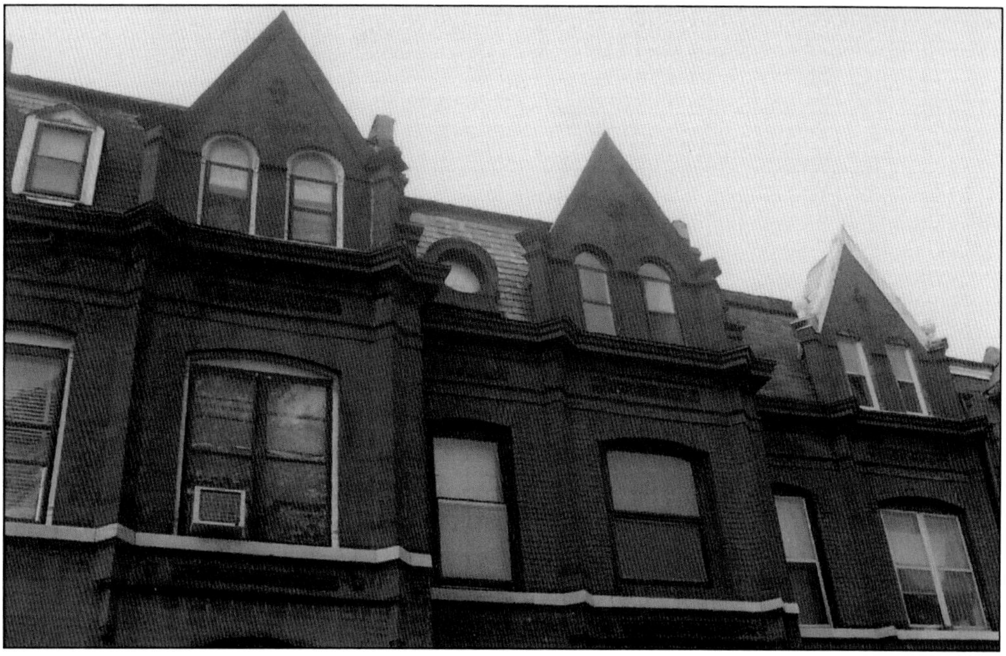

SITE A16: WODICKA ROW, 3017, 3019, AND 3021 CALIFORNIA. The residents of Wodicka Row in 1900 were working class families. Edward Meyers, a jail guard, lived at 3017 in one of the units with his wife and a daughter. The second unit was occupied by Mr. and Mrs. William Hamtil and six children. In 3019 lived a widow, Emma Luschenberg, and her five children. One of the units at 3021 was occupied by Theresa Hof and her three daughters, while the four Hanshild sisters lived in the other unit.

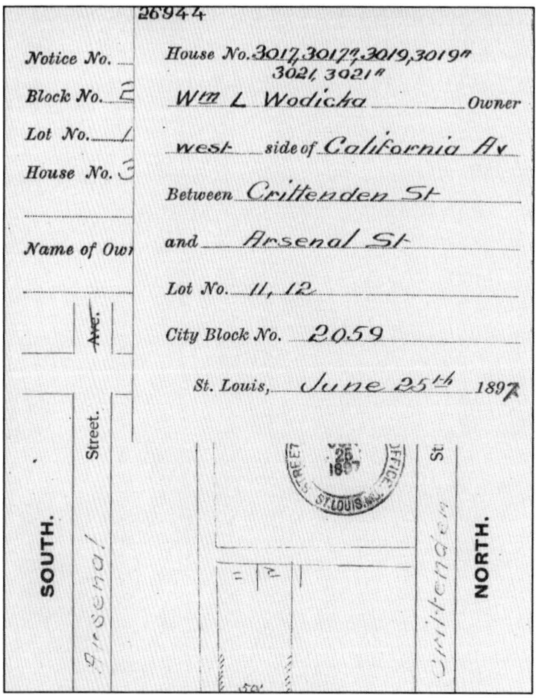

26944

Notice No.
Block No.
Lot No.
House No.
Name of Own

House No. 3017, 3017a, 3019, 3019a
3021, 3021a
Wm L Wodicka Owner
west side of California Av
Between Crittenden St
and Arsenal St
Lot No. 11, 12
City Block No. 2059
St. Louis, June 25th 1897

BUILDING PERMIT FOR WODICKA ROW. In 1897, William Wodicka, a butcher had these three-story brick dwellings built at a total cost of $5,000. Mr. Wodicka built them as rental properties. His residence was at 1849 South Twelfth Street. According to the 1900, census there was a total of five families living at these addresses. All of the residents were either born in Germany or were of German descent. Those immigrating had come to America in 1851, 1870, and 1890.

Site A17: St. Wenceslaus Catholic Church, 3014 Oregon. The parish was organized as the second Bohemian church in St. Louis in 1895. The church was dedicated to the national saint of Bohemia. The original church building was destroyed in the 1896 cyclone. In 1925, a permit was issued for the present structure, but it was not completed until around 1936. Emil Frei designed some of the stained glass in the church.

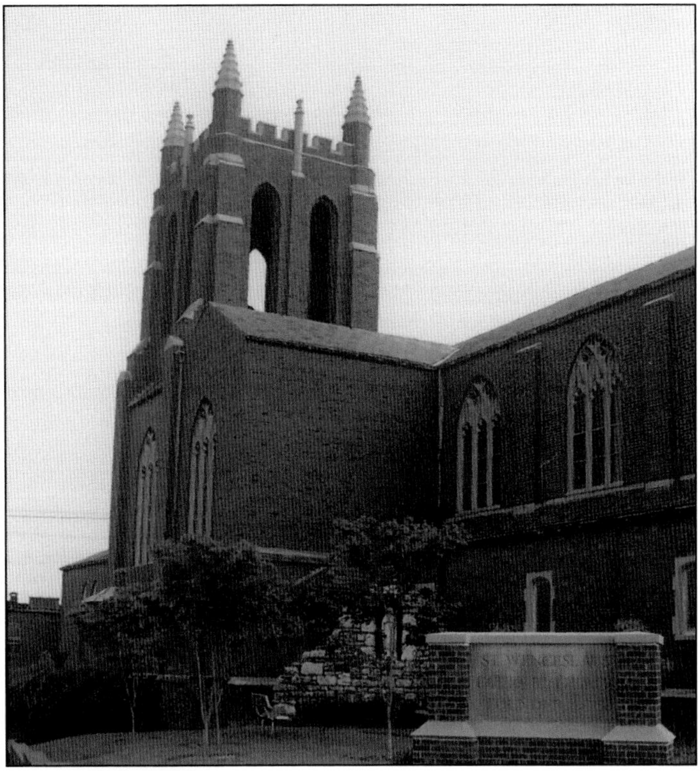

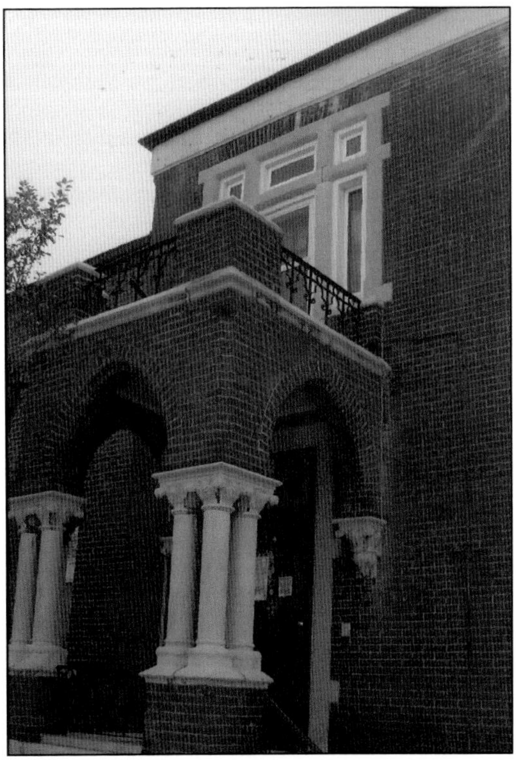

St. Wenceslaus rectory. The school started out in 1895 with 76 students and grew to 100 within a year. Now that there were four sisters instead of just two, they took up residence in the priest's former house, and he had to move to a rented residence. In 1897, Rev. Charles August Bleha was responsible for initiating the construction of a new residence for the priest. This rectory, still in use today, was completed in 1898.

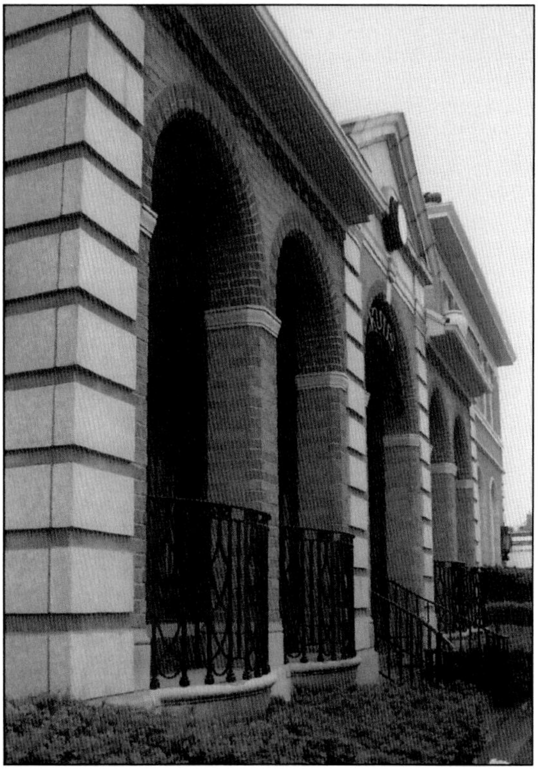

SITE A18: KUTIS FUNERAL HOME, 2906 GRAVOIS. Thomas F. Kutis was born in 1868 in St. Louis. After completing his education, he worked for 12 years in the cigar industry. By 1895, he opened his first cigar store at 210 North Sixth Street. In 1911, he set up as an undertaker at the same location. He married Mary M. Mares in 1901, and they had three children. In 1920, Thomas F. Kutis Jr. went to work in the family business.

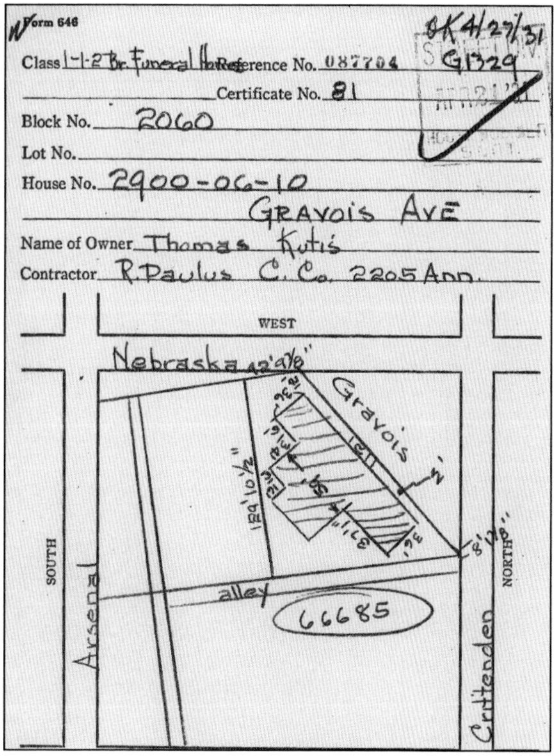

Form 646

OK 4/27/31
G1329

Class 1-1-2 Br. Funeral Home Reference No. 087704
Certificate No. 81
Block No. 2060
Lot No.
House No. 2900-06-10
GRAVOIS AVE
Name of Owner Thomas Kutis
Contractor R. Paulus C. Co. 2205 Ann.

BUILDING PERMIT ISSUED TO THOMAS F. KUTIS SR. Before the Kutis family moved their business to this location, they were located at 1006 Geyer. In the 1919 city directory, they were listed as Kutis & Mares Undertakers. The permit for the current building was issued in 1931. Thomas Sr. died in 1949, and Thomas Jr. became president. In 1977, Thomas Jr. passed away and Thomas III took over. He is still the president, and there are two more men of the same name in the Kutis family, Thomas IV and V.

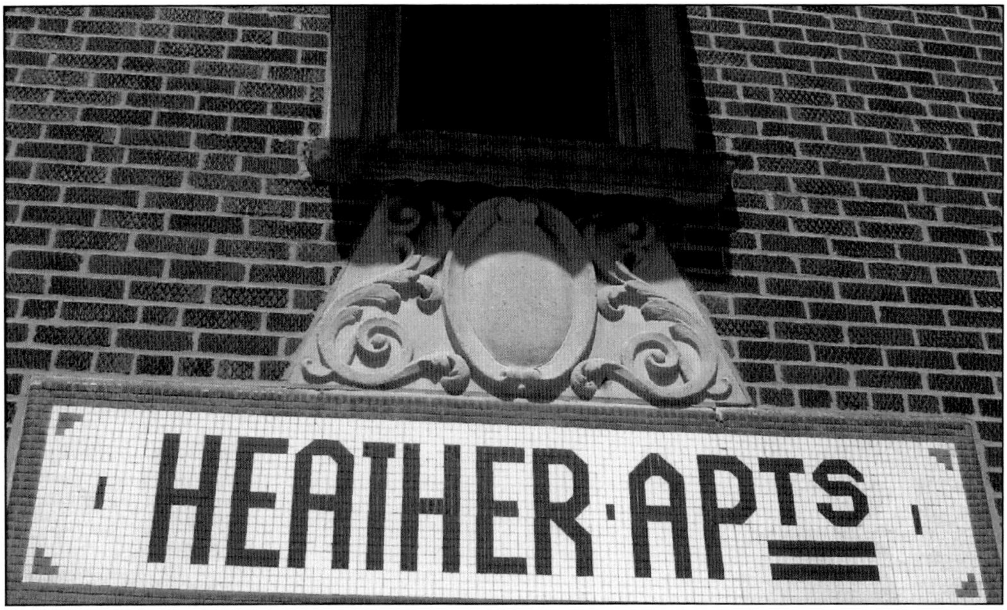

SITE A19: HEATHER APARTMENTS, 2749 PESTALOZZI. The Heather Apartments, consisting of 2747–2751 Pestalozzi, have housed many workers and their families. In 1930 and 1935 they were listed as Kressler Apartments, and in the early 1940s, they were known as Hediger Apartments, a name the buildings retained through 1980. In 1985, they were listed as vacant, and in 1990, there was only one resident listed. They were listed as simply apartments in 2000.

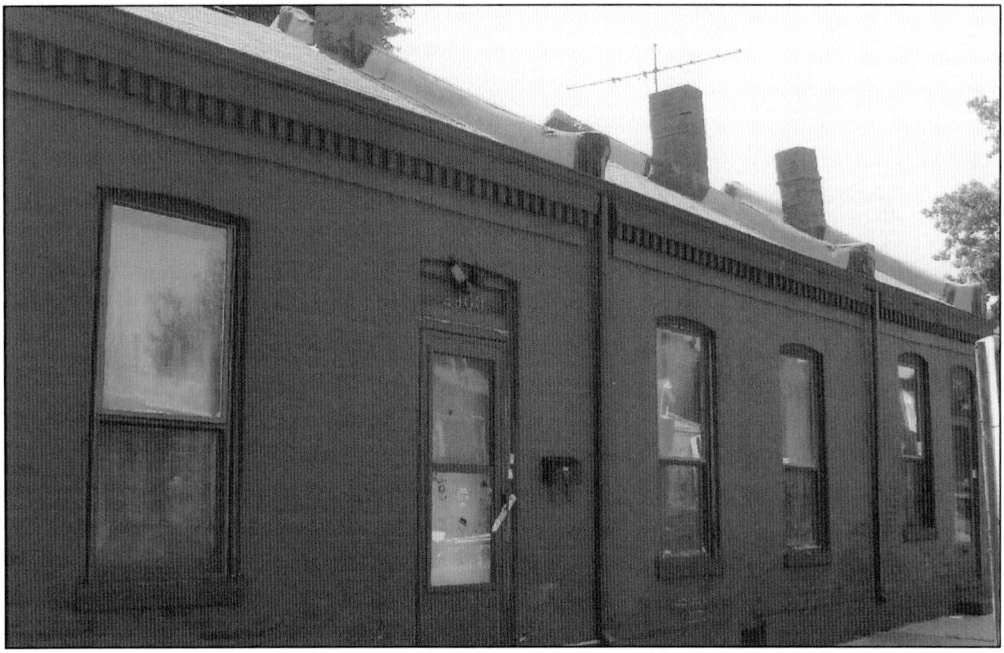

ACROSS THE STREET, 2900 AND 2904 CALIFORNIA. In 1900, this address was listed as 2900 California. There were three different families living here. Josh Grandwash was a tanner who came from Germany with his wife Maria in 1865. Catherine Hockenmeyer, a housekeeper, immigrated from Germany in 1860, and her son was a bricklayer. The other renters were a husband and wife.

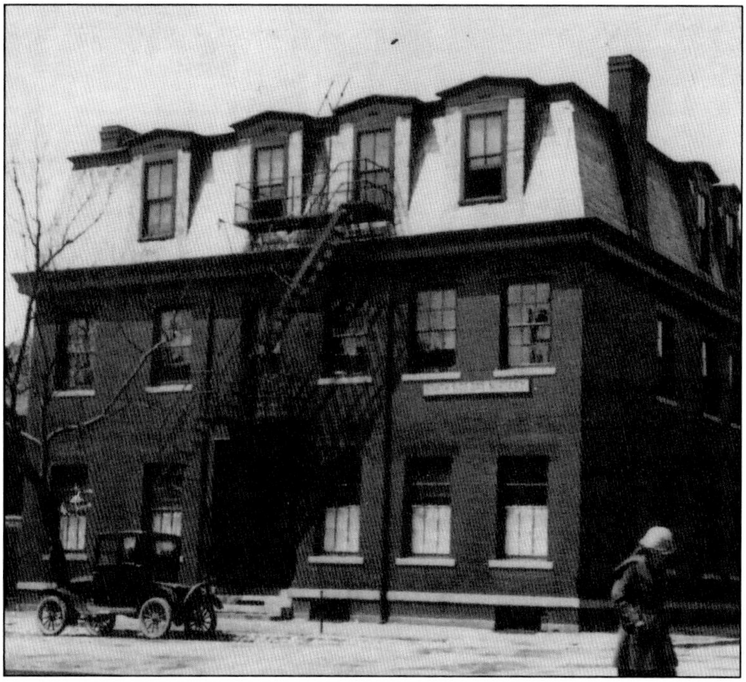

SITE A20: SOUTH SIDE DAY NURSERY, 2930 IOWA. This photograph shows the first permanent home for SSDN at 1621 Tenth Street on the corner of Julia Street. The nursery was founded in 1886, and their mission statement read, "The object of this Nursery shall be to prevent pauperism by assisting bread winners with young children on their hands, to earn an honest living." The nursery operated at the Tenth Street location until 1951.

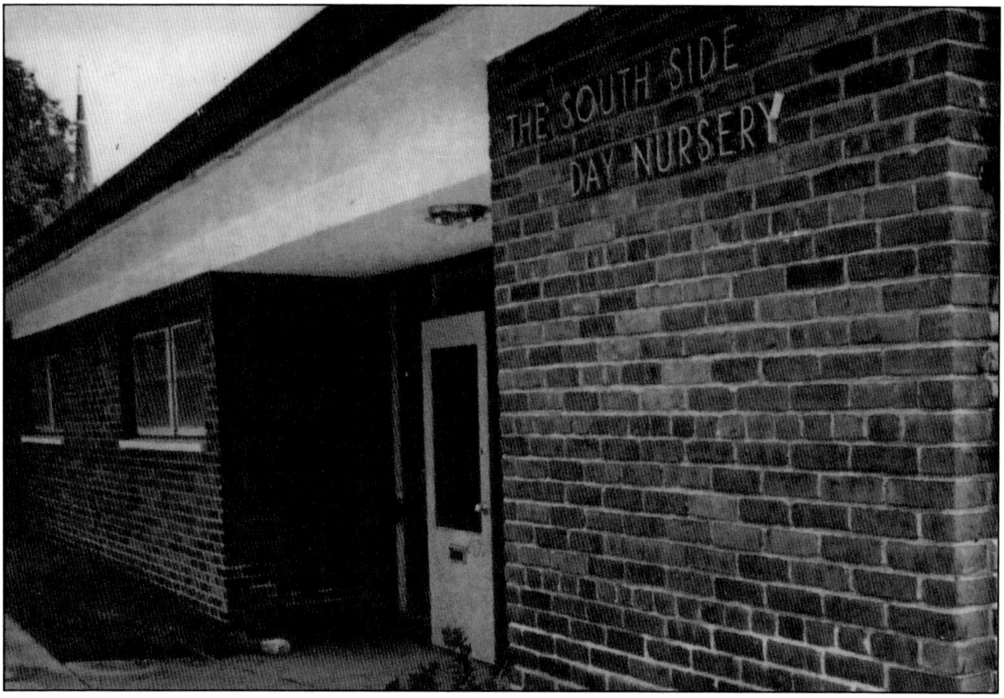

SOUTH SIDE DAY NURSERY TODAY. Started by 15 women, the nursery elected the first man to its board in 1910. During the Depression in 1932, times were hard, and nursery employees' salaries had to be cut by 10% as the nursery was providing relief work among the children's families. In 1938, student barbers gave the children haircuts. In December 1953, this new facility opened at 2930 Iowa, and in 1956, the nursery became a member of United Fund-United Way.

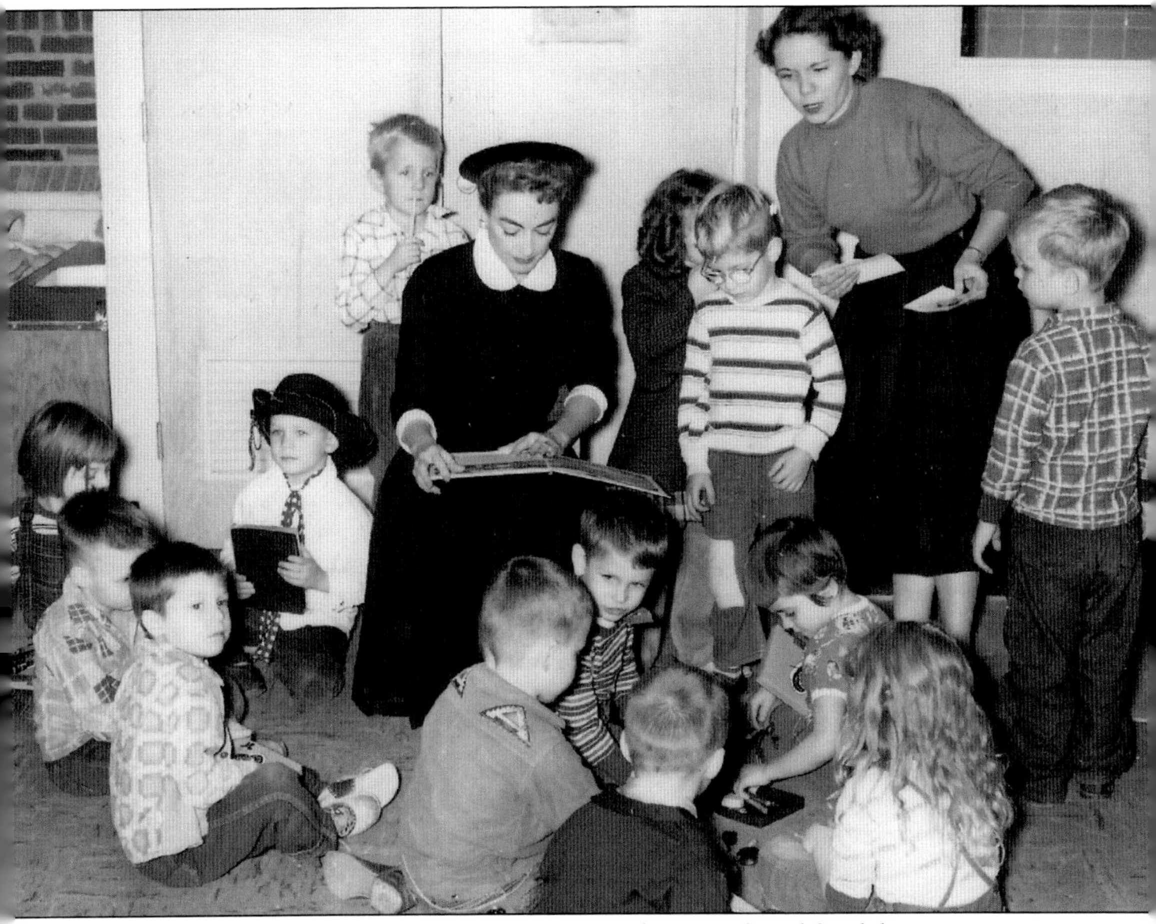

JOAN CRAWFORD VISITS THE SOUTH SIDE DAY NURSERY. The SSDN board faced discouragement in 1952 due to financial problems and the incomplete state of the new building. However, the Variety Club International was seeking a charity project to sponsor in St. Louis, and in January 1953, the board received a letter saying the Variety Club would help with the financing to complete the building. In 1954, the board met in the new building and on May 4, the structure was formally dedicated. On November 2, 1955, the St. Louis Variety Club arranged a visit by movie star Joan Crawford, who spent time with the children and gave out boxes of candy. After her visit, she sent a personal check for $100. The nursery still operates at this location, with offices at 2716 Pestalozzi, and is headed by CEO Marlene Levine. In 2002, South Side Outlet Store opened for business at 2720 Cherokee as part of SSDN's Business Incubator Project. Today there are more retail stores and office space across the street, helping to provide for the growing needs of the community.

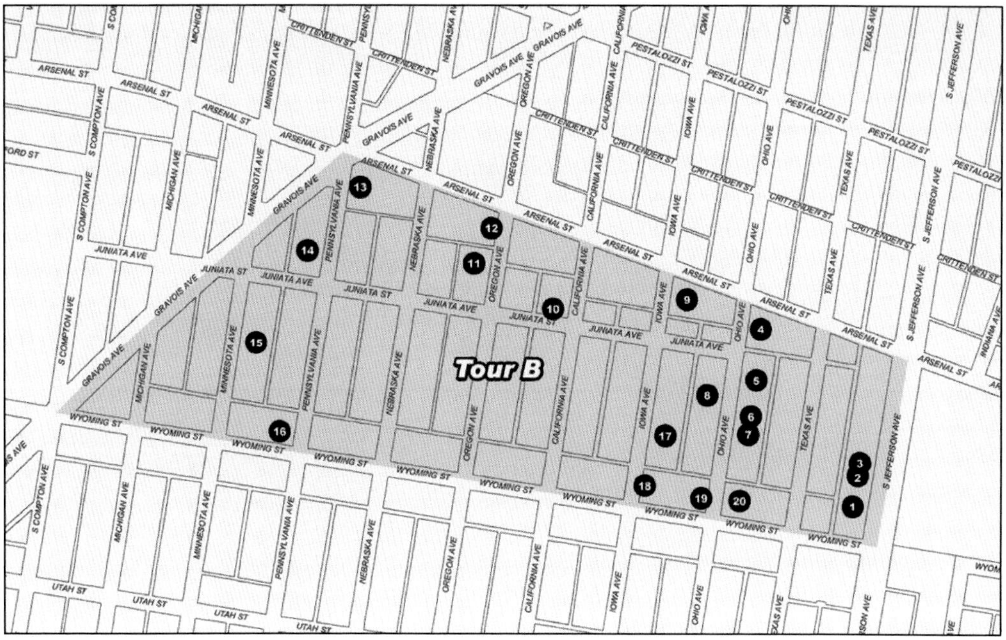
Tour B
ARSENAL ST
JUNIATA AVE
JUNIATA ST
WYOMING ST
UTAH ST
CRITTENDEN ST
PESTALOZZI ST
GRAVOIS AVE
S COMPTON AVE
MICHIGAN AVE
MINNESOTA AVE
PENNSYLVANIA AVE
NEBRASKA AVE
OREGON AVE
CALIFORNIA AVE
IOWA AVE
OHIO AVE
TEXAS AVE
S JEFFERSON AVE
1
2
3
4
5
6
7
8
9
10
11
12
13
14
15
16
17
18
19
20

MAP OF TOUR B.

Two

TOUR B

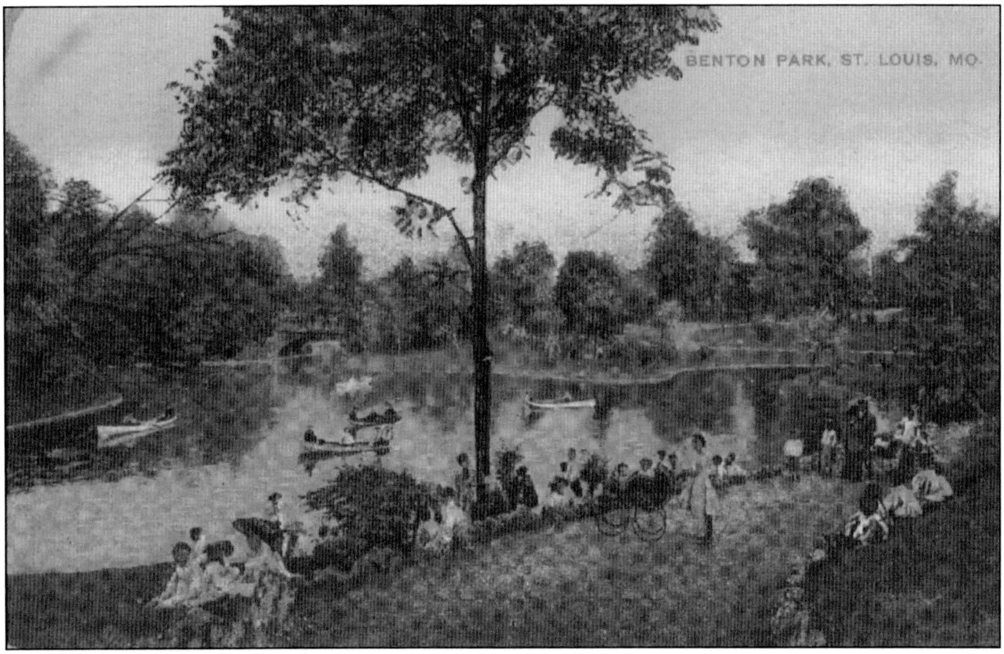

BENTON PARK. Benton Park stands across the street from 3155 South Jefferson where Tour B begins. This postcard was mailed to Mrs. W.J. Mills in Chicago, Illinois. Postmarked June 16, 1908, it has a one cent Ben Franklin stamp on it. Benton Park, named for Senator Thomas Hart Benton, became a city park in 1866; the area had been a cemetery from 1840 to 1865, but the bodies were exhumed and reburied on Arsenal Island. A monument dedicated to Friedrich Hecker, a leader of the St. Louis German community and colonel in the Union Army, sits on the hill. His first enlistment with the Union Army was as a private at age 50. Hecker died in 1881 and was buried in Illinois. 15,000 people attended the unveiling of the monument in 1882. There are two years inscribed on opposite sides: 1848 and 1861. The first is the year Hecker fled from the German Revolution as a political refugee, and the second is the year he joined the Union Army. The monument was designed by Ernst C. Jansen.

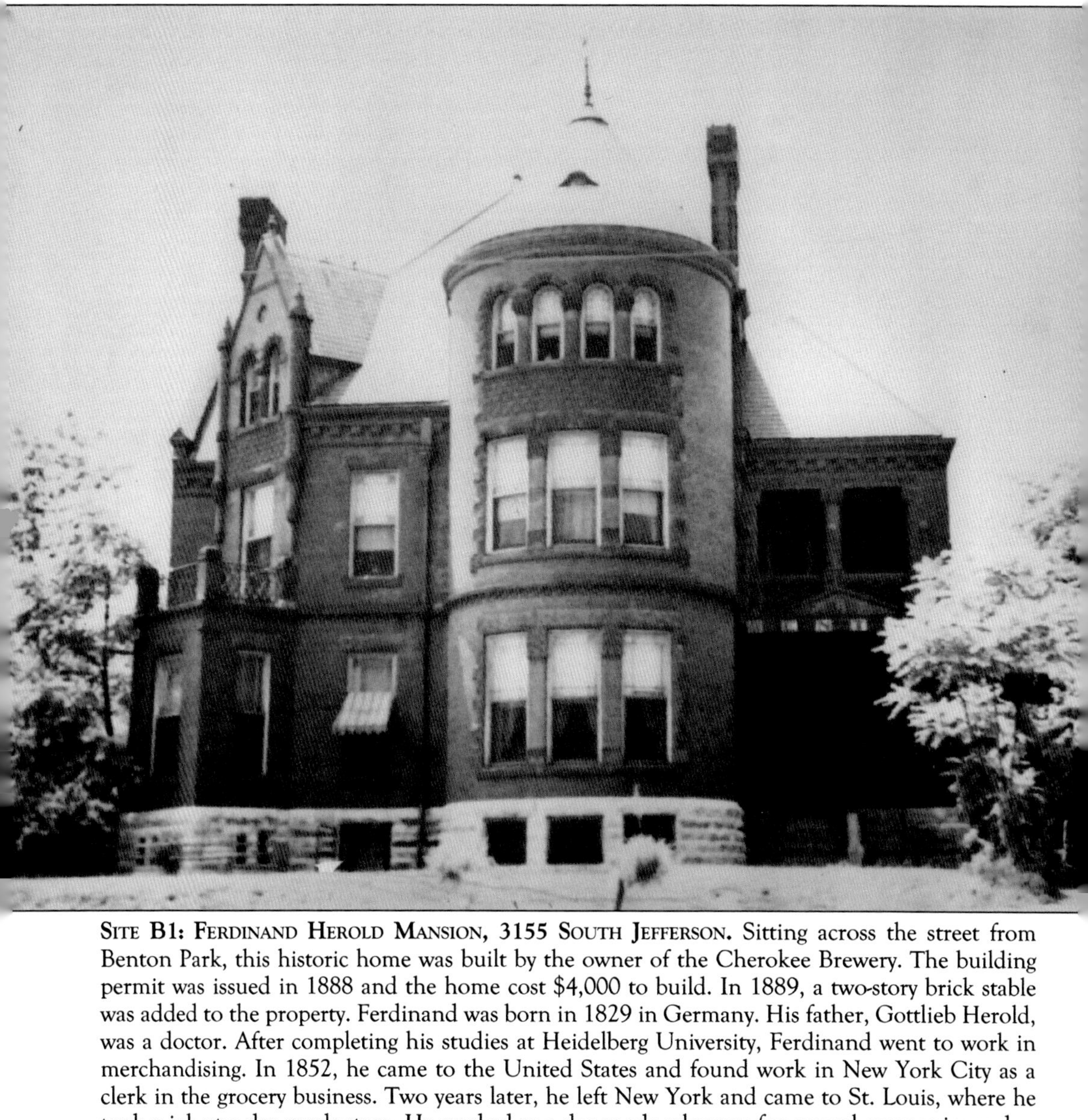

Site B1: Ferdinand Herold Mansion, 3155 South Jefferson. Sitting across the street from Benton Park, this historic home was built by the owner of the Cherokee Brewery. The building permit was issued in 1888 and the home cost $4,000 to build. In 1889, a two-story brick stable was added to the property. Ferdinand was born in 1829 in Germany. His father, Gottlieb Herold, was a doctor. After completing his studies at Heidelberg University, Ferdinand went to work in merchandising. In 1852, he came to the United States and found work in New York City as a clerk in the grocery business. Two years later, he left New York and came to St. Louis, where he took a job at a dry goods store. He worked as a dry goods salesman for several companies and as an assistant secretary for St. Louis Mutual Fire & Marine Insurance Company. Later he became a partner in a business in Mascoutah, Illinois, where he lived for ten years. While in Mascoutah, he also served as postmaster and owned and operated a soda factory. In 1866, he went to Europe, and when he returned, he bought the Meier Brothers' business, also known as the Cherokee Brewing Company. Before the brewery company was incorporated, it was known as Herold & Loebs. Eventually, Herold bought Robert Loeb's interest in the brewery and brought in his sons, Theodore and Robert, to help him manage the business. Mr. Herold died in the house on May 2, 1911, at the age of 83.

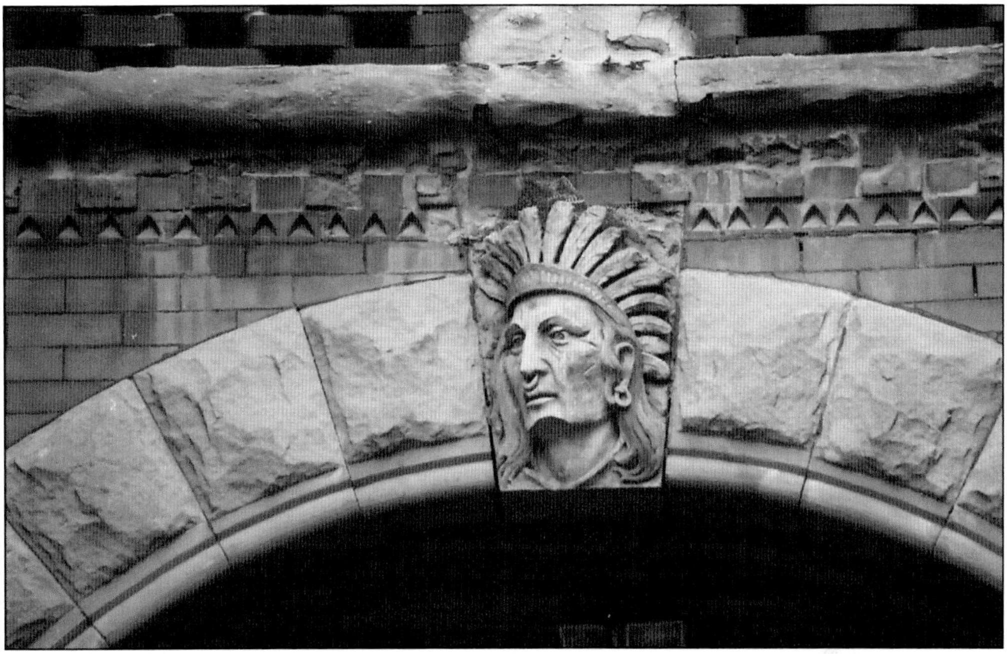

Herold Mansion Entrance. This head of a Cherokee Indian chief graces the arch at the front entrance of the mansion. Besides building his home in 1888, Mr. Herold also had Iowa Machine Works construct a freight and passenger steamboat he named *The Cherokee*. Mr. Herold was very fond of the Cherokee name: besides the brewery and the steamboat, he also owned Cherokee Tobacco and his son Theodore was called Cherokee at Christian Brothers Academy.

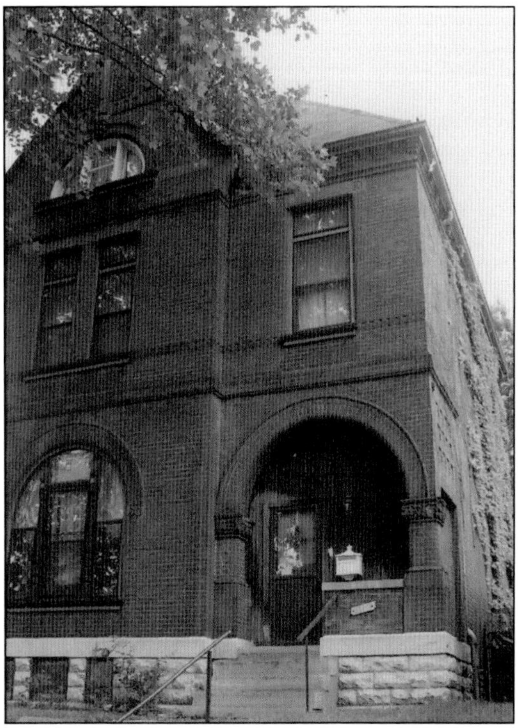

Theodore Herold Mansion, 3167 South Jefferson. In 1887, it cost $6,000 to build this house at what was known as 3159 until 1908. Theodore was the son of Ferdinand and Sophia Herold. At one time, he was employed by the Budweiser and Wine Company, and later became the secretary of the Cherokee Brewing Company. In 1890, he formed the Home Brewing Company and served as president until 1895. He then organized and became president of the Consumers' Brewing Company.

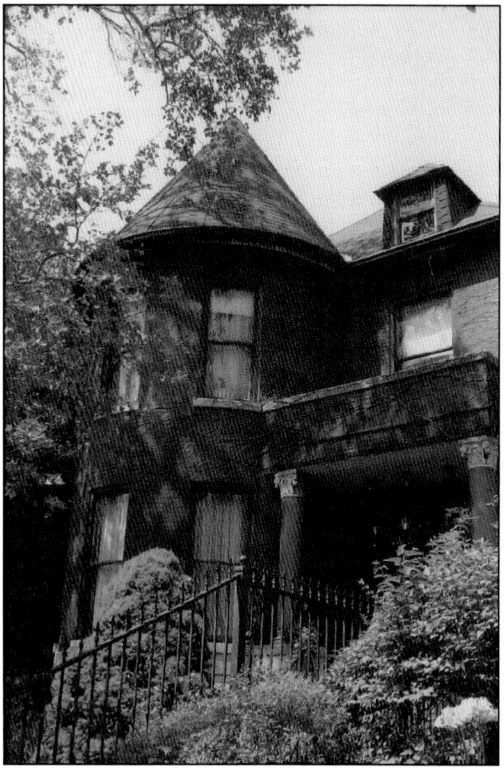

SITE B2: NEUDORF HOME, 3147 SOUTH JEFFERSON. D. I. Neudorf was a notary and an investigator of land titles. Though born in Missouri, Neudorf's father was a German immigrant. At the time of the 1900 census, he was 36 years old. The other residents of the house in 1900 were his wife, Minnie, and their daughter Meidy. Mrs. Neudorf's mother also resided here, as did a boarder and a servant.

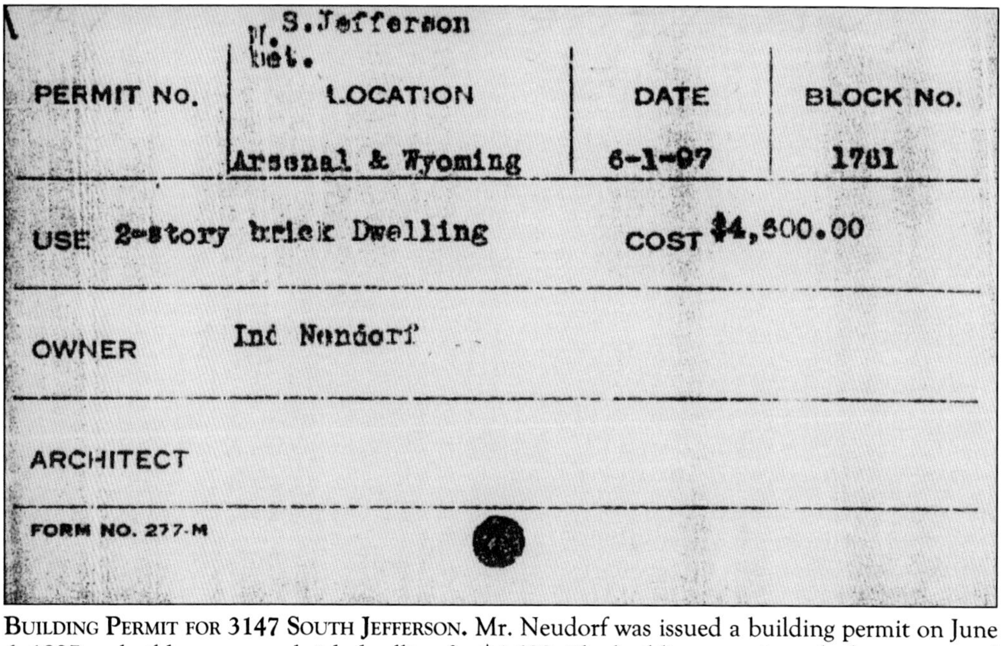

PERMIT No.	LOCATION	DATE	BLOCK No.
	S.Jefferson W. bet. Arsenal & Wyoming	6-1-97	1781

USE 2-story brick Dwelling COST $4,600.00

OWNER Ind Nendorf

ARCHITECT

FORM NO. 277-M

BUILDING PERMIT FOR 3147 SOUTH JEFFERSON. Mr. Neudorf was issued a building permit on June 6, 1897, to build a two-story brick dwelling for $4,600. The building permit cards that were typed for structures built before 1900 for the city of St. Louis did not list a number address, as is the case on this permit. However, the permits that were issued by the St. Louis Street Commission's Office did list the full address, but not the cost.

Site B3: Schollmeyer House, 3143 South Jefferson. Christian Schollmeyer built this house before 1886, but was issued a building permit that year to alter the brick dwelling at a cost of $4,400. Mr. Schollmeyer came to America from Germany in 1858. In 1900, he and his wife Barbara had been married 30 years. They had five children, but only two were still living at the time of the 1900 census. Their son, Christian Jr., who was 20 and still in school, resided with them.

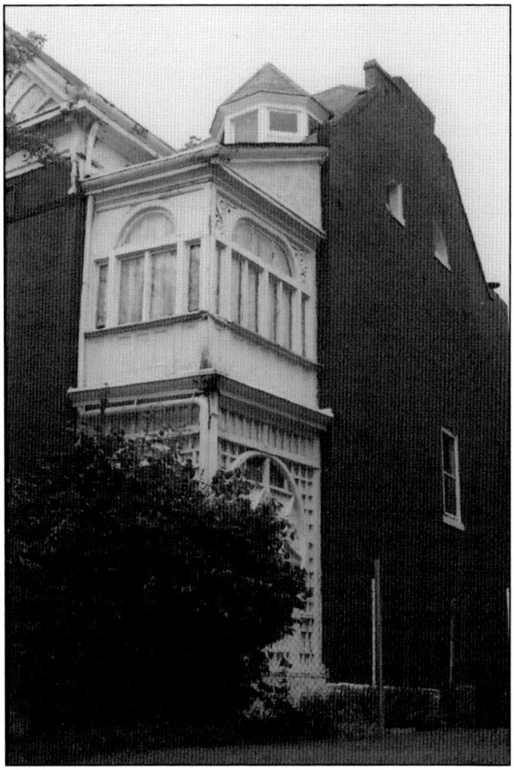

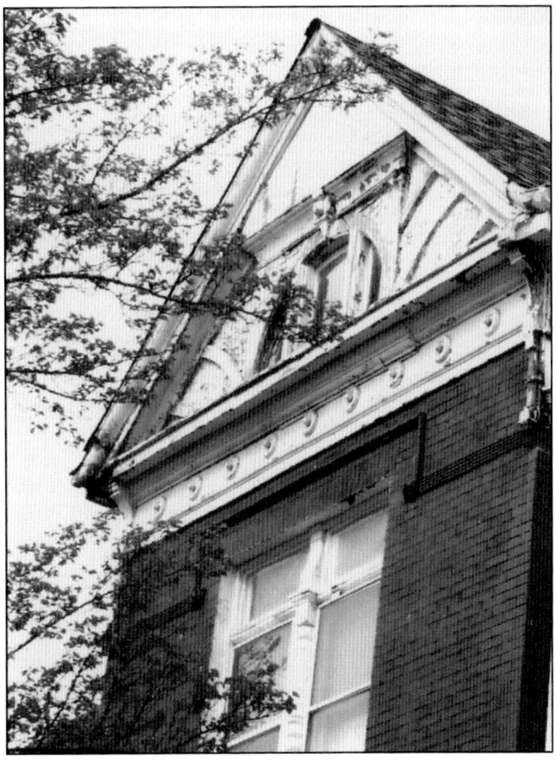

Businessman Schollmeyer. Christian Schollmeyer was a partner in the Hassendeubel Brothers Company with Gustave and Phillip Hassendeubel. Their company dealt in wholesale groceries. Phillip Hassendeubel was a neighbor at 2706 Wyoming. Phillip Hassendeubel and Christian Schollmeyer had several things in common they were near the same age: Christian was born in 1848 and Phillip in 1850. They both immigrated to the United States from Germany in the 1850s.

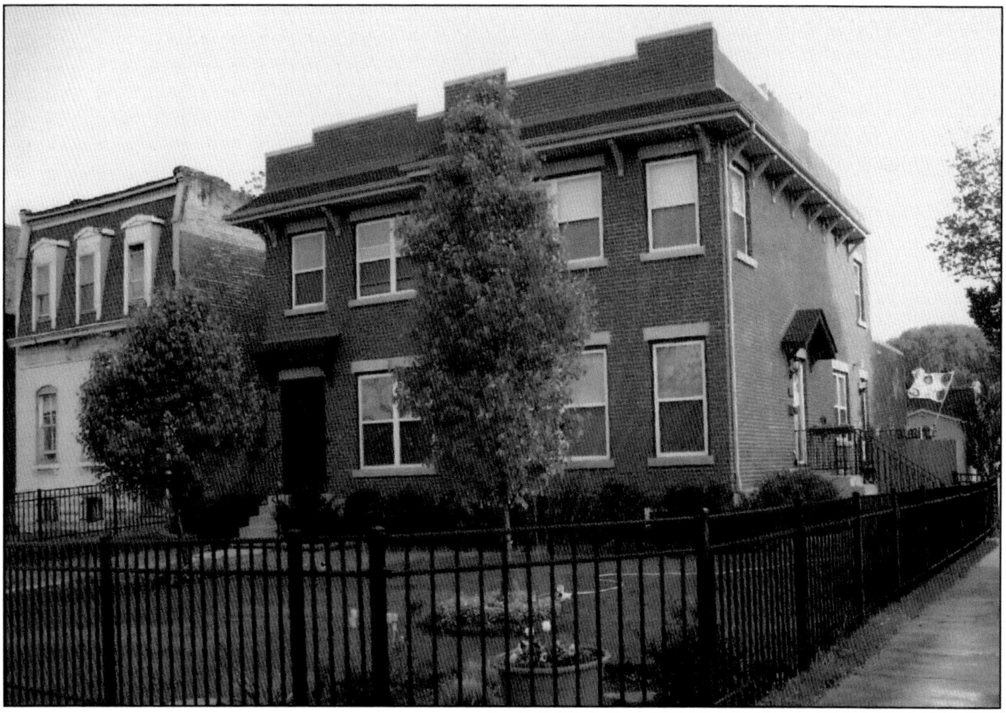

Site B4: New Townhouses at Arsenal and Ohio. These townhouses on the southeast corner of Arsenal and Ohio were completed in 2002; the addresses are 2646 Arsenal and 3100 Ohio. The construction of these new homes by Pyramid Construction Company was part of a long-range plan to revitalize the neighborhood. The revitalization continues in full force as Aldermen Ken Ortmann and Craig Schmid, CDA, the Benton Park West Housing Corporation, and private developers work together to bring new life to this historic neighborhood.

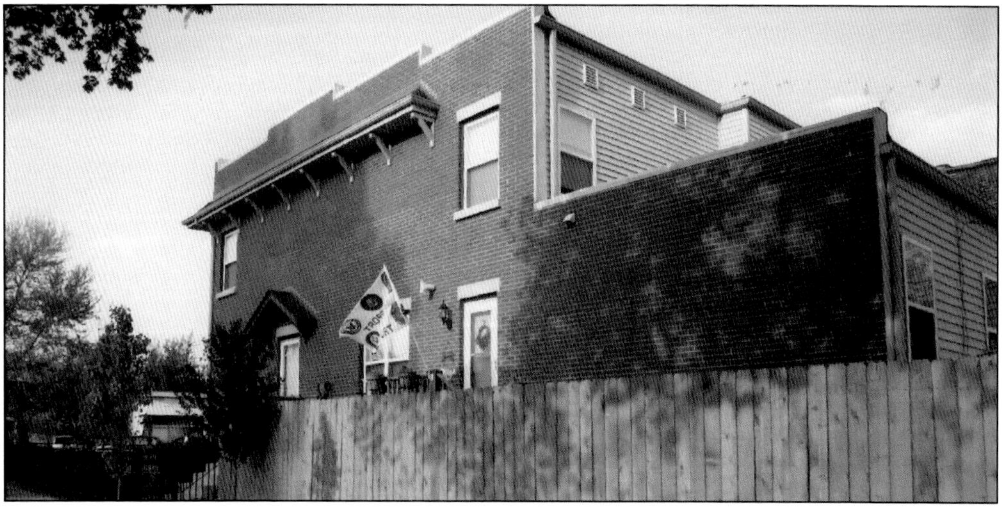

Frank H. Pedde Grocery Store. Prior to the new construction at Arsenal and Ohio, Mr. Pedde opened a grocery here around 1910. He was born in St. Louis in 1882 and was educated in parochial schools. His first job was with Middendorf Brothers Grocery Company. He worked there for at least 12 years before going into business for himself. A south St. Louis business journal commented that he had a nice store, stocked with basic and fancy foods.

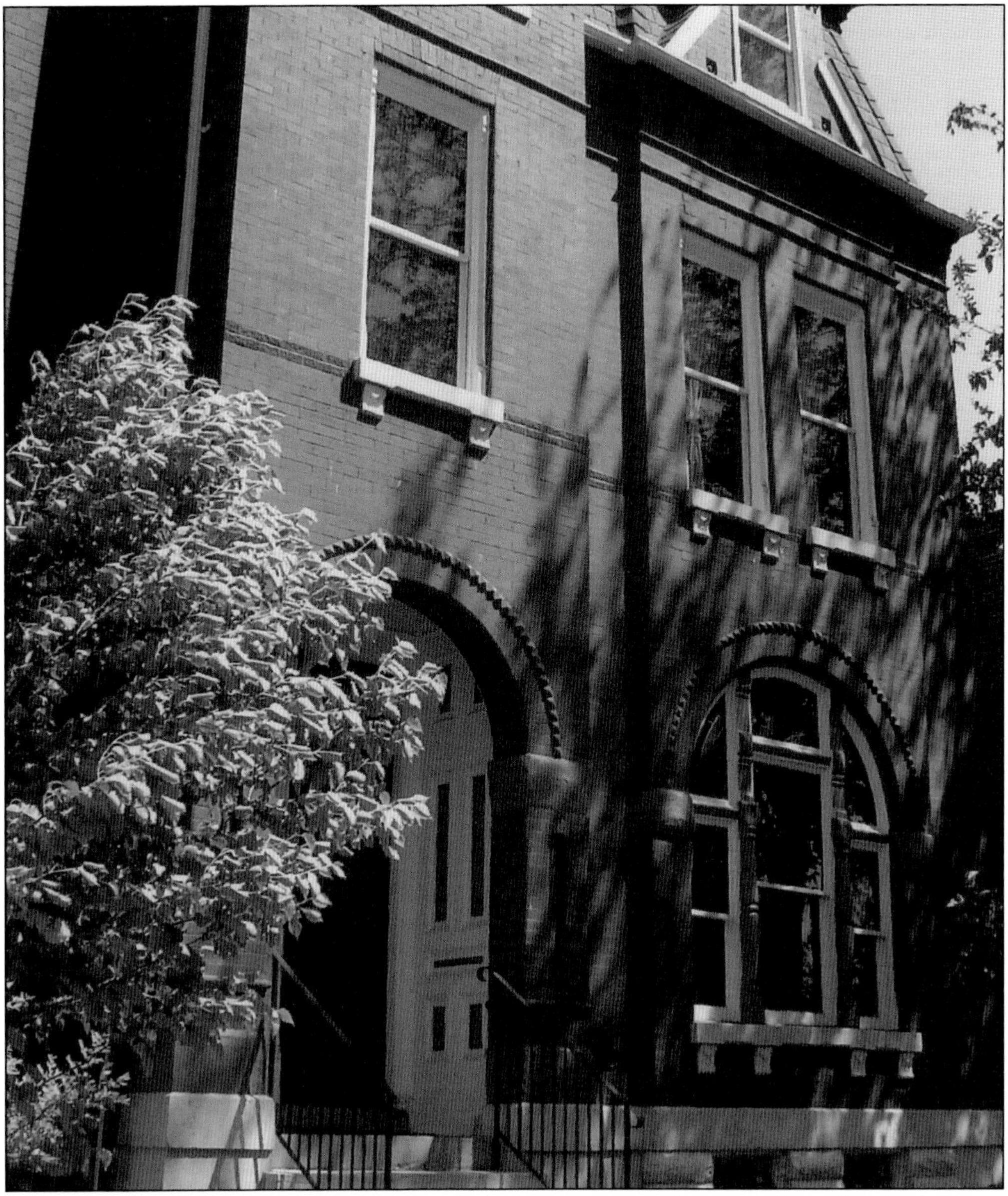

SITE B5: GABEL HOUSE, 3128 OHIO. Jacob Gabel was a carpenter who married Martha, the daughter of Gottlieb Eyermann. The Eyermann home was close by at 2906 Iowa. In 1882, Mr. Eyermann purchased the two lots that make up this address directly from the executor of the Delano Estate, after whom this addition is named. When Gottlieb Sr. died in 1888, the lots were first inherited by Gottlieb Jr. In 1891, he signed them over to his sister Martha Gabel, and in 1892, the Gabels built their house. After Jacob's death, Martha inherited the house, and in 1939, she added her sister Pauline Argurieo to the title as a joint tenant. By 1946, Martha had passed away and the title was transferred to Harry Eggers; the house had been in the same family for 54 years. The title would change hands several times before it was bought in 1982 with plans by the new owners to fully rehabilitate the house. The restoration was never completed, and the house was left in a gutted state until LRA took it over in 2001 and sold it to Millennium Restoration & Development, Inc. in 2002. In 2003, the rehab was completed and sold to a private owner.

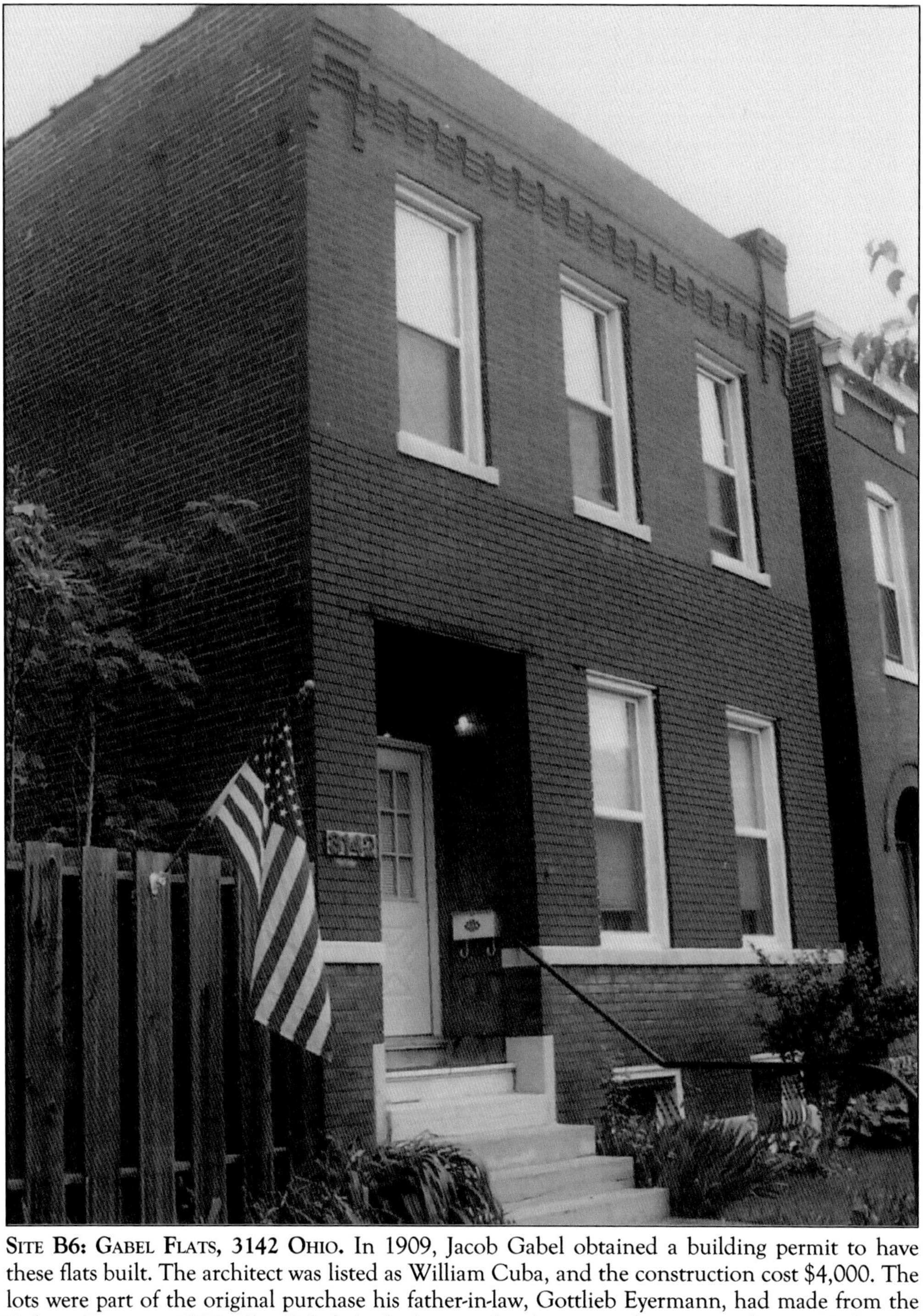

Site B6: Gabel Flats, 3142 Ohio. In 1909, Jacob Gabel obtained a building permit to have these flats built. The architect was listed as William Cuba, and the construction cost $4,000. The lots were part of the original purchase his father-in-law, Gottlieb Eyermann, had made from the Delano Estate in 1882. The Gabels built this two-family as rental property; they resided a few doors down at 3128 Ohio. The architect, William Cuba, was well known in the neighborhood as he had several real estate investments including 3007, 3009, 3011, 3015, and 3017 Ohio and 3304 Texas. Mr. Cuba had established his own business in 1905.

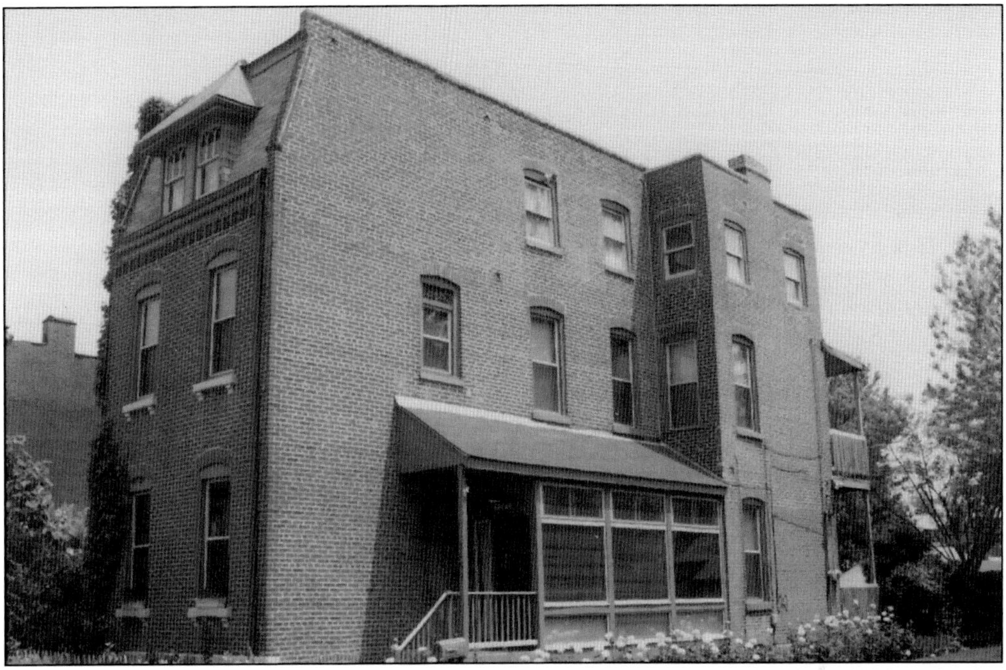

SITE B7: MERKEL HOUSE/GRAVENHORST HOME. On October 23, 1886, Richard Merkel bought this house for $3,350. Richard and Elizabeth Merkel had two young daughters, Emily and Pauline, and four grown sons who all resided with them. Charles H. Merkel was a partner in a bookbinding business. His brothers, Anton, Frances, and August, were also bookbinders, and in 1909, they formed their own company. The Merkel Brothers' business offices were located at 215 Locust. The home is now owned by the author and her husband, who reside here.

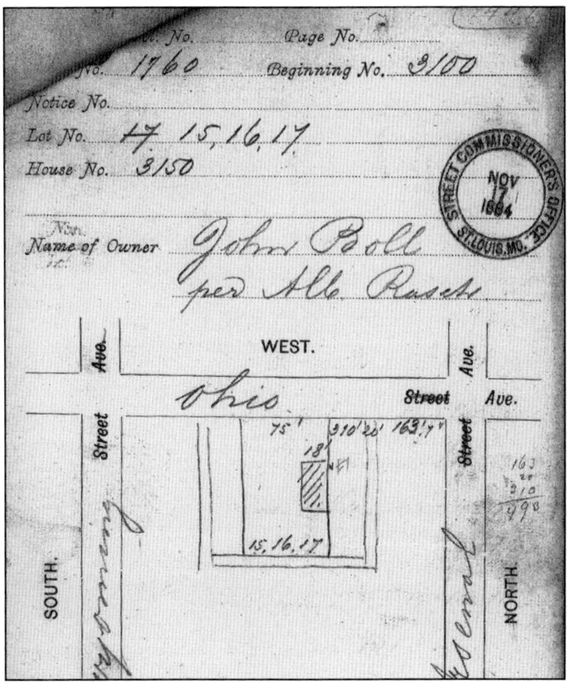

BUILDING PERMIT FOR 3150 OHIO. The building permit for the house was issued on November 17, 1884, to the owner, a jailor named John Boll, who was never listed at this address. Richard Merkel appeared at this address in 1888. In the 1890 Civil War Census of Union Veterans, Richard Merkel was listed as having served for one year and his disability read, "blind in right eye." Richard died on January 3, 1892. The house remained in the Merkel family until 1929.

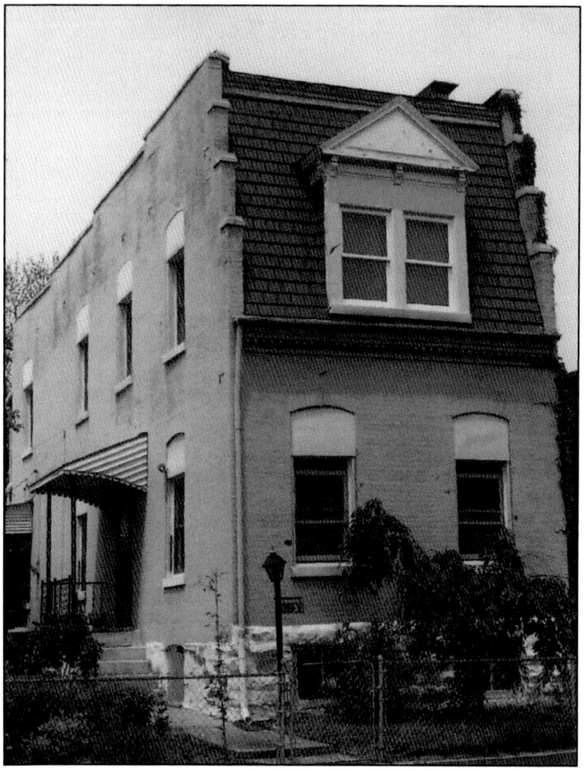

SITE B8: ENGER DAIRY HOUSE, 3153 OHIO. According to the computer records at the tax assessor's office at city hall, this house was built in 1883. The Enger family had another dairy in the area at 3234 California. After the Engers, the Restige family took over the dairy, followed by the Kramer family. Cow sheds on the 3100 block of Ohio were a common sight. This location continued to be a part of the dairy industry until the early 1940s.

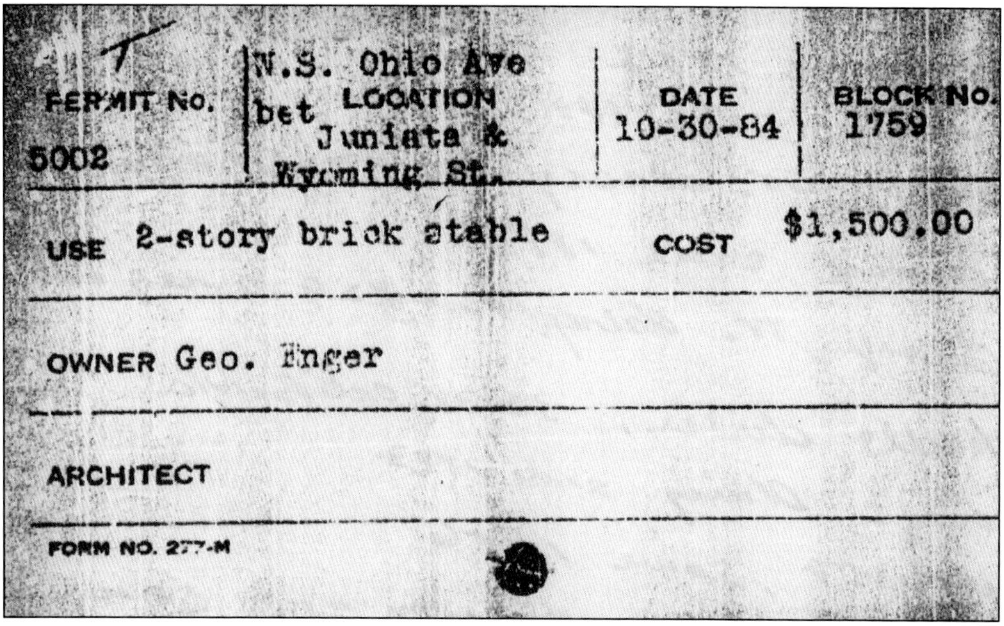

PERMIT No. 5002
LOCATION N.S. Ohio Ave bet Juniata & Wyoming St.
DATE 10-30-84
BLOCK No. 1759
USE 2-story brick stable
COST $1,500.00
OWNER Geo. Enger
ARCHITECT
FORM NO. 277-M

BUILDING PERMIT FOR THE DAIRY STABLES. This building permit for the dairy stables was issued to George Enger, though Charles Enger was the one who actually resided at 3153 Ohio. George lived at 3234 California. The dairy was called Enger & Son. On the same block, across the street and a few doors down from the dairy, Dr. Amalie Napier lived at 3158 Ohio. That house was built in 1889, and the doctor appears there in the 1916 city directory.

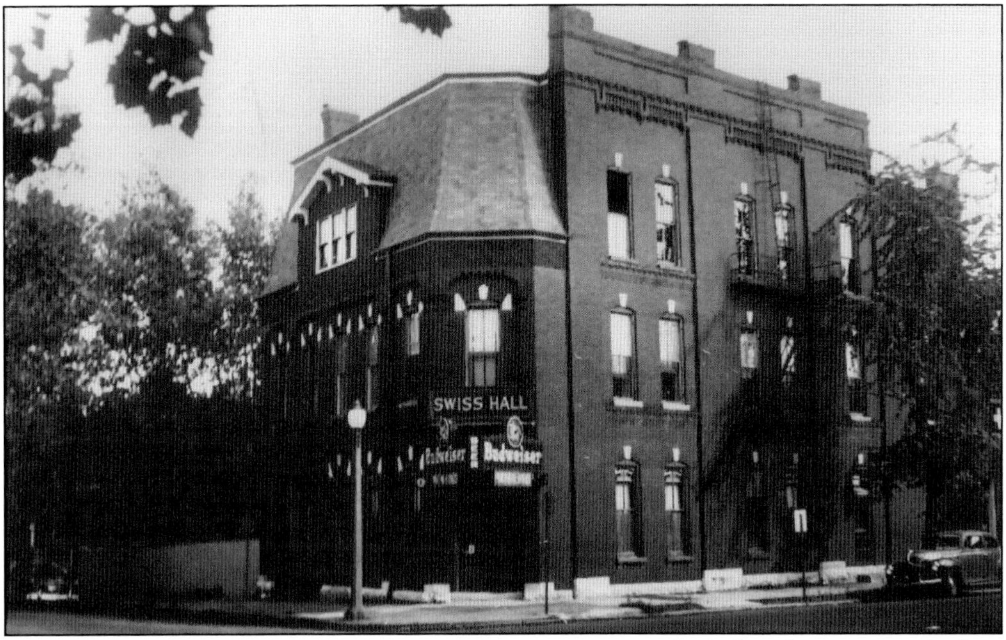

SITE B9: SWISS HALL AND BEER TAVERN, 2724–2726 ARSENAL. The hall and tavern were built in 1888 by Conrad Ebner. The Swiss Society bought the hall in 1910, along with two vacant lots to the east of the building. They constructed a new *turnverein*, or gymnastics club, in 1913 at the location then known as 3110 Iowa. In 1945, a bowling alley was added. The building was torn down in 1960, and is currently a parking lot for the Salvation Army, who built their structure at 2740 Arsenal.

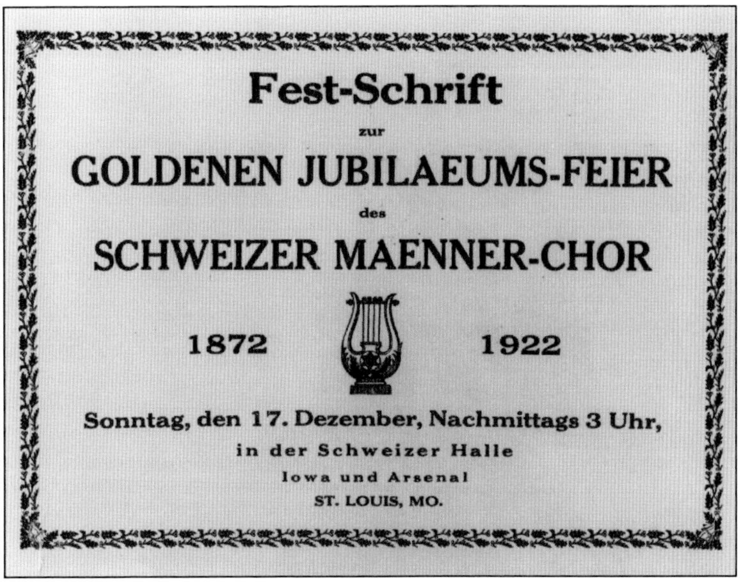

Fest-Schrift

zur

GOLDENEN JUBILAEUMS-FEIER

des

SCHWEIZER MAENNER-CHOR

1872 **1922**

Sonntag, den 17. Dezember, Nachmittags 3 Uhr,

in der Schweizer Halle

Iowa und Arsenal

ST. LOUIS, MO.

SWISS SOCIETY GOLDEN ANNIVERSARY CELEBRATION. This program was an elaborate publication with several pages of advertisement, many for neighborhood companies. One such advertiser, Witt Brothers Livery & Undertaking at 2929 South Jefferson (Tour A), stated in their ad, "Free use of Chapel and Rest Room." Schumacher Undertaking's ad read, "The Schumacher Funeral Home at Your Service without Cost." A jeweler, Fred Halter, also advertised himself as an optometrist.

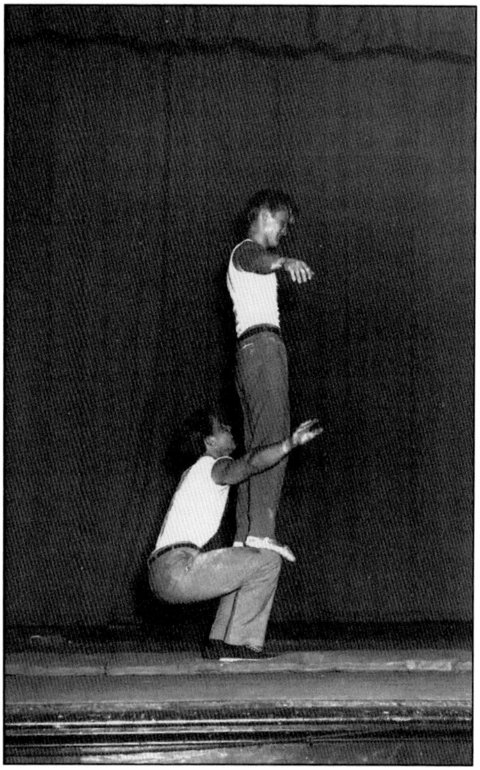

SWISS TURNER SOCIETY POSTCARD. St. Louis had many German-Swiss Turner Societies, a group which had chapters around the country. The society was a place to gather socially and athletically. During the Civil War, society members in St. Louis were trained secretly in case the war broke out locally. The Germans were supporters of the Union Army. When Captain Nathaniel Lyon was allowed to enlist volunteers in St. Louis, more than 80% of the four infantry regiments he formed were of German descent.

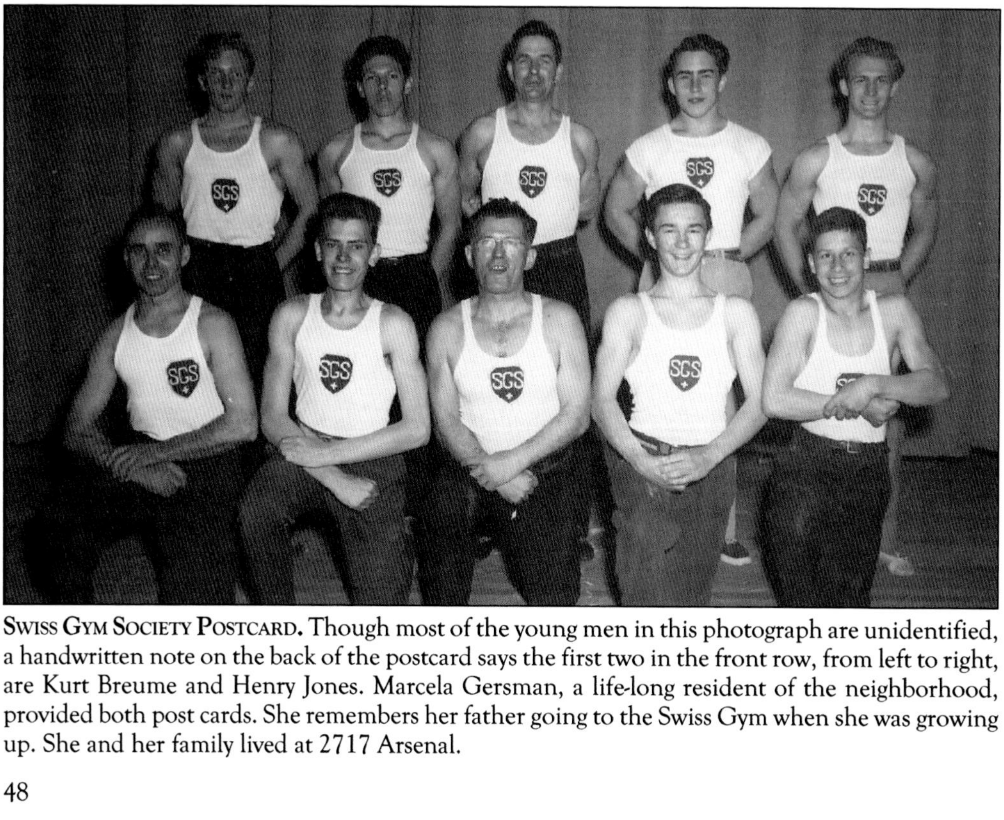

SWISS GYM SOCIETY POSTCARD. Though most of the young men in this photograph are unidentified, a handwritten note on the back of the postcard says the first two in the front row, from left to right, are Kurt Breume and Henry Jones. Marcela Gersman, a life-long resident of the neighborhood, provided both post cards. She remembers her father going to the Swiss Gym when she was growing up. She and her family lived at 2717 Arsenal.

MRS. HASSENPFLUG'S CONFIRMATION CERTIFICATE. This certificate was found at 3120 Iowa. In the 1910 census, the Hassenpflug family was listed at 3120A. Mr. Hassenpflug, Missouri-born with German immigrant parents, was 45 and shoed horses for a living. His wife, Helen, was born in Germany and came to America in 1890. They had two children, Christian Jr. and Helen, who lived at this address all her life. The West family bought the property in 2001 and is the second owner in 98 years.

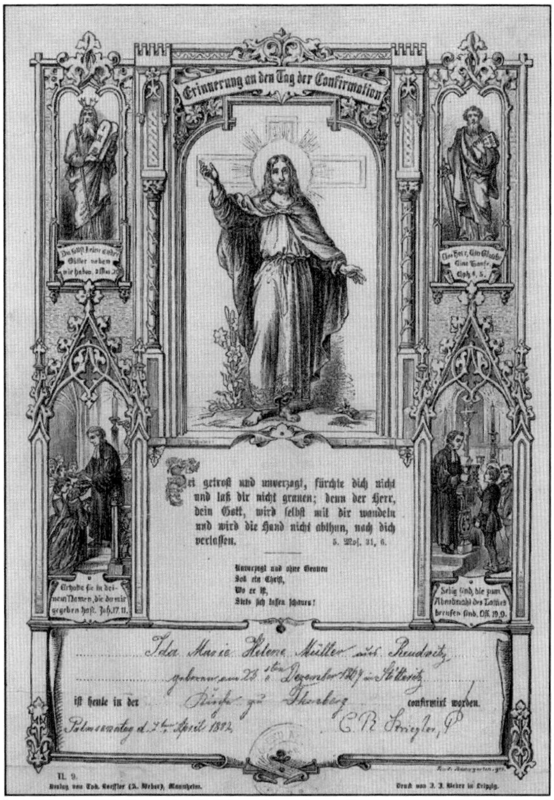

Erinnerung an den Tag der Confirmation

Sei getrost und unverzagt, fürchte dich nicht und laß dir nicht grauen; denn der Herr, dein Gott, wird selbst mit dir wandeln und wird die Hand nicht abthun, noch dich verlassen. 5. Mos. 31, 6.

Unverzagt und ohne Grauen
Soll ein Christ,
Wo er ist,
Stets sich lassen schauen!

Ida Marie Helene Müller aus Reudnitz

ist heute in der … confirmirt worden.

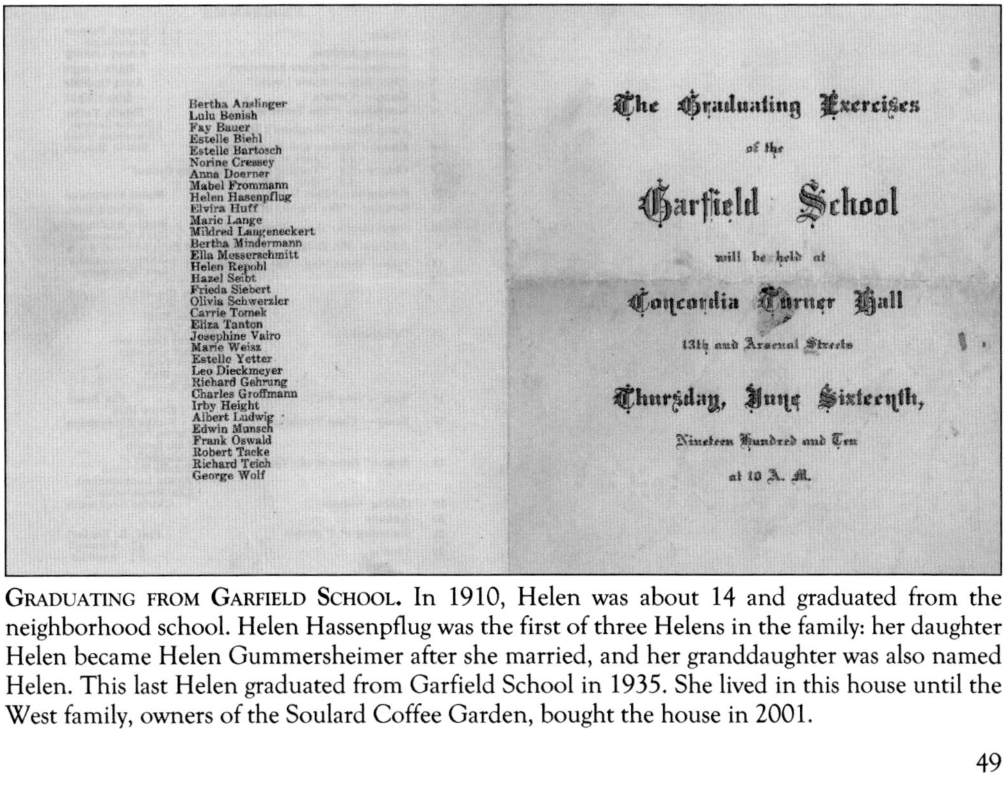

Bertha Anslinger
Lulu Benish
Fay Bauer
Estelle Biehl
Estelle Bartosch
Norine Cressey
Anna Doerner
Mabel Frommann
Helen Hasenpflug
Elvira Huff
Marie Lange
Mildred Langeneckert
Bertha Mindermann
Ella Messerschmitt
Helen Repohl
Hazel Seibt
Frieda Siebert
Olivia Schwerzler
Carrie Tomek
Eliza Tanton
Josephine Vairo
Marie Weisz
Estelle Yetter
Leo Dieckmeyer
Richard Gehrung
Charles Groffmann
Irby Height
Albert Ludwig
Edwin Munsch
Frank Oswald
Robert Tacke
Richard Teich
George Wolf

The Graduating Exercises
of the
Garfield School
will be held at
Concordia Turner Hall
13th and Arsenal Streets
Thursday, June Sixteenth,
Nineteen Hundred and Ten
at 10 A. M.

GRADUATING FROM GARFIELD SCHOOL. In 1910, Helen was about 14 and graduated from the neighborhood school. Helen Hassenpflug was the first of three Helens in the family: her daughter Helen became Helen Gummersheimer after she married, and her granddaughter was also named Helen. This last Helen graduated from Garfield School in 1935. She lived in this house until the West family, owners of the Soulard Coffee Garden, bought the house in 2001.

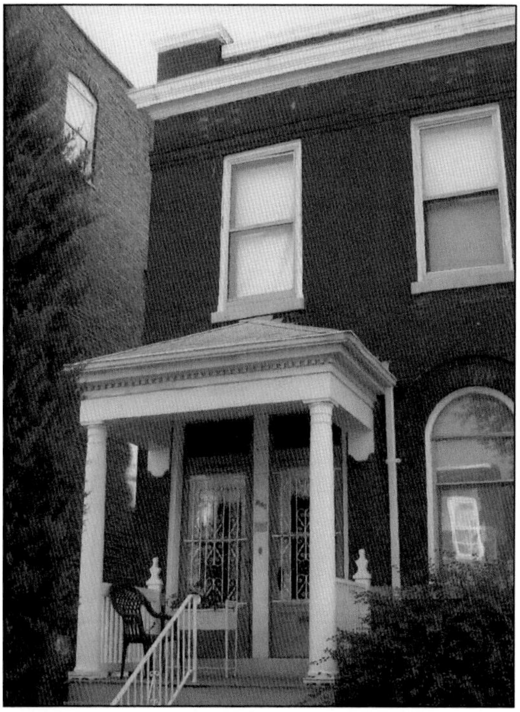

Two-Family Flats, 3120 Iowa. It cost $4,600 to build this two-family dwelling in 1906. Christian Hassenpflug and his family had lived at 3116 Iowa before they moved to 3120. He had built their former home for $2,500 in 1893. At that time, his horse shoeing shop was located at Lemp & Shenadoah, where it remained from 1888 to 1915.

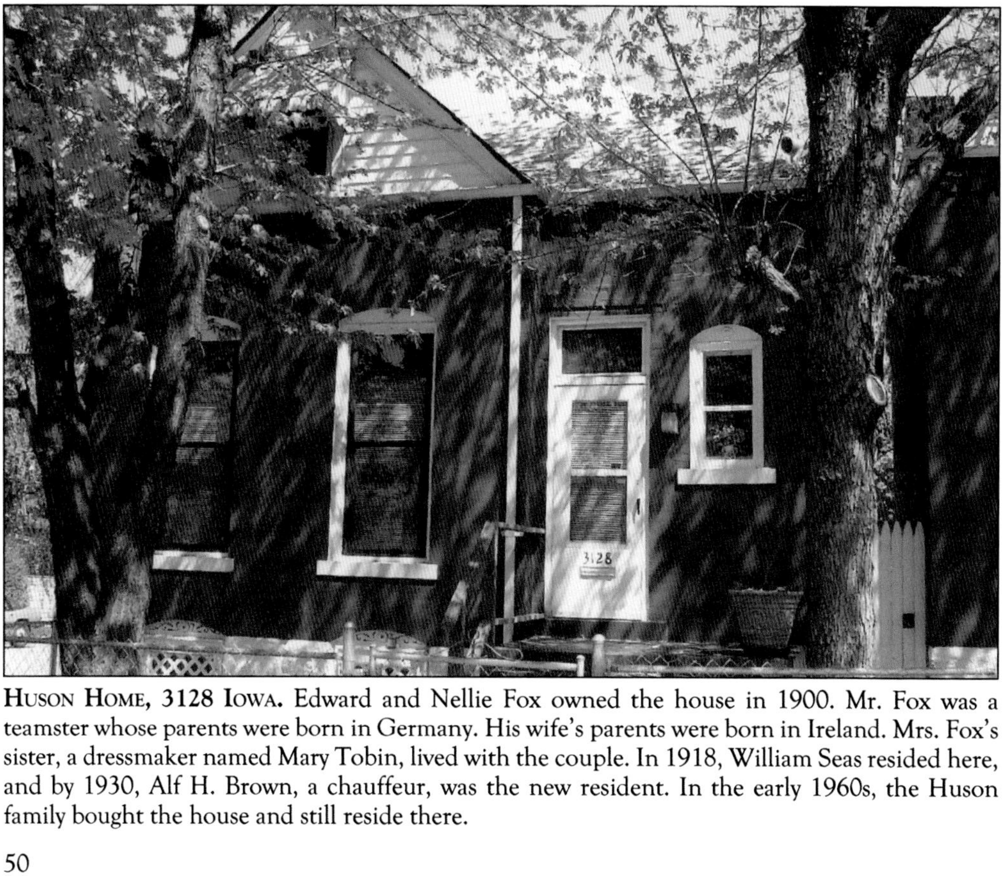

Huson Home, 3128 Iowa. Edward and Nellie Fox owned the house in 1900. Mr. Fox was a teamster whose parents were born in Germany. His wife's parents were born in Ireland. Mrs. Fox's sister, a dressmaker named Mary Tobin, lived with the couple. In 1918, William Seas resided here, and by 1930, Alf H. Brown, a chauffeur, was the new resident. In the early 1960s, the Huson family bought the house and still reside there.

Site B10: Calvary Cross Mission Baptist Church, 3127 California. This church was originally built as a Lutheran church. In 1908, that congregation moved to a different location in the neighborhood at the corner of Utah and Oregon. St. Andrew's German Evangelical Church was the next resident in this building. They later became a United Church of Christ. In 1964, the Calvary Cross Missionary Baptist Church took up residence and is still here today.

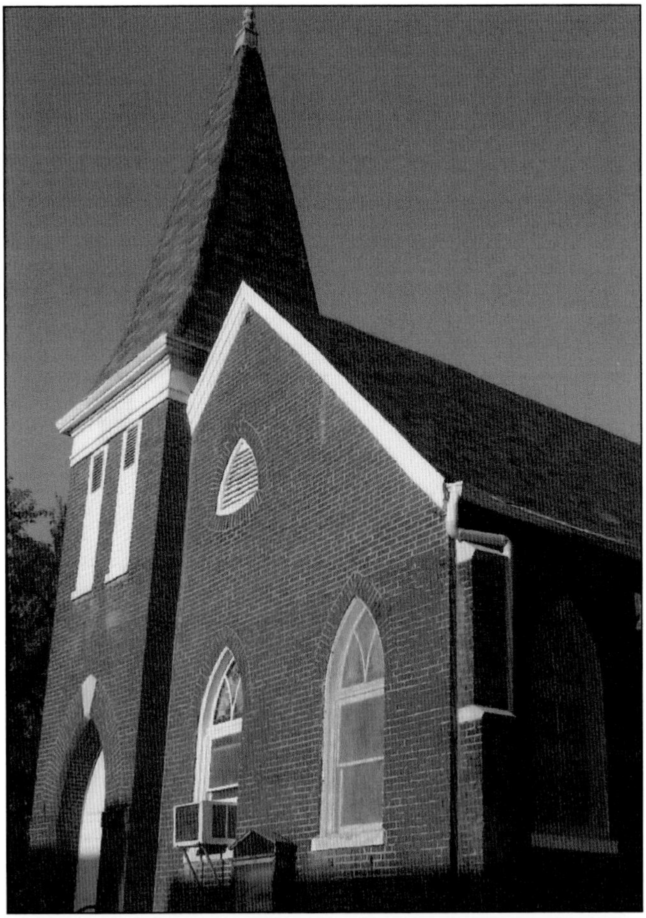

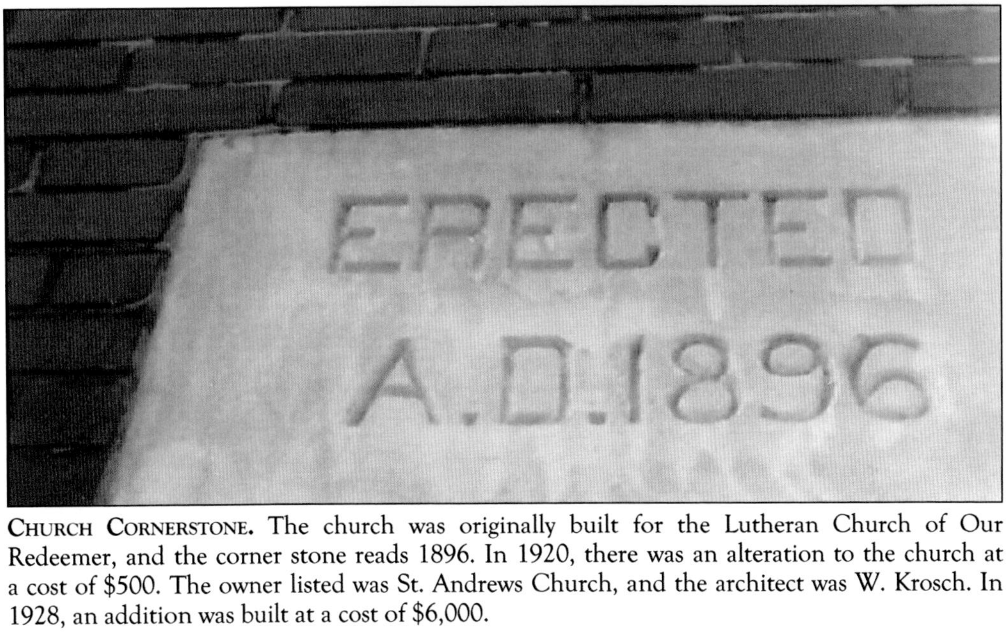

Church Cornerstone. The church was originally built for the Lutheran Church of Our Redeemer, and the corner stone reads 1896. In 1920, there was an alteration to the church at a cost of $500. The owner listed was St. Andrews Church, and the architect was W. Krosch. In 1928, an addition was built at a cost of $6,000.

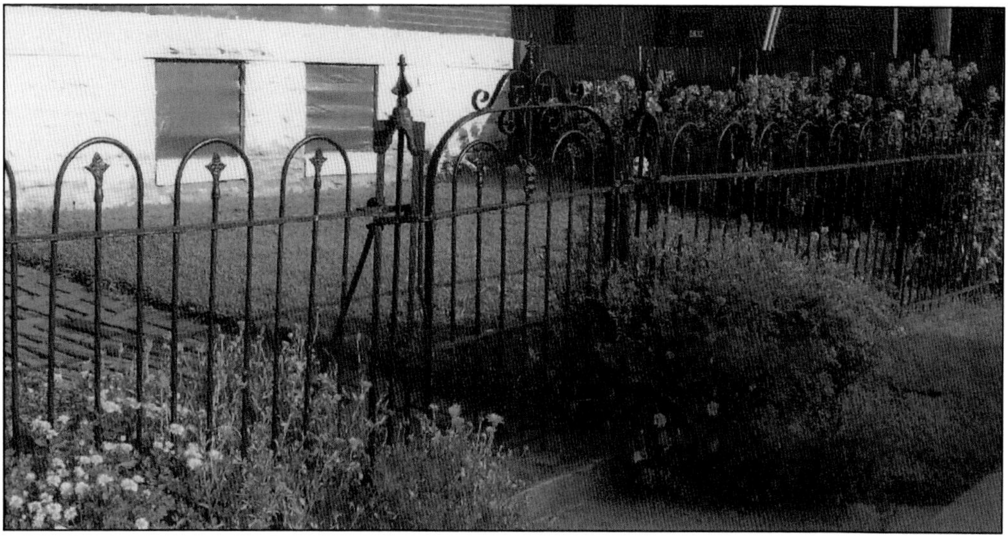

Site B11: Original Wrought Iron Fence, 3121 Oregon. This fence was manufactured by St. Louis Wire & Iron Company, founded by German-born R. Tiesler in the mid-1880s. The company manufactured fences, rails, crests, balconies, chairs, signs, screens, fixtures, stairs, and sidewalk lights. The store and factory were located at 516–522 Chouteau. The company used the latest machinery powered by steam and stocked many of their goods for sale, but they also worked on custom orders.

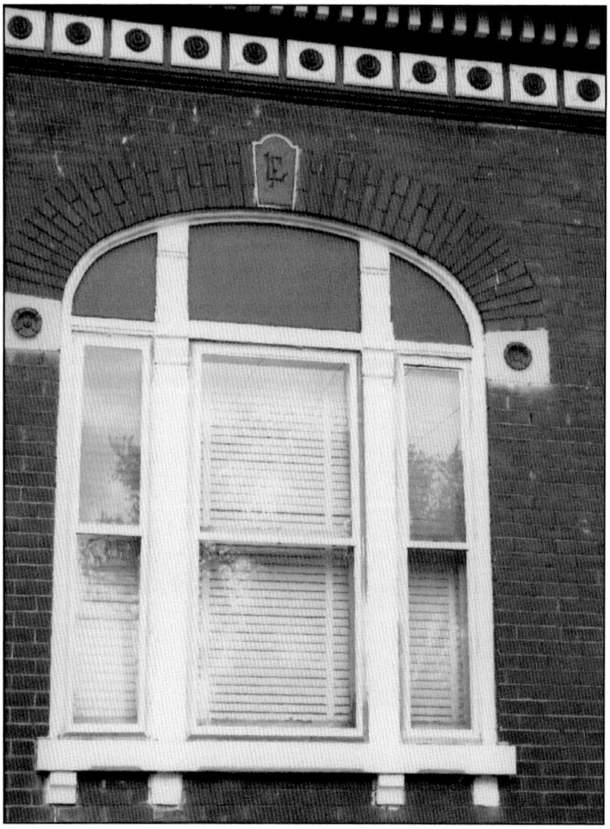

Window Crown. The initials "FL" over the arch of the front window belong to the original saloon owner, Franz Lendi, who built his house for $2,000 in 1887. The listed owner in 1900, Louis Schumacher, also operated a saloon. In 1921, Mrs. Schumacher was listed as the owner when a permit was issued to build a one-story frame shed for $175. The architect was J. Alt.

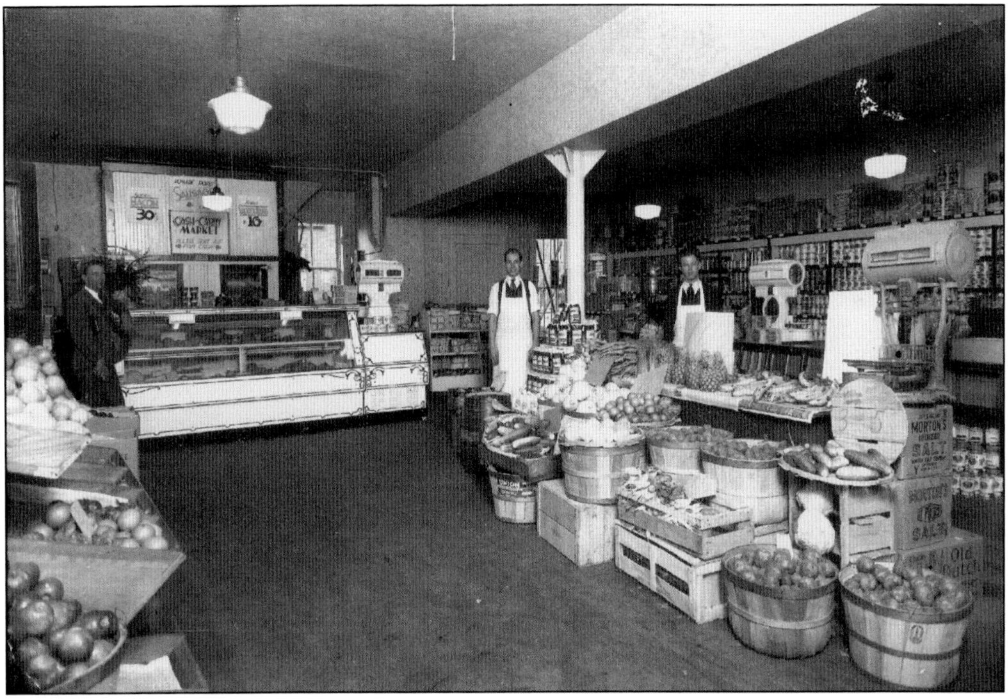

SITE B12: HEJLEK MARKET. This c. 1936 image shows the interior of Hejlek's Market, which operated from 1936 to the 1977. In 1900, it was the home and business of Herman and Agnes J. Neunuebel. Herman and son Frank worked in the grocery store. In 1918, this location was the saloon of George H. Zuver, and in 1930, Herman Setzer had an upholstery business here. After Hejlek's closed, the building became Rhinehardt's Market, and in 1990, it was H & K Furniture.

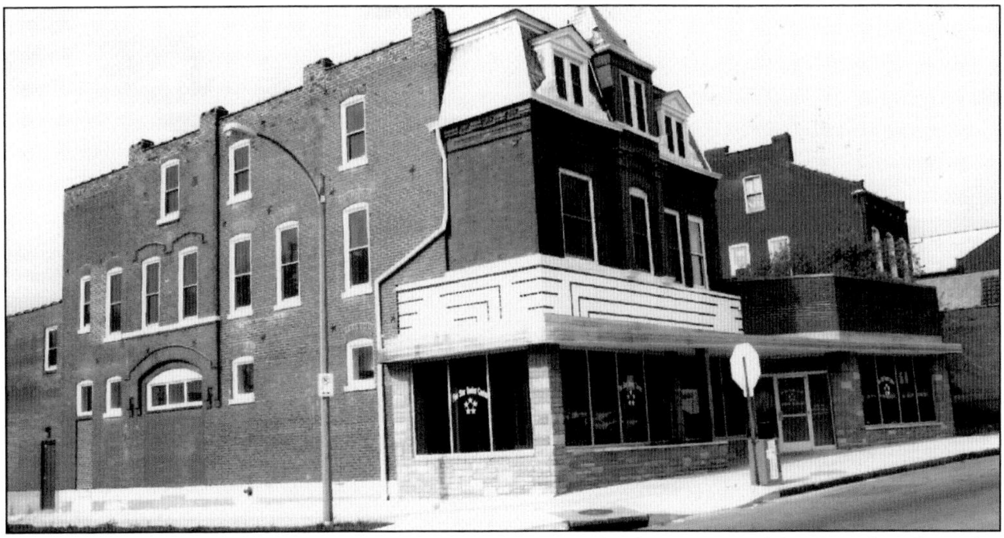

FIVE STAR SENIOR CENTER, 2832 ARSENAL. The center, which was started by five churches who wanted to provide a ministry to seniors, serves as a place where seniors come for meals. It also provides an activity center for people 60 years of age and older. Alderman Ken Ortmann was instrumental in bringing this historic building back to life after a fire which could have easily earmarked this neighborhood gem for demolition.

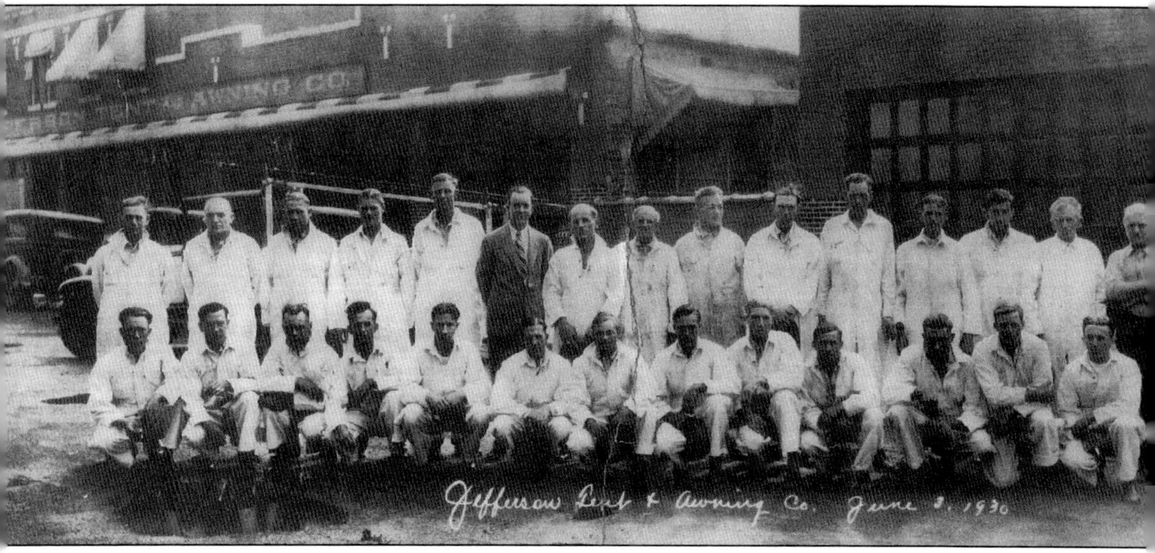

SITE B13: JEFFERSON TENT & AWNING COMPANY, 2930 GRAVOIS. The company was established at this location in 1911 by Henry L. Rauss. A year later, the company was listed as a seller of wagon, horse, and dray covers at 2624 Arsenal.Today the address is listed as 2930 Gravois. The address was listed as the business and residence of H. L. Rauss. Mr. Rauss was already in the business before 1911; in 1893 he sold awnings at 3755 California, and in 1900, he worked the same job at 2809 Texas. The current owner is Beatrice Heinz.

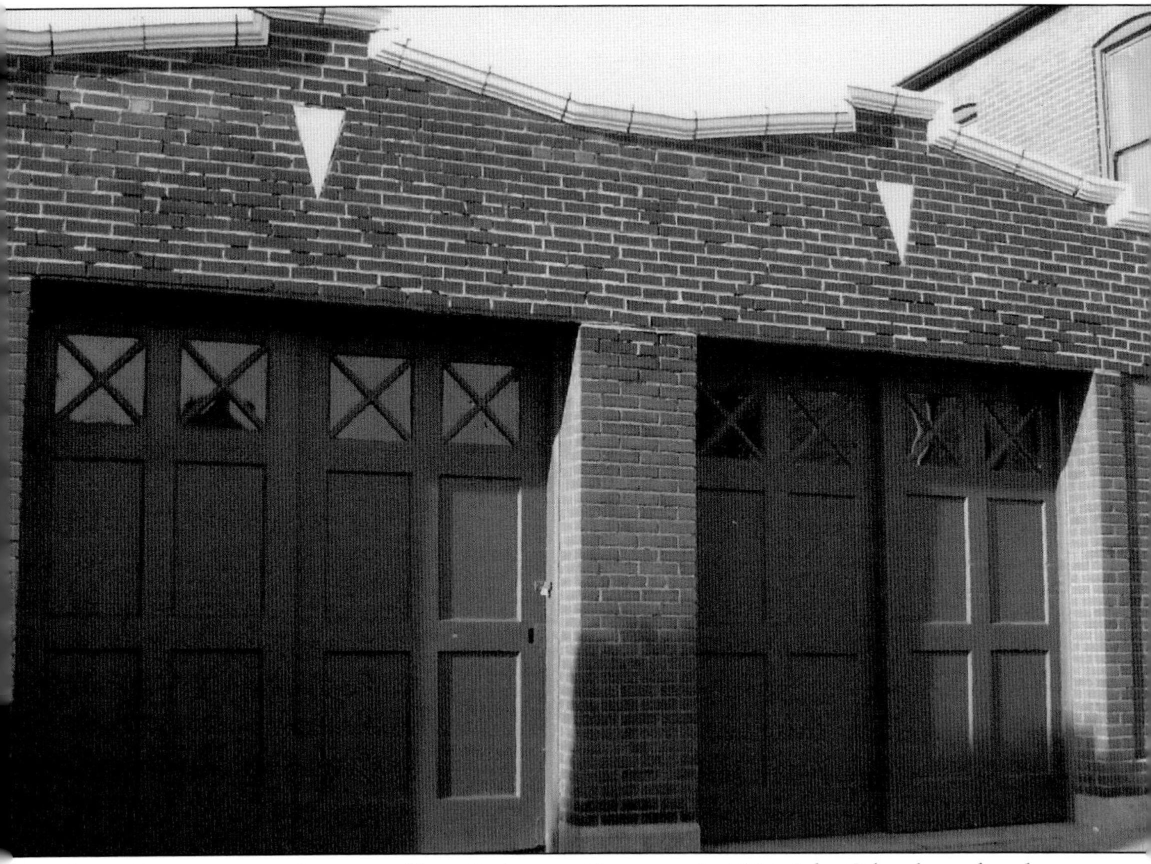

EARLY GARAGES OF THE JEFFERSON TENT & AWNING COMPANY. In 1914, John Schwob was listed as the owner of the structure at 2930 Gravois. He built a one-story brick dwelling for $1,400 at what was then known as 3128 Pennsylvania. In 1916, Mr. Schwob was listed as a machinist. In 1917, he added a one-story frame shed and a frame porch. A building permit was issued to the Jefferson Tent & Awning Company in 1919 for a one-story steel shed at a cost of $500 on this property.

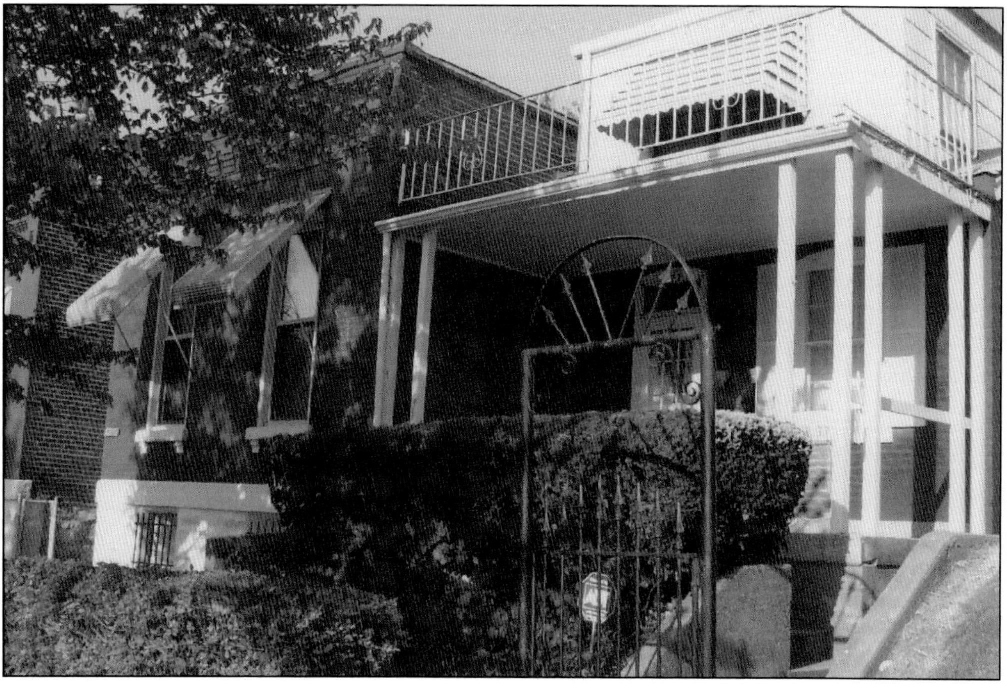

Site B14: Peter Kaufmann House, 3135 Pennsylvania. This house was built in 1889 by carpenter and owner Peter Kaufmann at a cost of $1,300. In 1893, John F. Schlag and his wife Christine bought the house. Mr. Schlag was a salesman for the Ideal Coffee & Tea Company at 1700 South Broadway. It was the Schlag family business. Other family members were Charles, George, Henry, and Julius Schlag.

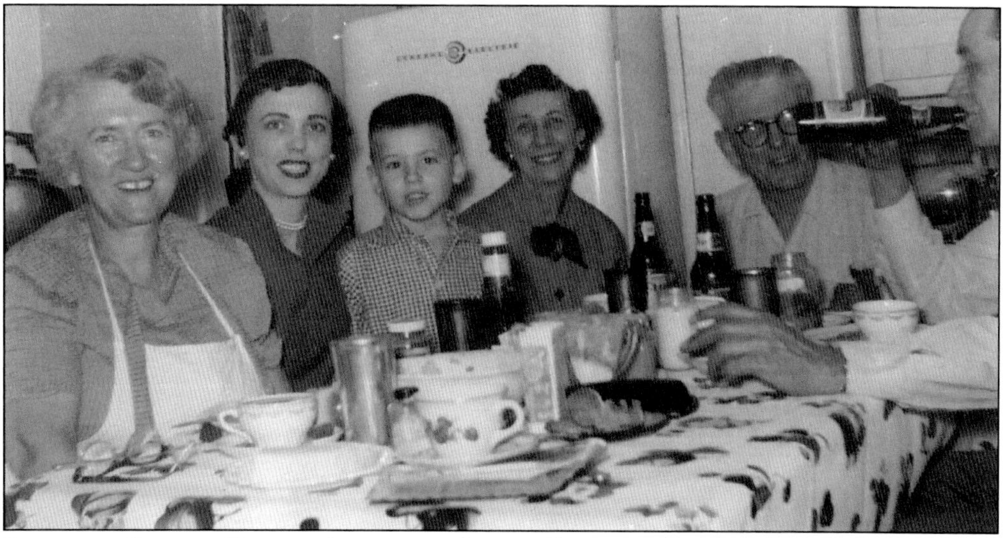

Zeiler and Gersman Families Gather for Sunday Dinner. Edward and Cecilia Zeiler bought the house in 1962, and in 1965, they transferred the title to Robert and Marcela Gersman. The Zeilers were Marcela's parents. Robert was an office manager at Ed F. Mangoldorf & Brother, Inc., a wholesale seed company. Marcela would spend her whole life in this neighborhood. She was raised at 2717 Arsenal and her grandparents lived at 2721. Today, she resides close by at Beauvais Manor.

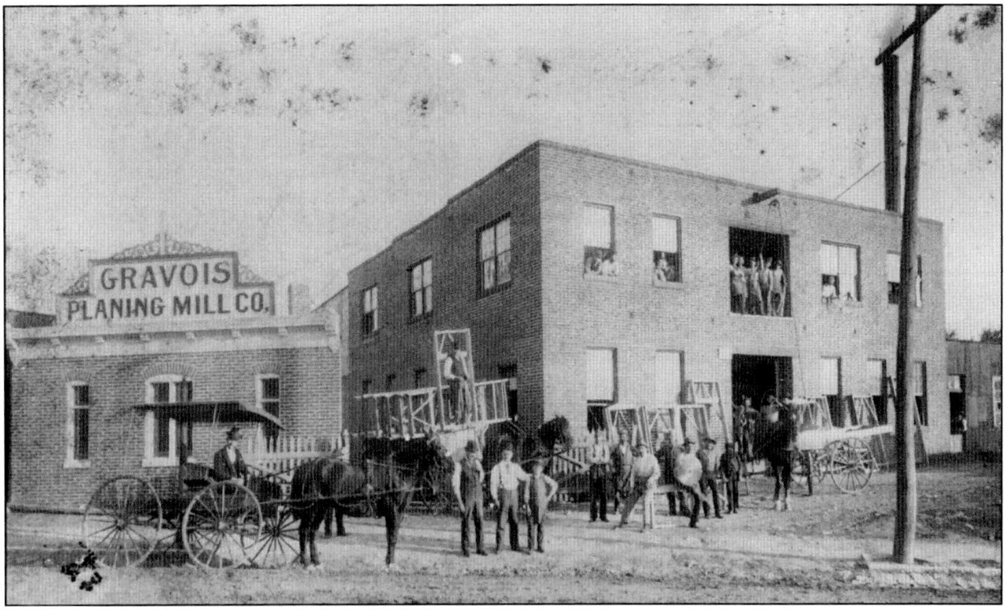

Site B15: Gravois Planing Mill, 3026 Juniata. One of the first building permits issued for the mill was granted in 1892. The next year, a two-story brick dry house and engine room were added. While the original owner was building his business, Christian C. Beckemeier Jr.,the second owner of the mill, was gaining experience. In 1894, Mr. Beckemeier worked for Andrew Kuenzel, a sash company. In 1897, he was employed by the Great Western Planing Mill, and by 1901, Mr. Beckemeier was listed as the secretary of the Gravois Planing Mill.

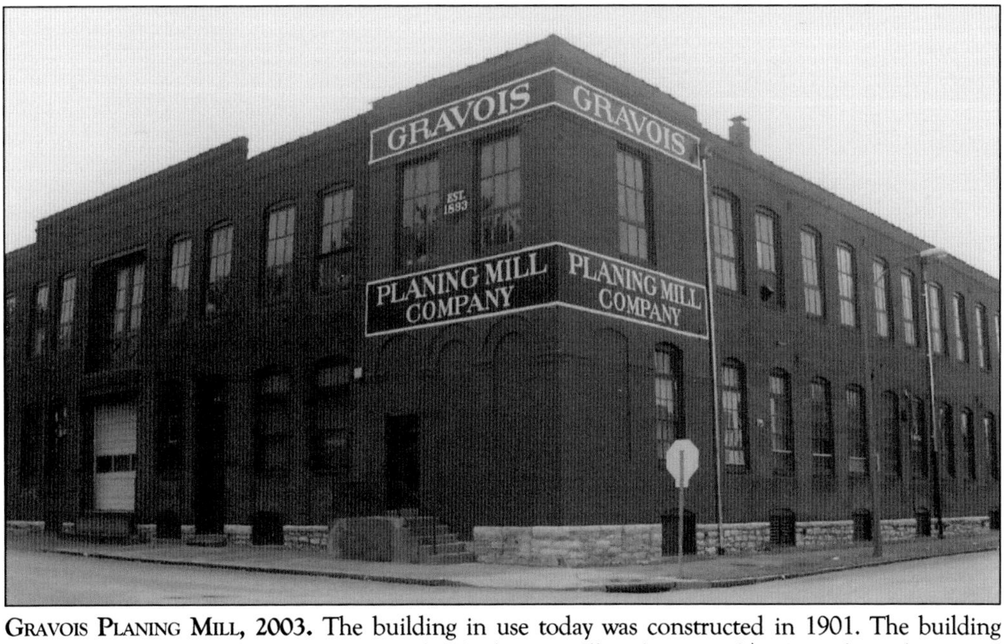

Gravois Planing Mill, 2003. The building in use today was constructed in 1901. The building permit was issued in 1900 for a two-story brick planing mill at the cost of $6,500. The architect was Henry Schaumburg Jr. In 1903, Mr. Schaumburg was hired to design a one-story brick dry kiln costing $250. A two-story brick stable was added in 1910 for $877. In 1923, another one-story brick dry kiln was added. The company would stay in the Beckemeier family until 1969.

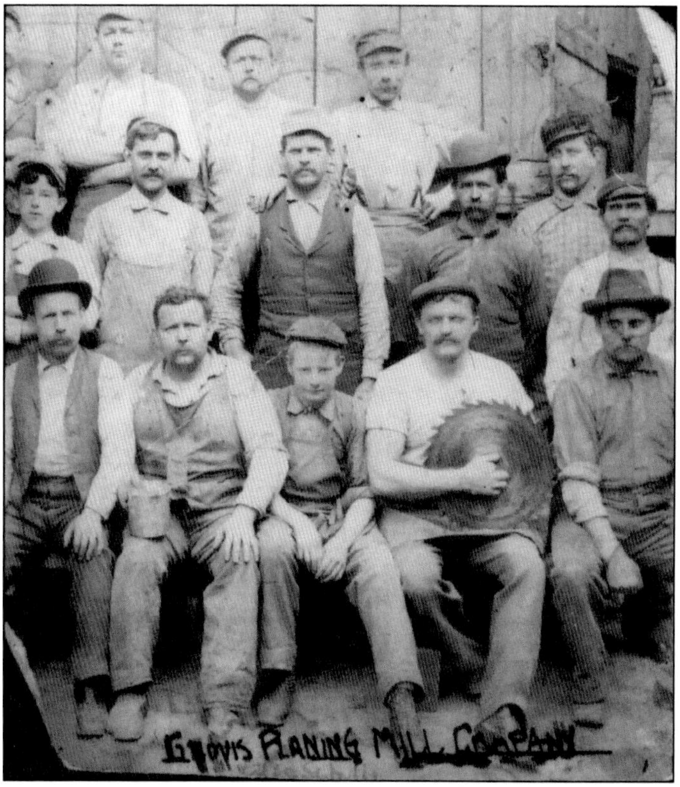

Gravois Planing Mill Employees. In 1969, the Beckemeier family sold the company's assets to their employees. By 1972, the company was resold to Leo Paradoski and Russell Emmenegger. As of 2005, the company was still owned by the Paradoski family with Jim Paradoski as president. After a century of turning out quality millwork, the mill still provides a much needed service in the renovation of historic homes.

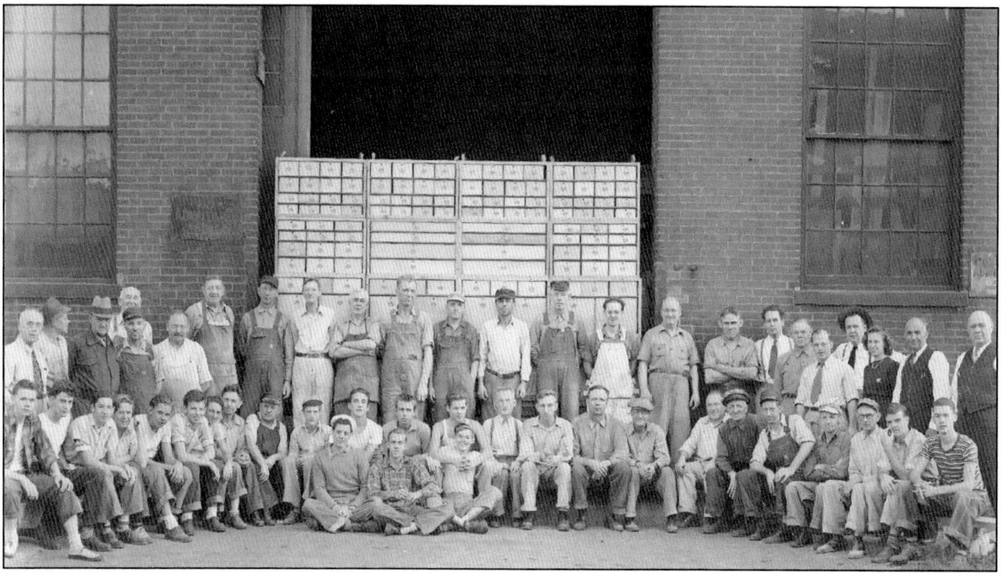

Planing Mill Employees, 1943. The large case sitting across the entrance to the building is a piece that was made for a university research lab. Today the mill is known for its custom architectural millwork. It provides window parts, door parts, and wood molding. Developers try to salvage as much of the original wood work as possible, but when wood work is missing entirely or pieces need to be matched to the original, they depend on the Gravois Planing Mill for their millwork.

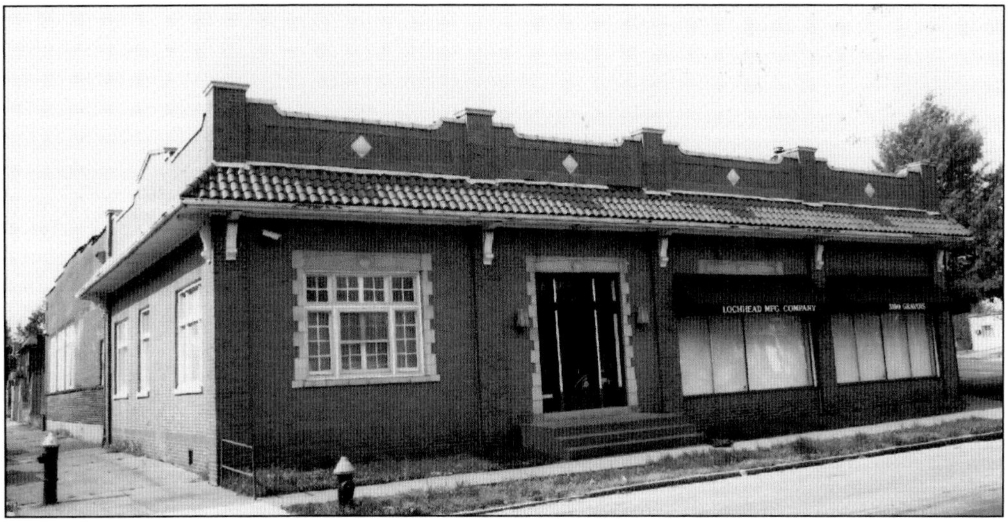

LOCHHEAD MANUFACTURING COMPANY, 3100 GRAVOIS. This building was part of the Gravois Planing Mill, built in 1927 for $17,000. In 1999, the Lochhead Manufacturing Company bought the building. The Lochhead family has been producing vanillas and flavors for three generations, since 1918. The company is run by the Lochhead brothers and has two locations, this one in St. Louis and one in Evergreen, Colorado. This location is run by John, while the location in Colorado is run by George.

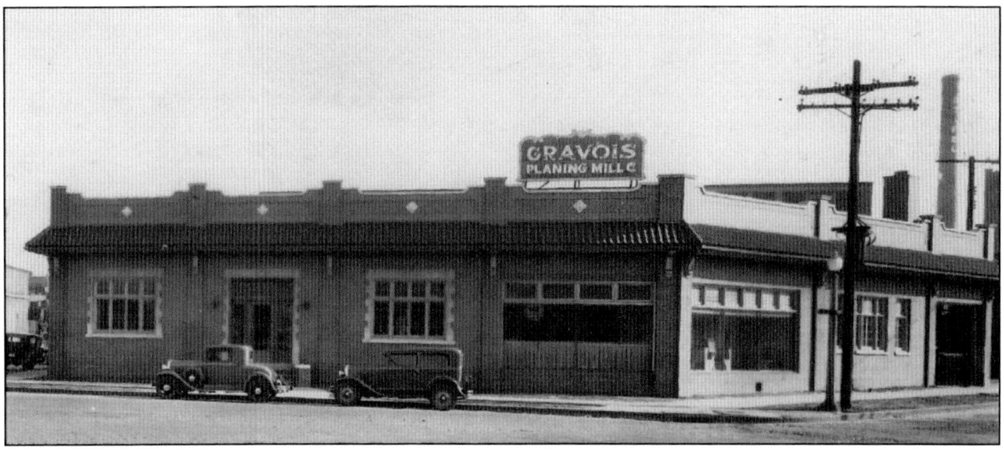

HOME TO MANY BUSINESSES. In 1934, Falstaff Brewing Company was listed as the owner of this building. In 1935, Triangle Auto used it as a showroom. From the mid-1940s to the mid-1970s, it housed the John Fabrick Tractor Company. In 1976, Charles Equipment used it in the sales and service of industrial engines and generators. By 1980, Sam Brown Generator Sales & Parts had taken over, followed by Phase 2 Air Brake in 1990 and Andrews Interiors in the mid-1990s.

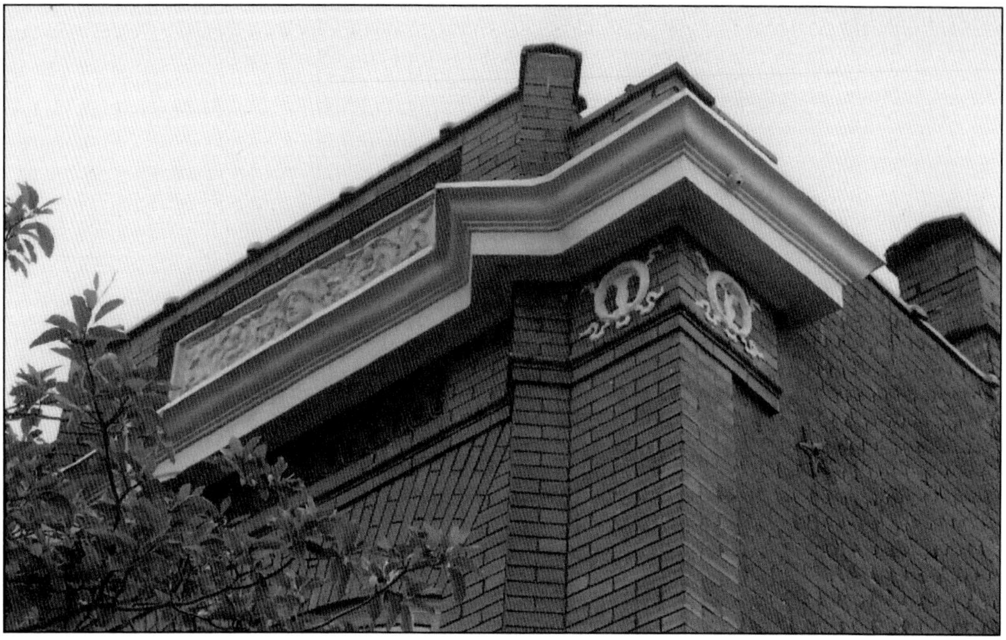

SITE B16: STEIMKE HOUSE, 3007 WYOMING. This house, rich with architectural details, was built in 1886. The permit was issued to Emma Steimke. Take a look at the front of the building toward the roof. The decorative plaques across the front with the woman's face in the middle are rare finds in this neighborhood. The wood work in the front entrance was probably milled at the Steimke Manufacturing Company, which was located at 3016–3018 Gravois.

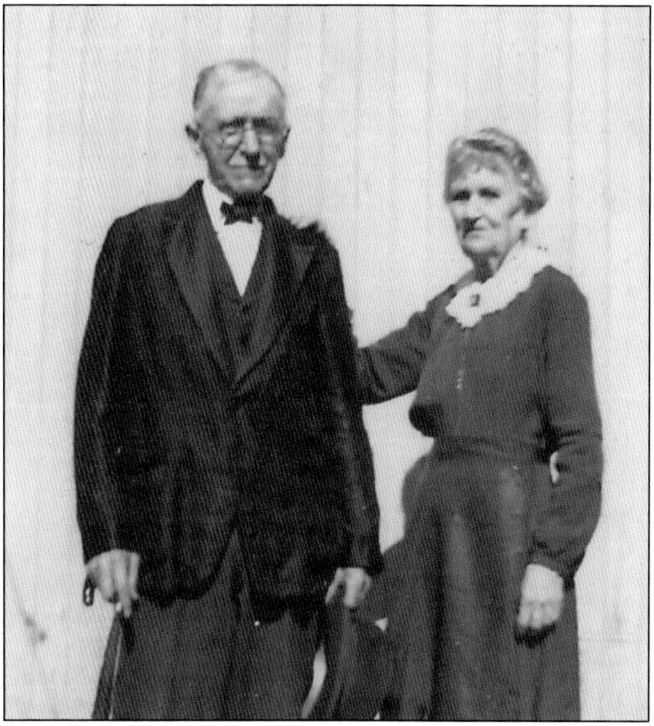

THE STEIMKES, 1935. Emma and Dietrich Steimke pose by what is now the back porch. They were the original residents of this house. Today, Chris Hoffman resides at 3007; her father, Carl Hoffman Jr. lives in the house to the right; and her brother, Carl III, lives next door to the left. Chris and Carl III are the fourth generation of the Steimke/Hoffman family to reside here. Carl Hoffman Sr. married Elise Steimke, daughter of Emma and Dietrich.

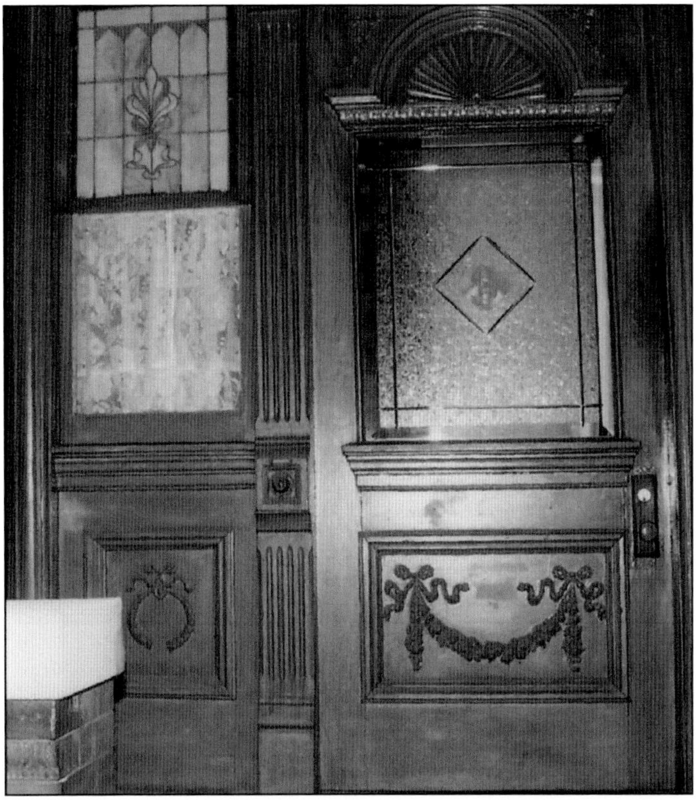

Quality German Craftsmanship. The entrance to the Hoffman residence is very fancy for this neighborhood. There are many fine examples of custom architectural millwork and glass. Look closely at the frosted glass panel on the door. The initials "DS" are etched in the glass. The decorative woodwork on the door and side panel shows off the skills of the Germans who settled in St. Louis. The stained-glass window adds to the overall elegance of this well-preserved home.

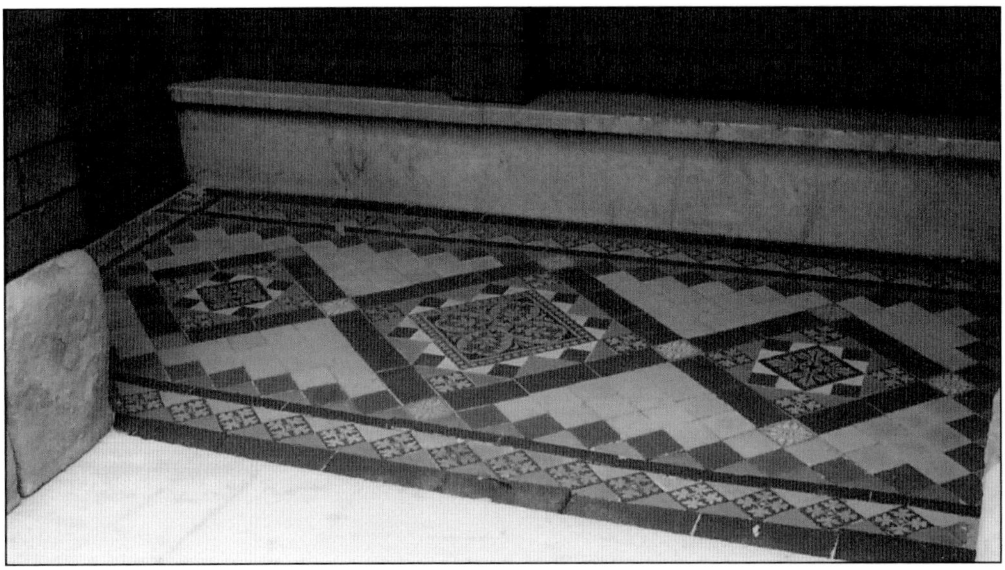

Fancy Tile Work. There are several tiled entrances that can be seen during the walk tours in this book, but take a good look at the one above, as it is one of the fanciest in this neighborhood. It shows off several colors of tiles and has a patterned design. There are other examples with only two or three colors of tiles. Some of the storefronts on Cherokee have the business name in tiles at the store's entrance.

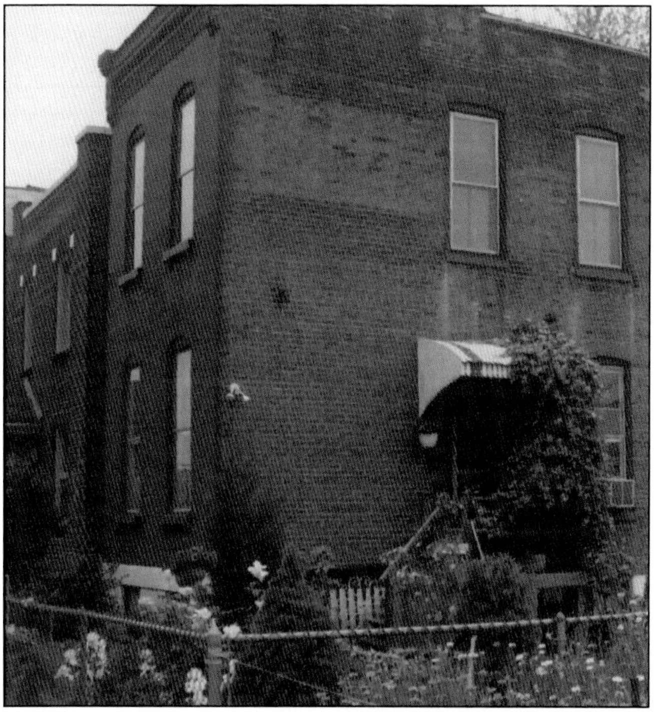

Site B17: Rental House, 3158 Iowa. Usually a building permit can be found for houses constructed after 1880, but in this case, no permit was located. In 1900, the house was a rental. The Filsner family showed up there in the 1900 census. John and his wife Laura had five children: John, Jessie, William, Jean, and Walter. John was of Scottish descent. In 1920, the house was still a rental.

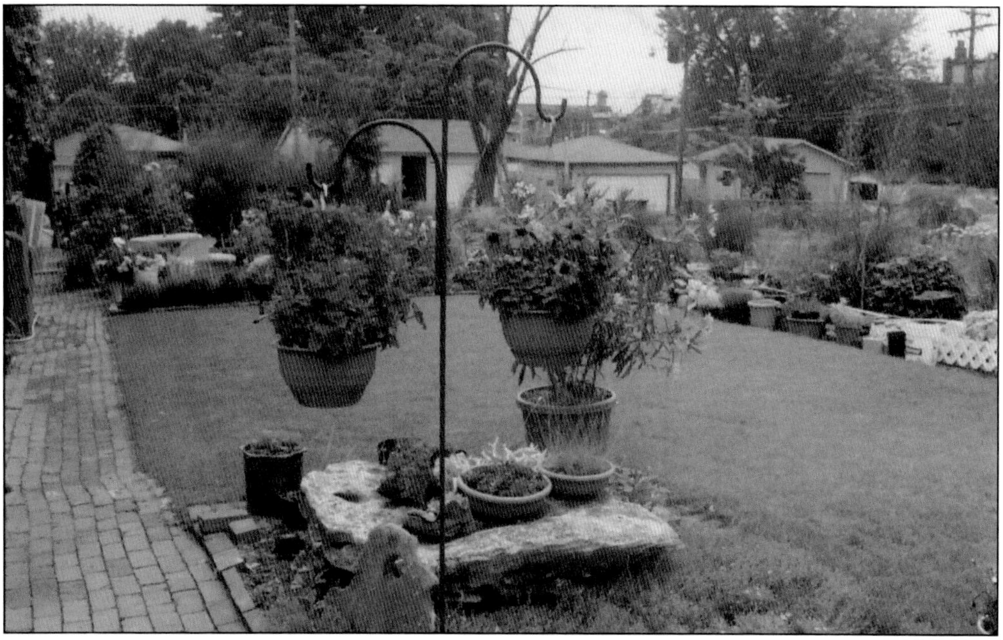

Bentley's Garden Next Door. German immigrants were the first to build homes in Benton Park West. Today there is a diverse mix of may different people, which brings a nice balance to this historic neighborhood. The current owners of 3158 Iowa are Natividad Brejot and her daughter, Wendy. Natividad is from the Philippines and has created a garden that reminds her of her homeland. The garden is named for Bentley, a cancer survivor, and the beloved dog of Mark Cartwright and Gerhardt Gern.

SITE B18: FRANK L. SCHMITTGENS HOUSE, 2727 WYOMING. Police sergeant Frank Schmittgens did not live in this house long. He died on March 17, 1894, at the age of 52, and his funeral took place in the house on March 19 at 2:00 p.m.. In attendance were acting police chief Reedy, all the captains, and many sergeants and patrolmen. Schmittgens' wife Theresa and his children were listed at this address in the 1910 census. A childless couple rented part of the house.

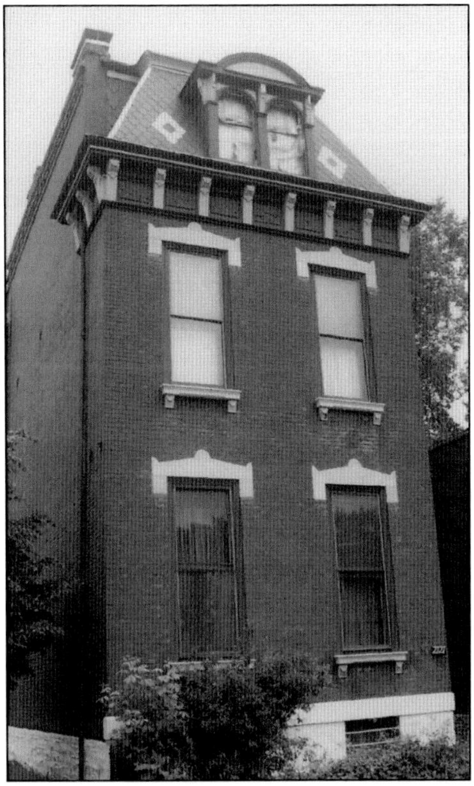

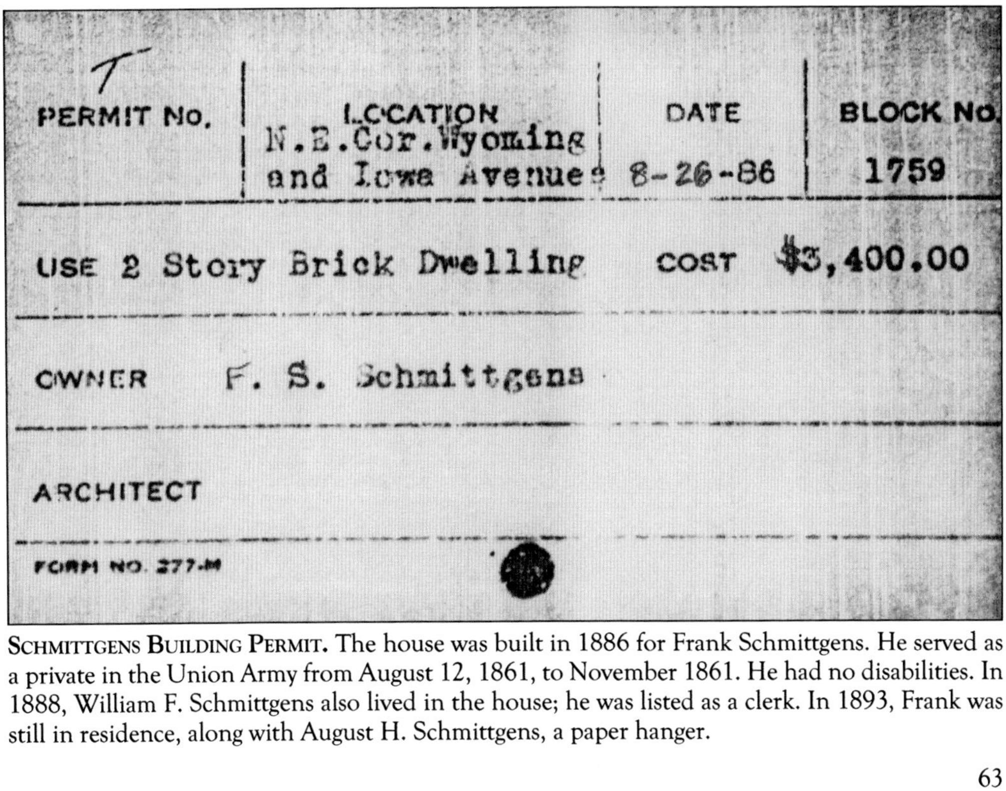

T

PERMIT No.	LOCATION	DATE	BLOCK No.
	N.E.Cor.Wyoming and Iowa Avenues	8-26-86	1759

USE 2 Story Brick Dwelling COST $3,400.00

OWNER F. S. Schmittgens

ARCHITECT

FORM NO. 277-M

SCHMITTGENS BUILDING PERMIT. The house was built in 1886 for Frank Schmittgens. He served as a private in the Union Army from August 12, 1861, to November 1861. He had no disabilities. In 1888, William F. Schmittgens also lived in the house; he was listed as a clerk. In 1893, Frank was still in residence, along with August H. Schmittgens, a paper hanger.

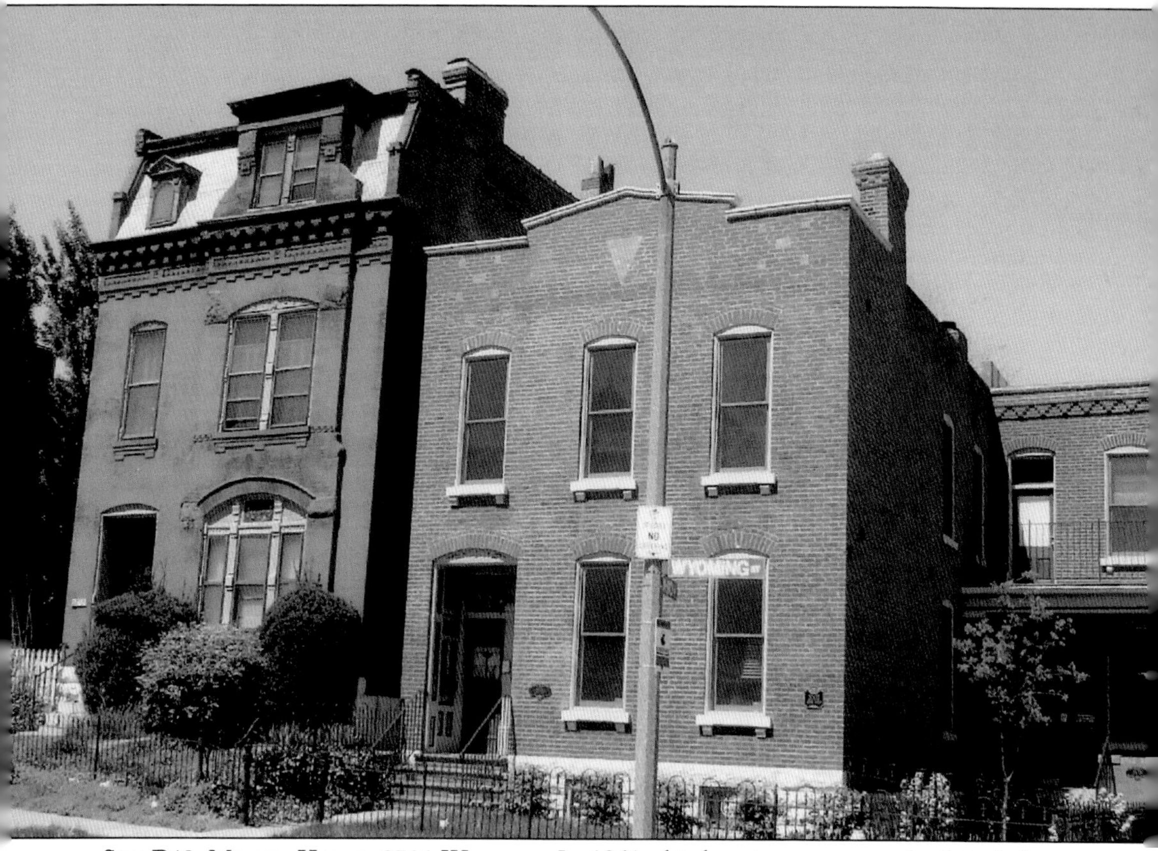

SITE B19: MERKEL HOUSE, 2701 WYOMING. In 1861, this location was part of a dairy belonging to Burkart Sebastian, who lived in the area of Iowa and Wyoming Streets. In 1888, Maria Merkel bought the lots and was granted a building permit to build the original structure, a two-story brick dwelling, at a cost of $2,700. Mrs. Merkel, her three daughters, and a son were the residents of this large house. From 1890 to 1900, Anna Merkel earned her living by teaching music at this address. In 1901, Clara, another old maid, joined her sister Anna in teaching music at the house. The following year, Julia joined her sisters in the music education profession. Through the 1920s, this address was known as Merkel's Music Studio.

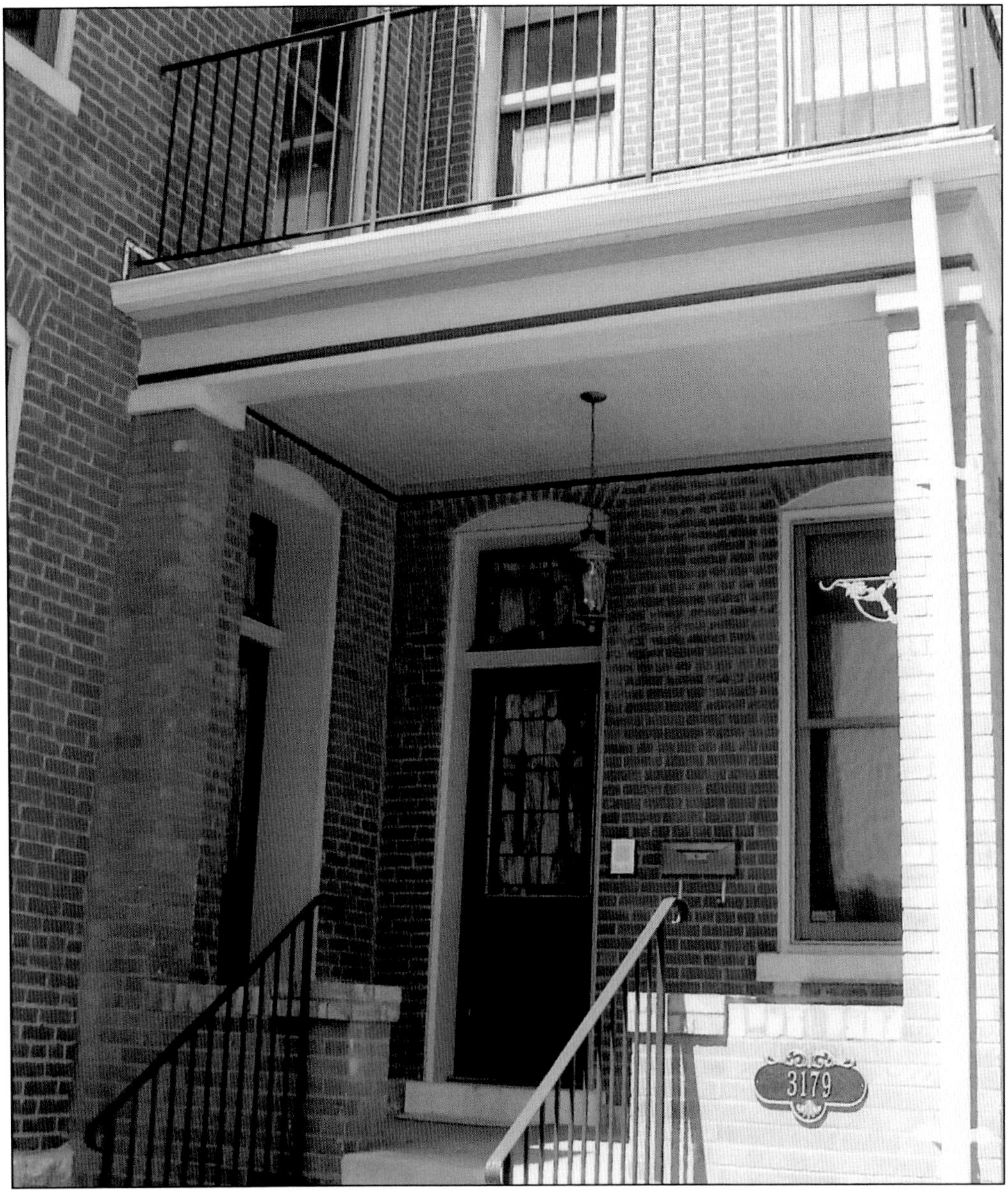

ADDITION TO THE MERKEL HOUSE (NOW 3179 OHIO). In 1897, a building permit was issued to Mrs. Merkel for a two-story addition at a cost of $900; today that addition is a separate townhouse. The big house that had started off as a single-family dwelling was turned into a two-family unit by the 1920s. The Merkel family lived in this house for 50 years. Through the 1940s, the residence became a three-family dwelling, and by the mid-1950s, there were four different families living here. In 1956, 2703 Wyoming became known as 2701 and 2703 Wyoming. In 2003, Millennium Restoration & Development Corporation turned what had been an eye sore at the corner, with ragged curtains flying out broken windows, into a set of urban gems. Millennium Restoration & Development Corporation is a family-owned business, run by Tim Vogt and his mother, Claire. The brothers involved in the business are Chris and John. When Millennium took over this property much of the original woodwork was missing or in such bad shape it could not be saved. John built the new stairway that is showcased in this townhouse.

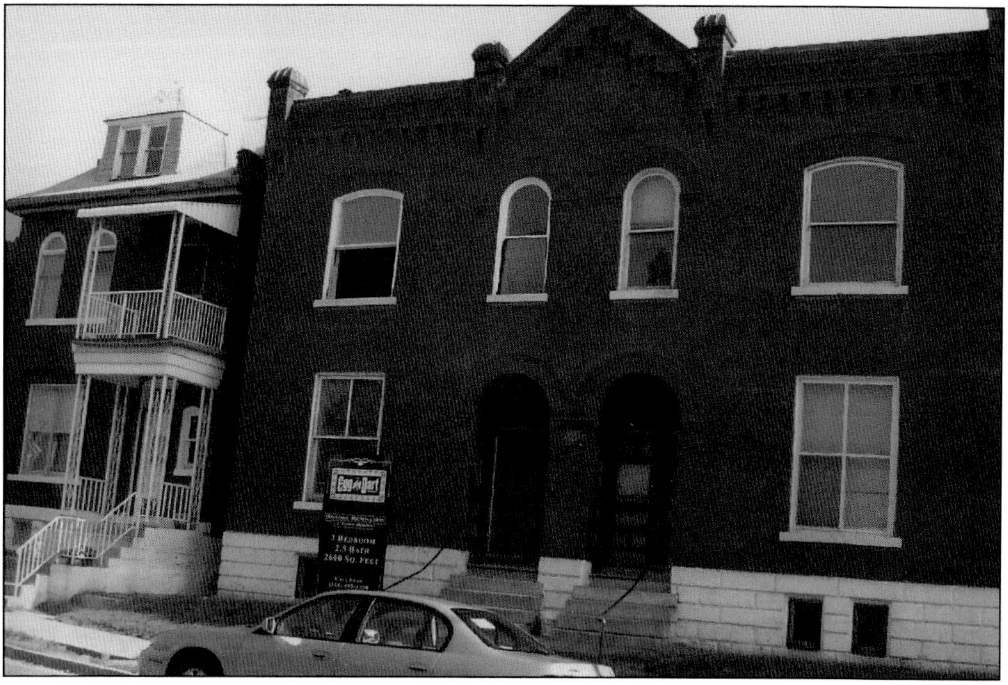

Site B20: Townhouses, 2641 and 2643 Wyoming. This structure started out as four family flats built in 1895 by Henry Kumpf for $5,000. Mr. Kumpf was a collector for Comstock Furniture and lived at 2641A. His son Henry Jr. resided at the same address and worked as a clerk at George West Perry & Company. Today the four units have been rehabilitated into two townhouses by Egg & Dart Properties, a family owned business operated by Norm, Sean, and Andy Zalmanoff and Jeff Marnati.

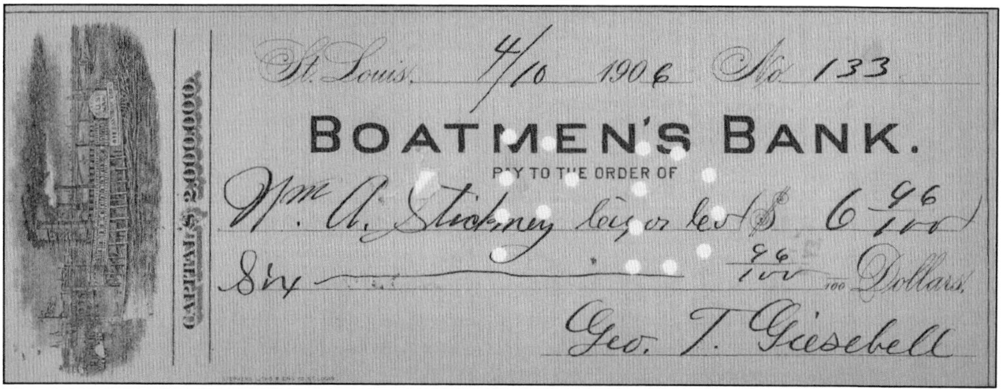
St. Louis, 4/10 1906 No. 133
CAPITAL $ 2,000,000.
BOATMEN'S BANK.
PAY TO THE ORDER OF Wm. A. Stickney $ 6 96/100
Six 96/100 Dollars
Geo. T. Giesebell

If Walls Could Talk. In 2004, when Norm Zalmanoff of Egg & Dart Properties, LLC and his crew were rehabilitating this location, they found a stack of cancelled checks hidden in a wall of the unit known as 2641A. The checks were used for laundry services, cigars, mustache wax, and other barber supplies. Mr. George T. Giesebell, whose signature was on the checks, was indeed the owner of a barber shop at 712 Washington and resided at 2641A Wyoming.

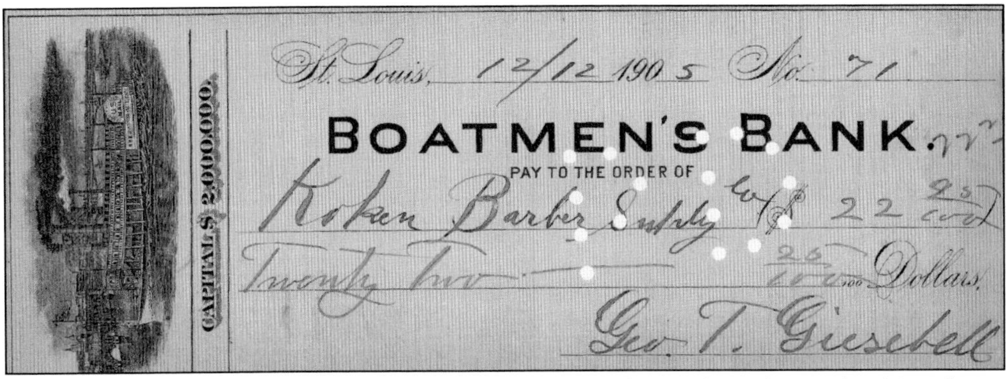

PAY TO THE ORDER OF KOKEN BARBER SUPPLY COMPANY. The factory for Koken Barbers' Supply was located at 2500–2598 Ohio. The company was started by E. E. Koken, who served as president. In 1881, the company changed the name to Koken & Boppert. When Mr. Boppert died in 1886, the company name reverted to E. E. Koken. In 1889, the company incorporated and became Koken Barbers' Supply Company. Besides stocking supplies for barbers, the company began to import cutlery and glassware.

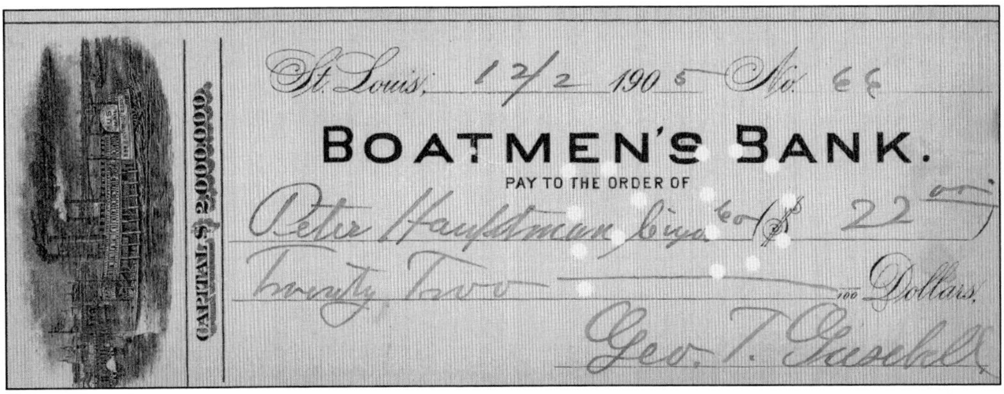

PAY TO THE ORDER OF PETER HAUPTMANN CIGAR COMPANY. National Cigar from Frankfort, Indiana, acquired Hauptmann Cigars from St. Louis in the early 1960s. Cigar smokers called the Hauptmann brand, "the cigar of St. Louis." Hauptmann Perfecto was packaged and sold in tin containers holding 25 cigars; in the early 1980s, the tin was replaced by a red carton. The tin containers are now collectors' items. The Hauptmann label is still popular and available today.

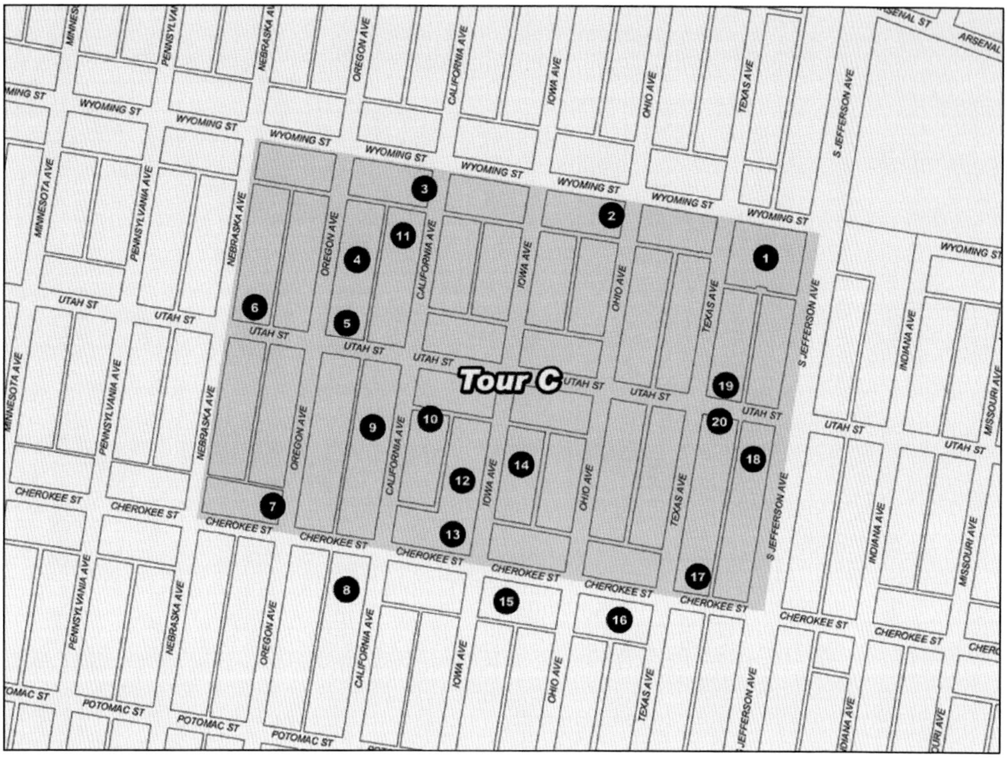

Map for Tour C.

Three

Tour C

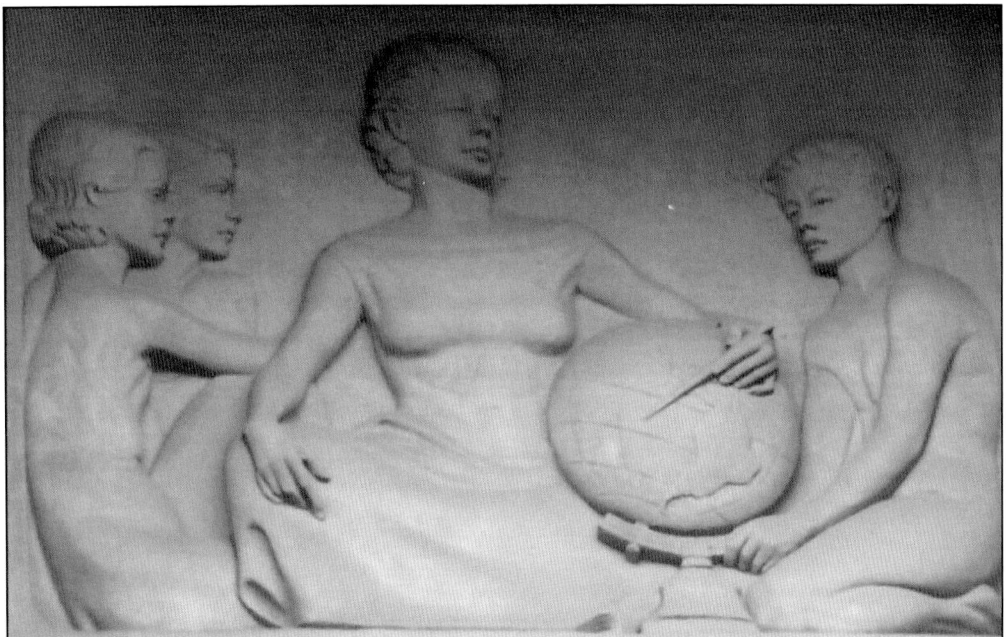

German Influence and Cultural Diversity. Most of the neighborhoods in south St. Louis, including Benton Park West, were established by German immigrants who were anxious to start their new lives in America. The low cost of property in these subdivisions, where most of the lots measured 25 feet across and 120 feet long, attracted many immigrants. A lot could be bought for $200 to $300. With a small down payment and terms of three to six years to pay, the area attracted skilled workers such as carpenters, stone masons, brick makers, bricklayers, and iron workers. During the walk, notice front entrances with intricate brickwork and ceramic tiles laid in a pattern. There are many examples of wrought iron fences. Some of them still have plates or stamps bearing the manufacturer's name. While there are still many families of German descent in the community, there is also a diverse mix of many cultures, which brings a nice balance to this historic neighborhood. There are people of other European heritage, Asians, African Americans, and Hispanics. This tour is a great example of how much Benton Park West has changed.

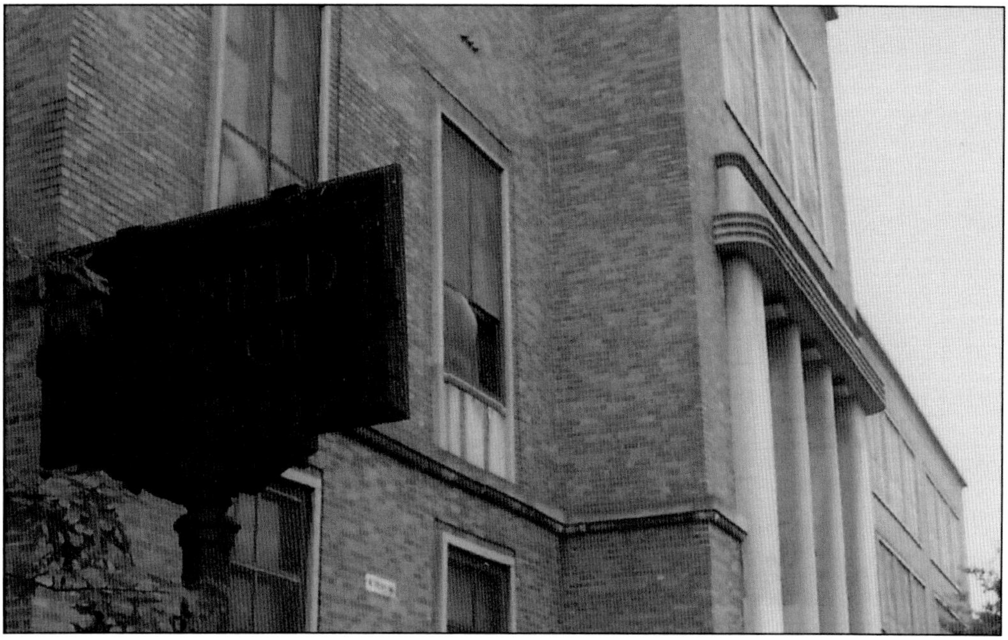

SITE C1: GARFIELD SCHOOL, 2612 WYOMING. The building standing today was constructed in 1936 and is the second Garfield School; the first school opened at this location in 1883. Around 1950, the population of St. Louis started declining and "urban" became associated with "problems." Families kept moving to the suburbs and student population declined. From 1967 to 2002, student enrollments in city schools dropped by more than 64%. Garfield School closed in 2003.

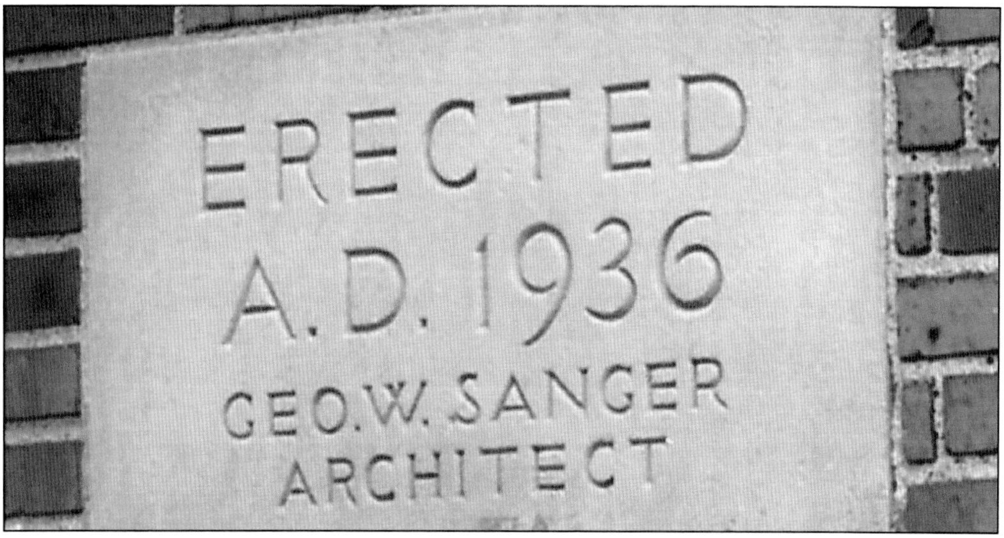

GARFIELD SCHOOL CORNERSTONE. The building was designed by Board of Education architects. George West Sanger was the commissioner of school building at the time. In May 1939, he was revived after taking an overdose of sleeping powders. He took a leave of absence, and in August, he returned to his job. On September 12, 1939, however, he formally resigned his position. The next day, Mr. Sanger took his life by locking himself in the garage while he left the motor of his car running.

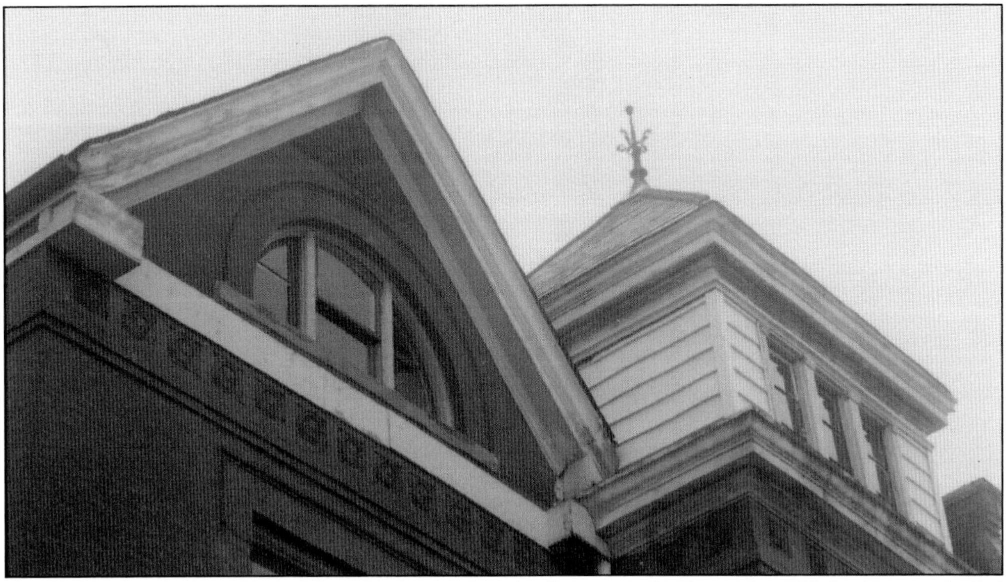

Site C2: Hassendeubel House, 2706 Wyoming. This home was built in 1887. Philip Hassendeubel and his brother Christian Schollmeyer, who lived at 3143 South Jefferson, were partners in the Hassendeubel Brothers Company. They were commission merchants who dealt in provisions and groceries. Mr. Hassendeubel was in business from 1880 until his death in 1939. On his 90th birthday, he was asked to what he attributed his longevity. He replied "that he had always worked, slept, and smoked regularly, ten cigars daily."

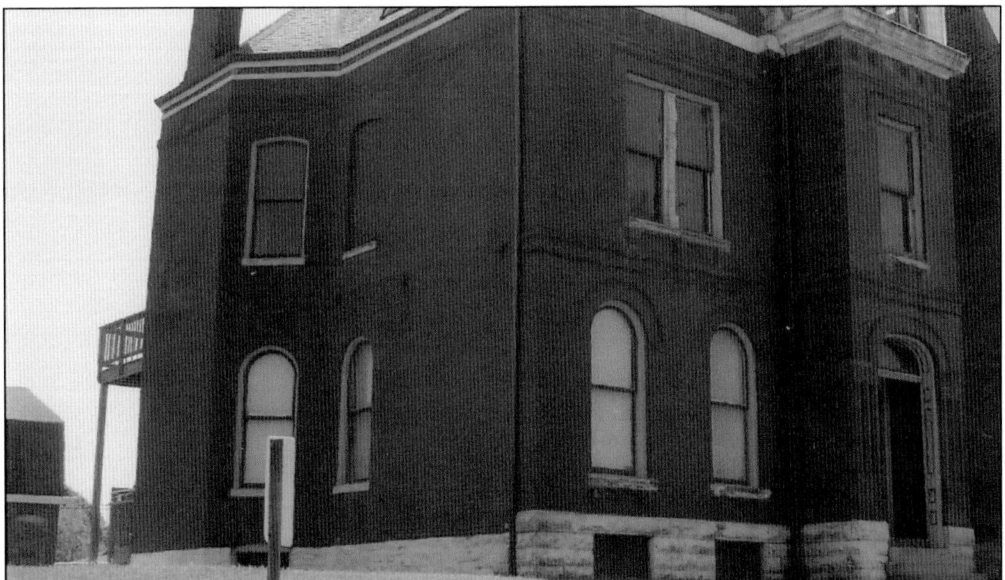

Corner Lot, Wyoming and Ohio. In 1886, Mr. Hassendeubel bought the lots from Louise Barbara Kraft for $1,050. Today there is a great advantage in having the house sit up on the lot. The views from the second and third floors of the Gateway Arch, the national monument, and downtown are breathtaking. Michael Kaul is in the process of rehabilitating this house where its original owner lived from 1888 to 1939, a span of 52 years.

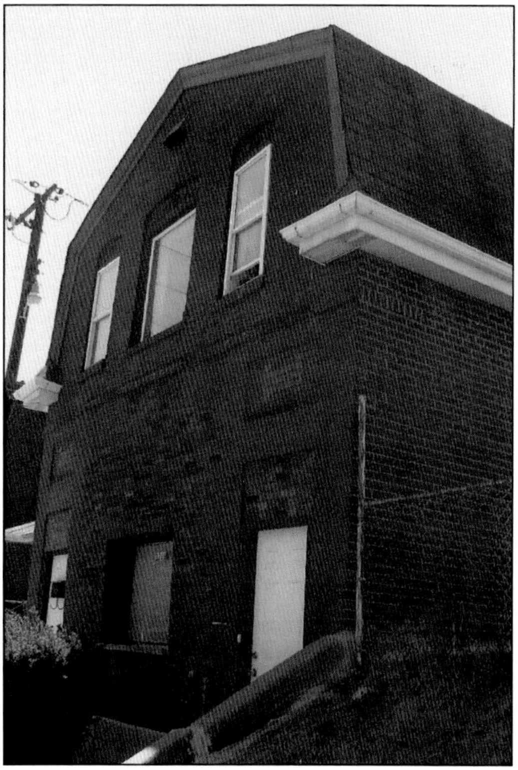

Former Hassendeubel Garage, 3211 Ohio. This address was originally part of 2706 Wyoming and was known as 2700 Wyoming in 1911. The private garage with living quarters was built for Philip Hassendeubel in 1911 at a cost of $2,500. In 1914, Theo Ratz built an addition to the garage for $900. The earliest resident found at this address was Charles Roschenshuh; in 1914 he was listed as a driver. He was probably employed by Hassendeubel Grocery Company.

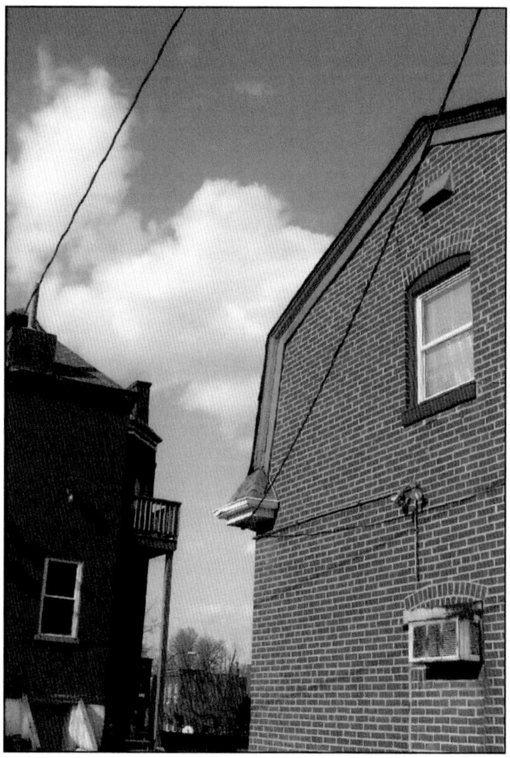

Separate House. In 1939, Mr. Hassendeubel passed away and left the main house and garage/apartment to his children. In 1954, the property was sold to Henrietta M. Erle. Two months after the purchase, Miss Erle sold the properties separately, splitting the garage/apartment from the main house. This dwelling was part of 2706 Wyoming for more than 40 years. The people in the neighborhood are hoping that one day the properties will be reunited and become a single property again.

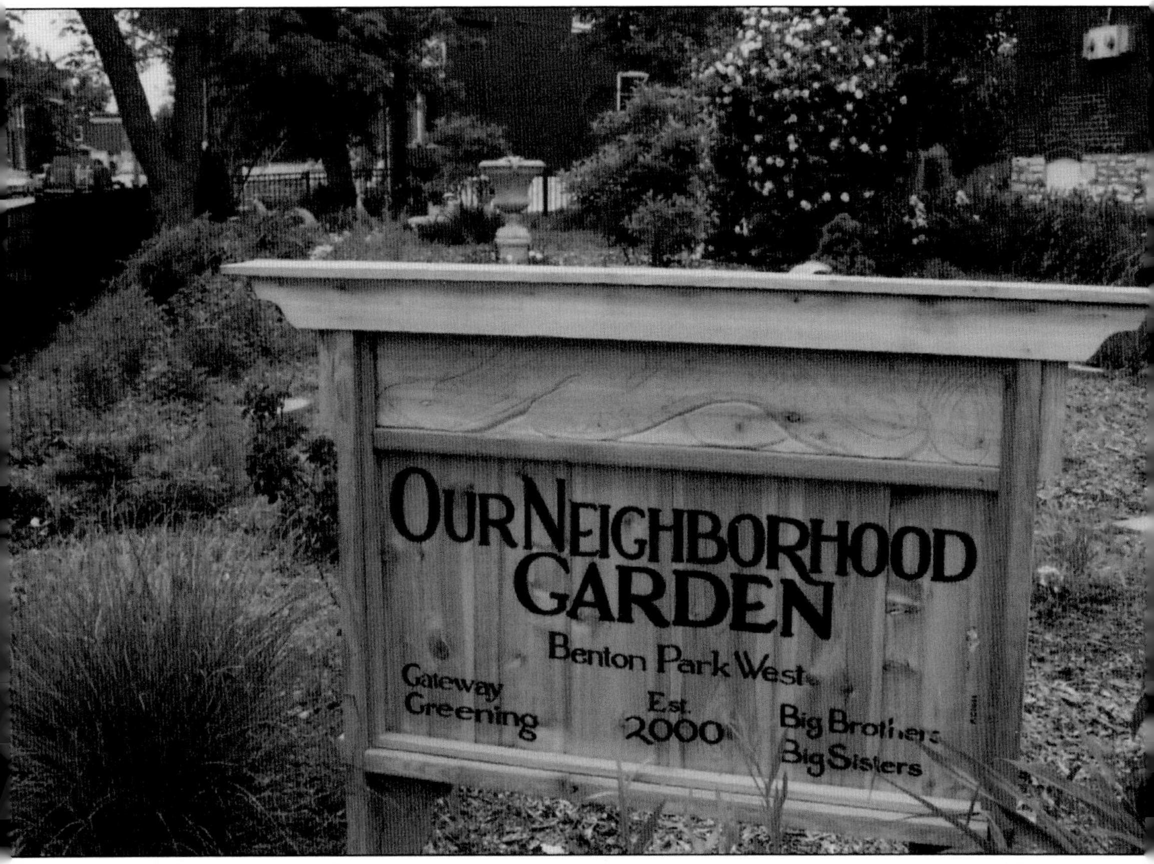

SITE C3: NEIGHBORHOOD GARDEN, SOUTHWEST CORNER OF WYOMING AND CALIFORNIA. In 1891, Philip Sauerwein built a two-story store and dwelling for $2,900. Mr. Sauerwein and his son Philip Jr. were both carpenters. This address was listed as 2800 California when the building permit was granted. In 1920, the resident was East J. Boehm, who owned a dry goods store. He was still listed in 1930. By 1940, William F. Reifeiss had taken over ownership of the store, and in 1952, it was listed as Louis Bartoni, liquors. In 1960 and 1970 it was listed as Magnolia Tavern and in 1980 it was known as the Kitty Kat Tavern. By 1990, the address was no longer listed, and in 2000, this corner became the Benton Park West Neighborhood Garden.

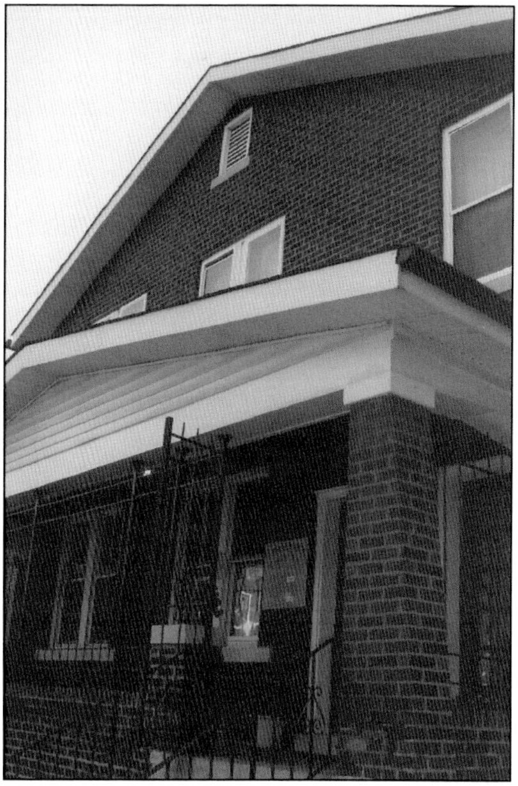

SITE C4: EDMOND'S CHILE, 3236 OREGON. Herman Schulte came to America in 1892, and in 1900, this was the location of his home and dairy. The household consisted of Schulte's wife, Katie; his sister Ana; his stepbrother Herman Winkler, who drove the dairy wagon; and his step siblings, Maggie, Willie, and Tillie Winkler. There were also two boarders—the dairy laborer and a dairy driver. By 1922, Frank Biermann owned the dairy and had a store at 3240 Oregon.

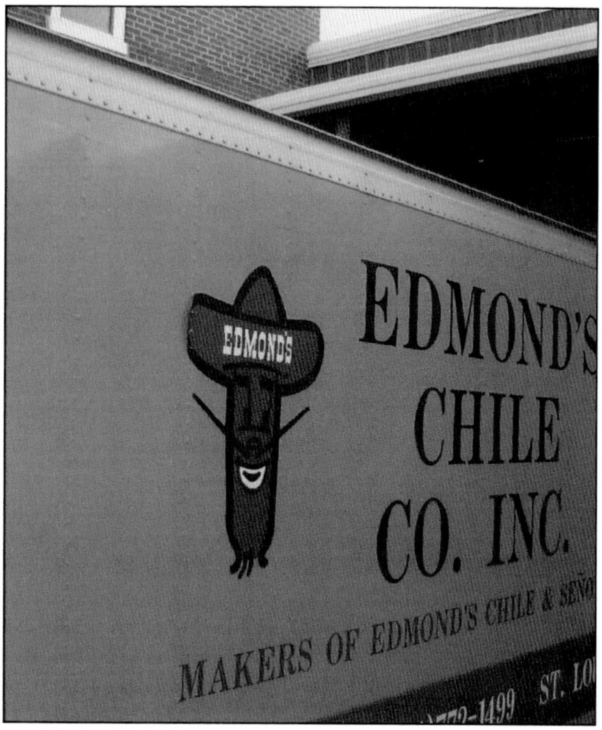

FIFTY YEARS OF CHILI. Business partners Edmond Williams and Harry Brunsen established the company in East St. Louis around 1948 to provide products for O. T. Hodges Chile Parlors. Edmond was O. T. Hodges' son-in-law. In 1950, they moved their business to its present location, which had been part of Biermann's Dairy. Today the company is owned by Mark Adelman.

Site C5: Our Redeemer Evangelical Lutheran Church, 2817 Utah. This congregation was formed in 1894. Their original church was built at 3127 California, the first English Lutheran congregation in south St. Louis. This location was "the site of the first Conference for Institutional Chaplains of the LCMS." It was also the home congregation for Mayor Henry Kiel.

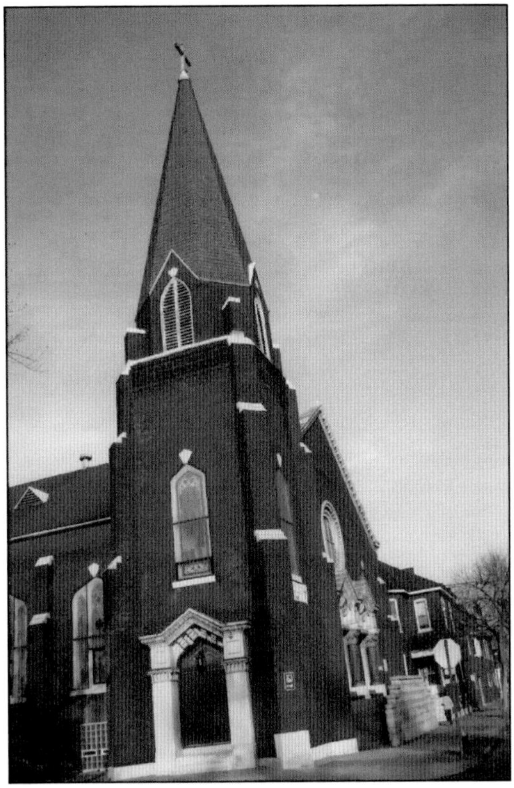

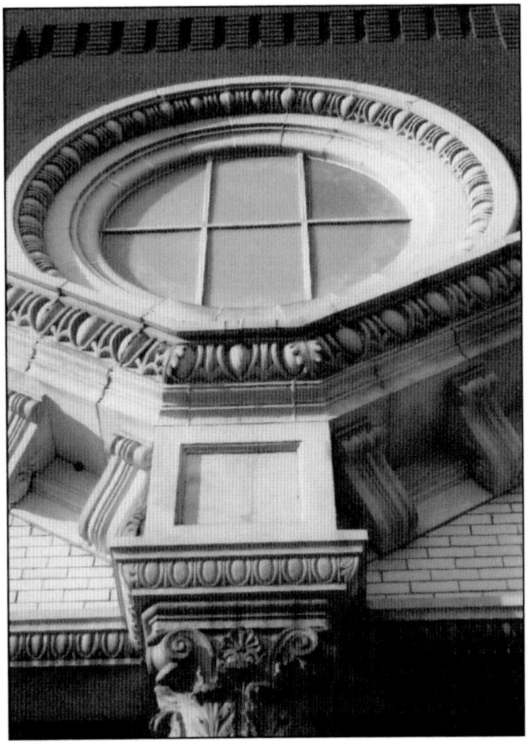

Egg and Dart Design. Our Redeemer has wonderful architectural details, and the exterior exhibits the egg and dart design. This decorative detail can be found across doorways, on columns, above and below cornices, and over or around windows. It can be seen throughout the Benton Park West Neighborhood and south St. Louis. Many of the storefronts on Cherokee used the design along with decorative bricks. It is even possible to find the egg and dart design on iron storefronts.

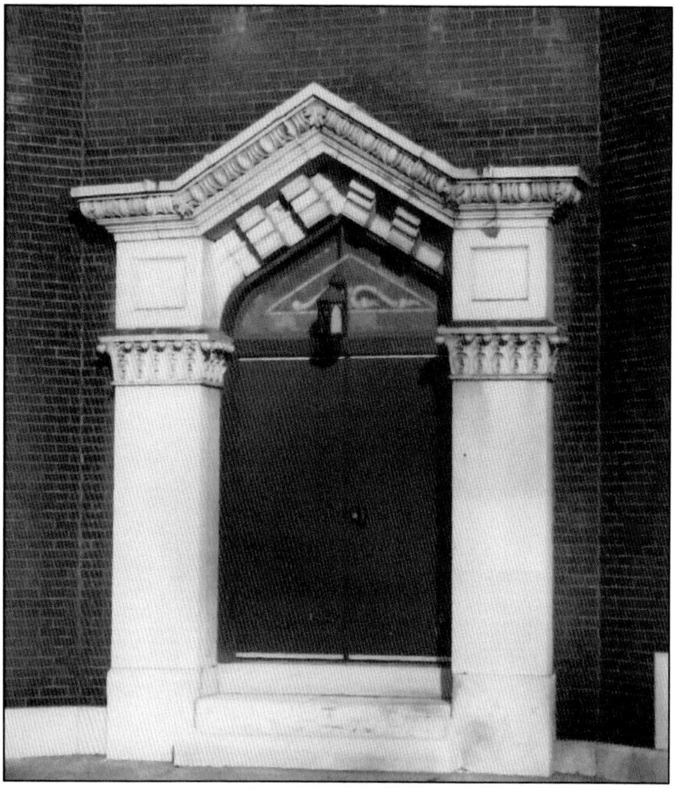

THROUGH THESE DOORS. Mayor Henry Kiel was born in 1871 in St. Louis. He was the first mayor to serve 3 four-year terms. He was elected mayor in 1913 after serving as a ward committeeman. During his administration, the Municipal Auditorium, later named Kiel Auditorium, was constructed. Mayor Kiel was called "father of the Municipal Opera." After retiring from the mayor's office, he became the St. Louis Police Board President. Former Mayor Kiel passed away in 1942.

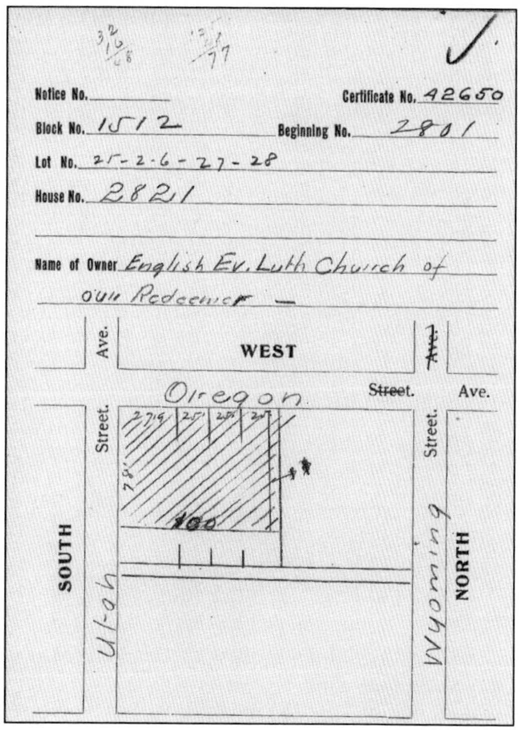

Notice No.
Certificate No. 42650
Block No. 1512
Beginning No. 2801
Lot No. 25-26-27-28
House No. 2821

Name of Owner English Ev. Luth Church of our Redeemer —

BUILDING PERMIT FOR OUR REDEEMER. The church was built in 1908 for $30,800. The parsonage had already been constructed in 1901 at 2815 Utah for $4,000; it was designed by Foell Architectural Company. August Foell was an architect and builder who had his offices at 3349 California. He was born and raised in St. Louis and went into business in 1881; in 1894 he was named president of the company.

SITE C6: WILLIAM G. MERKEL HOME, 2855 UTAH. This four-family consisting of 2855 and 2857 was built in 1895 for Frederick W. Kunst. In 1900, the Eckerick family and the Merkel family were renting 2855. William G. Merkel resided here with his wife, Susia, and six of their seven children. Mr. Merkel was born in New York in 1856. He was 43 in 1900 and worked as a piano tuner in the family business, Merkel Pianos.

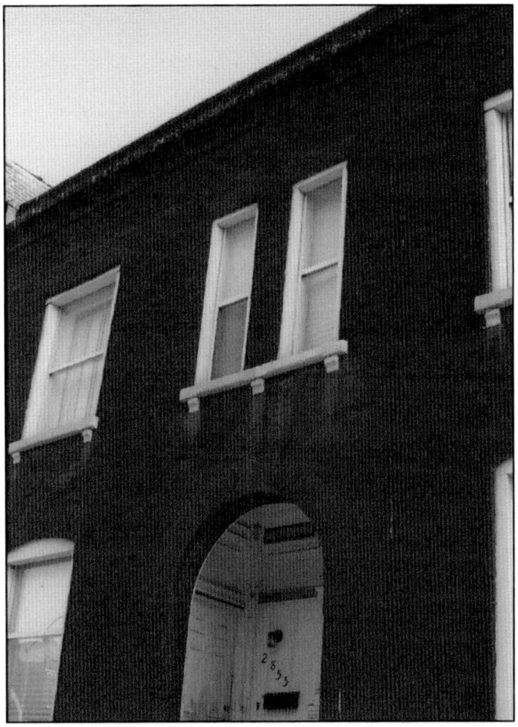

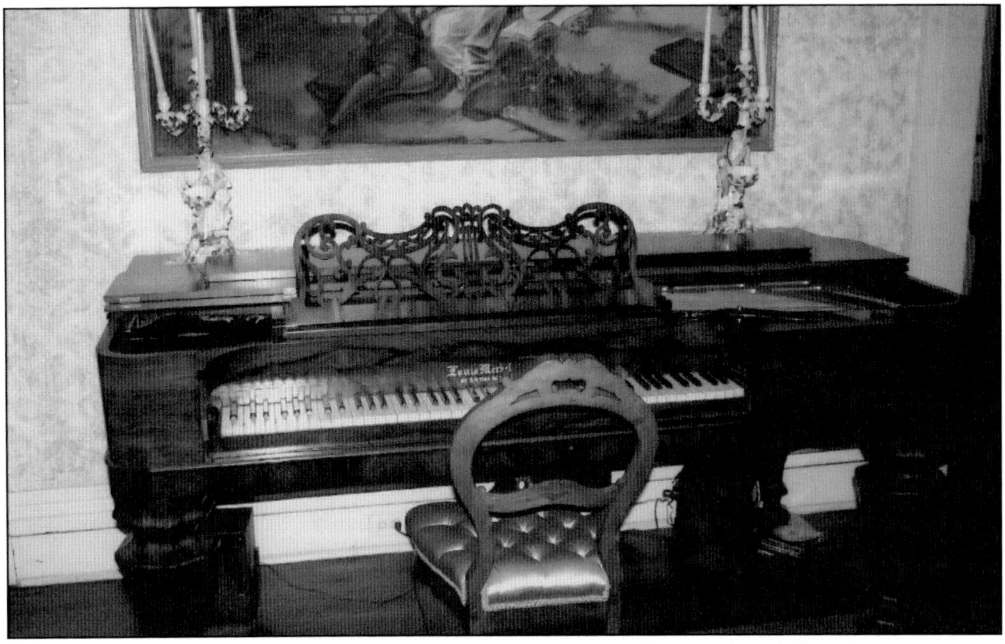

MERKEL PIANOS. Louis C. Merkel, a piano maker, and his family were already listed in St. Louis in the 1860s census. The Merkel family manufactured pianos in St. Louis for more than 100 years. The Merkel piano in this photograph is at the Chatillon-DeMenil Mansion at 3352 DeMenil Place, right off Cherokee Street in the Benton Park Neighborhood. The original parts of the mansion date to the 1840s, when it was a farmhouse.

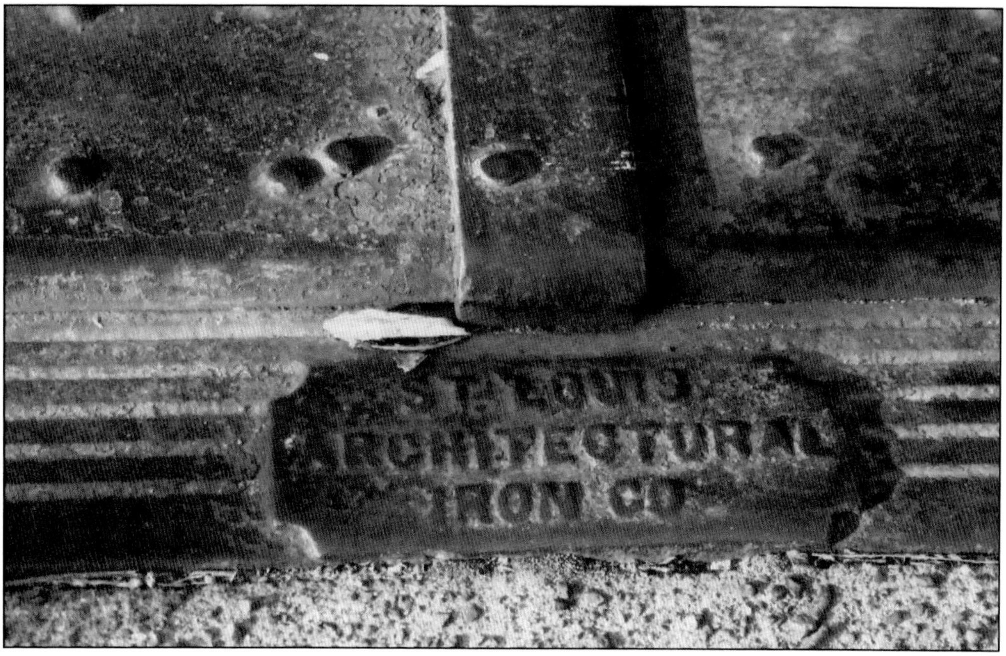

St. Louis Architectural Iron Company. While walking the neighborhood, look for metal plates in sidewalks, metal doors, coal chutes, and iron fences and gates. These tell a story. The St. Louis Architectural Iron Company was listed in the city directories from 1901 to 1928. In 1923, C. A. Simon was president, George J. Simon was vice president, E. P. Simon was secretary, and Walter C. Simon was the treasurer.

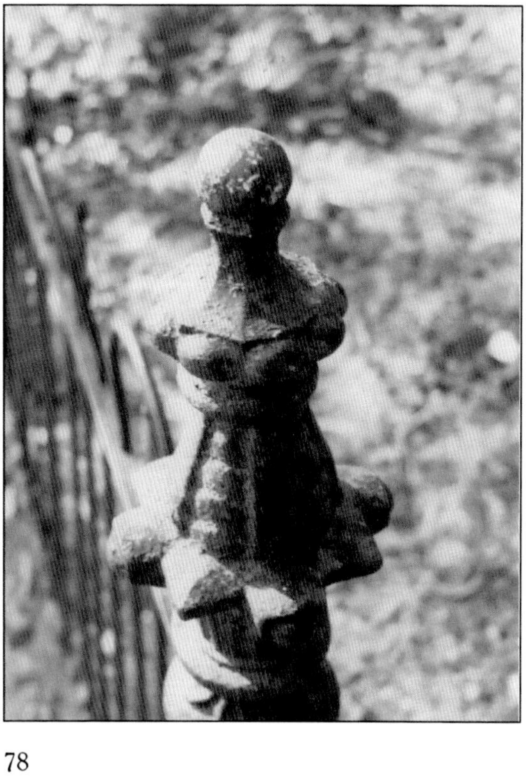

St. Louis Iron and Foundry Industry. When visiting other cities around the country, look for iron store fronts. Who manufactured the historic iron works? Many of these iron storefronts were made in St. Louis. The iron goods could be shipped down the Mississippi River or anywhere in the country by rail. The foundries manufactured fancy architectural pieces such as balconies, storefronts, and fencing or basic works used in jails, vaults, and fire escapes.

SITE C7: BUTCHER'S SHOP, 2831 CHEROKEE. The storefront was built in 1895 by Jeremiah Thompson. Mr. Thompson was a butcher. In 1900, the property was owned by provision dealer, Emil Trolley. This was also the Trolleys' residence. Mr. Trolley was born in Switzerland in 1862 and came to America in 1883 at the age of 16. His wife, Bertha, was born in Illinois, though her parents were born in France. Mr. Trolley's stepson, also named Emil, was a beer brewer.

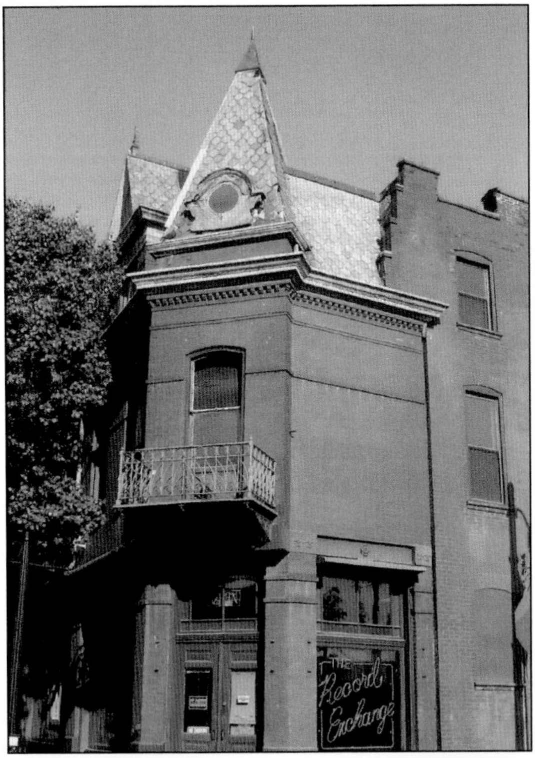

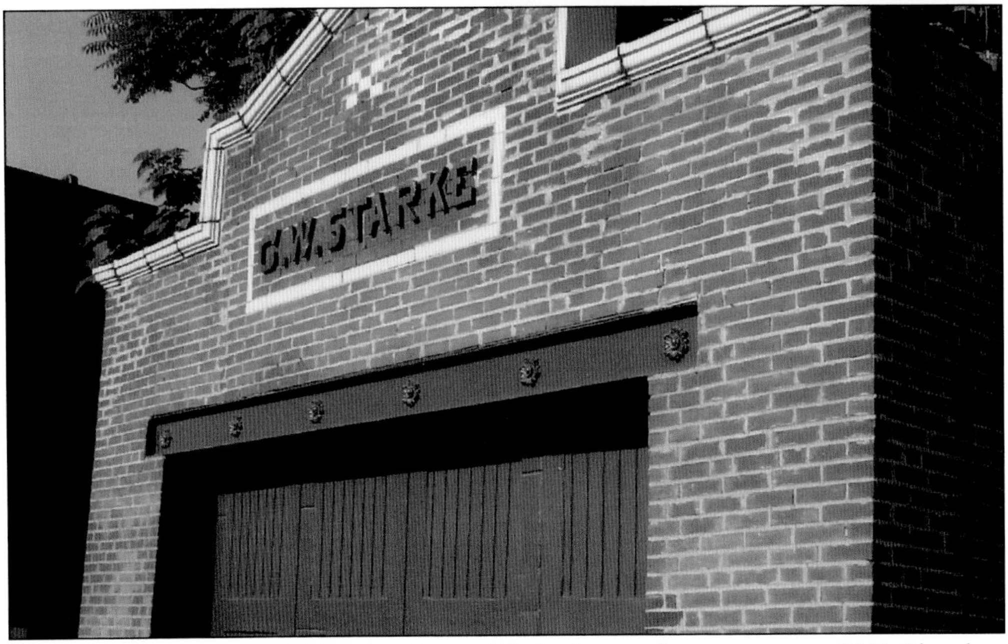

BUTCHER'S GARAGE. By 1915, butcher George W. Starke was the new owner at 2831 Cherokee, and in the early 1920s, the storefront was the George W. Starke Market. By 1927, however, the grocery was listed as Starke & Son. Mr. Starke made several changes to the property: in 1915, he added a bath for $10; in 1925, he added a furnace for $585; and in 1927, he altered the brick garage for $500.

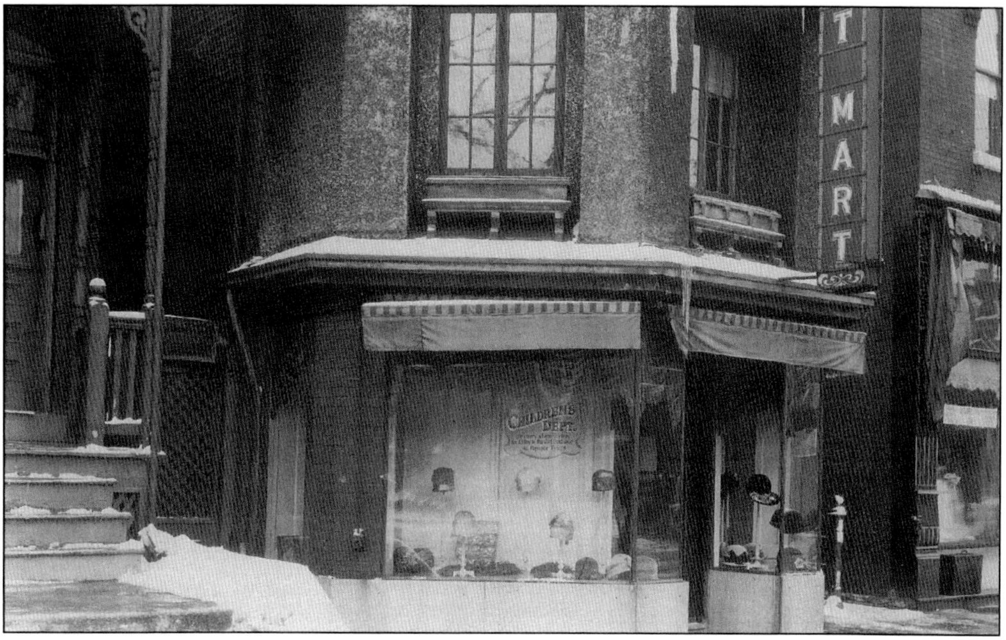

SITE C8: HAT MART, 3411 CALIFORNIA. In 1891, a permit was issued to owner A. Wiest to build a two-story brick dwelling. August Wiest and his son were barbers. This building was also home to August Jr. In 1903, a permit was issued to A. W. Riewe to alter the front of the store. In 1915, Amanda Dohrman moved into the house, and on July 5, she married Henry Maass. They opened the Hat Mart the same year.

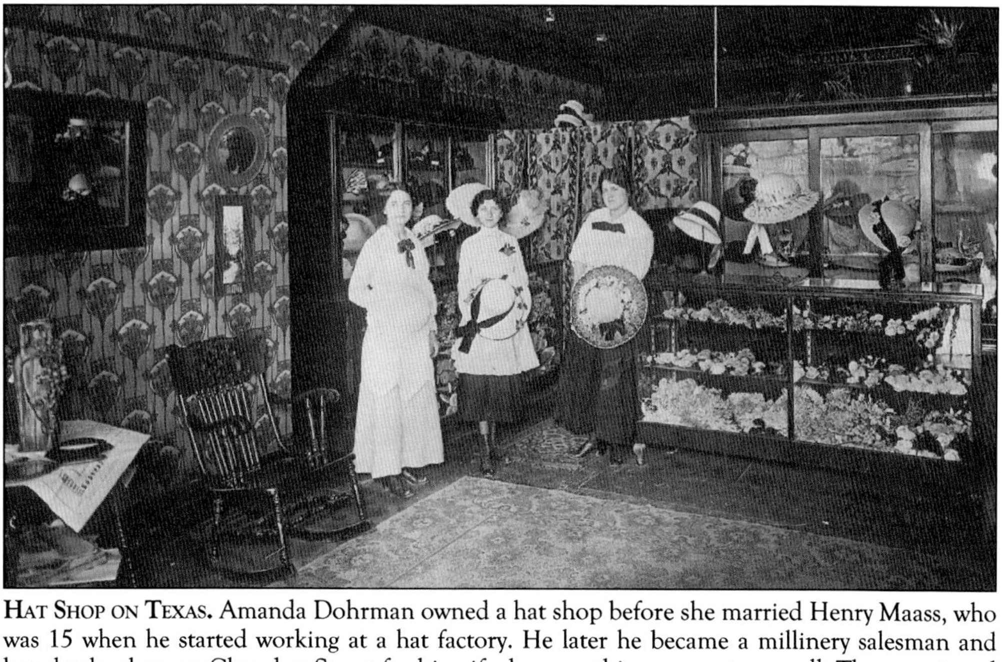

HAT SHOP ON TEXAS. Amanda Dohrman owned a hat shop before she married Henry Maass, who was 15 when he started working at a hat factory. He later he became a millinery salesman and bought the shop on Cherokee Street for his wife, because this one was too small. They continued to invest in the area, and in 1924, Mr. Maass built one-story brick stores at 2822 and 2824 Cherokee. In 1929, a store room was added to the Hat Mart.

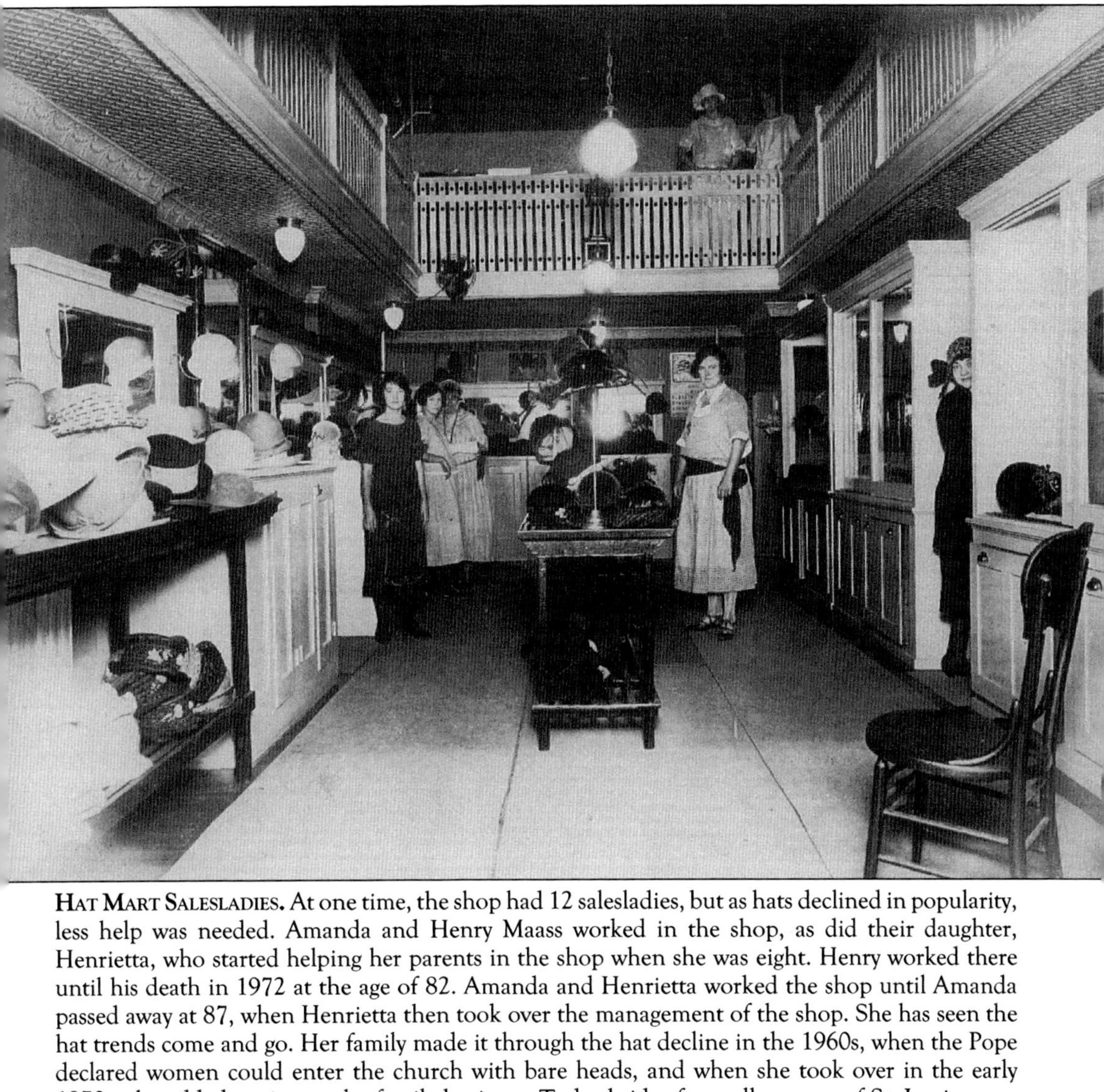

Hat Mart Salesladies. At one time, the shop had 12 salesladies, but as hats declined in popularity, less help was needed. Amanda and Henry Maass worked in the shop, as did their daughter, Henrietta, who started helping her parents in the shop when she was eight. Henry worked there until his death in 1972 at the age of 82. Amanda and Henrietta worked the shop until Amanda passed away at 87, when Henrietta then took over the management of the shop. She has seen the hat trends come and go. Her family made it through the hat decline in the 1960s, when the Pope declared women could enter the church with bare heads, and when she took over in the early 1970s, she added sewing to the family business. Today brides from all corners of St. Louis come to the Hat Mart for their wedding veils and headpieces for their bridesmaids. As long as the old customers keep coming in and new ones take an interest in this south St. Louis landmark, the sign in the window, "Open since 1915," stays up. Henrietta Kupferer's daughter, Jan Beekman, takes care of the everyday business, but a few days a month, Henrietta is still in the shop, waiting and visiting with new friends and long-time customers who are old friends.

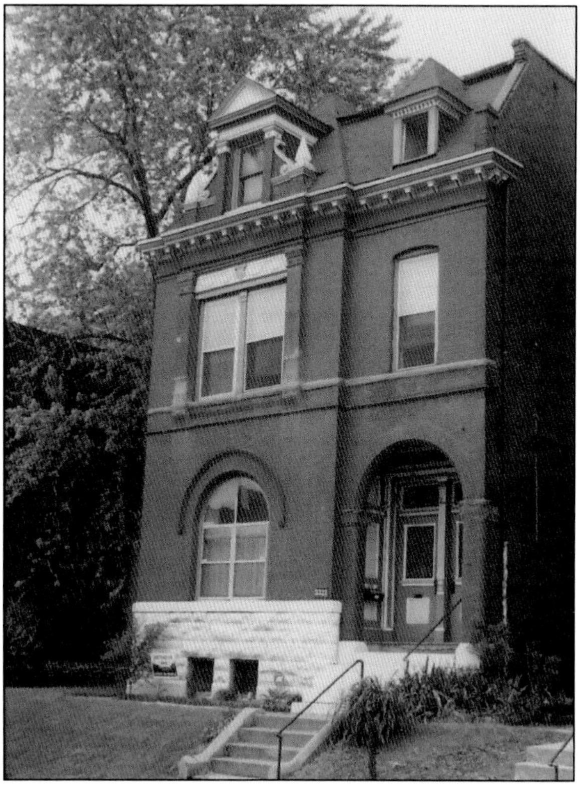

SITE C9: PAULINE EYERMANN RENTAL PROPERTY, 3321 CALIFORNIA. There were two couples renting from Miss Eyermann in 1900. Richard Spiendler and his wife, Margaret, were in one unit. Both born in Germany, Mr. Spiendler was retired and had come to America in 1873. Mrs. Spiendler came in 1851. Frank and Stella Warner lived in the other unit. Mr. Warner was of German descent and worked as a license inspector. Mrs. Warner's father was English, and her mother was Irish.

EYERMANN PROPERTY BUILDING PERMIT. The permit issued in 1892 for the property listed Pauline Eyermann as the owner. Pauline was the daughter of Gottlieb Eyermann, who built his house at the corner of Pestalozzi and Iowa in the 1860s. Miss Eyermann was also the sister of Gottlieb Jr., who lived in the family home at 2906 Iowa; George from 2901 Iowa; and Martha Gabel who lived at 3128 Ohio. Pauline would later marry Adam Arqurieo.

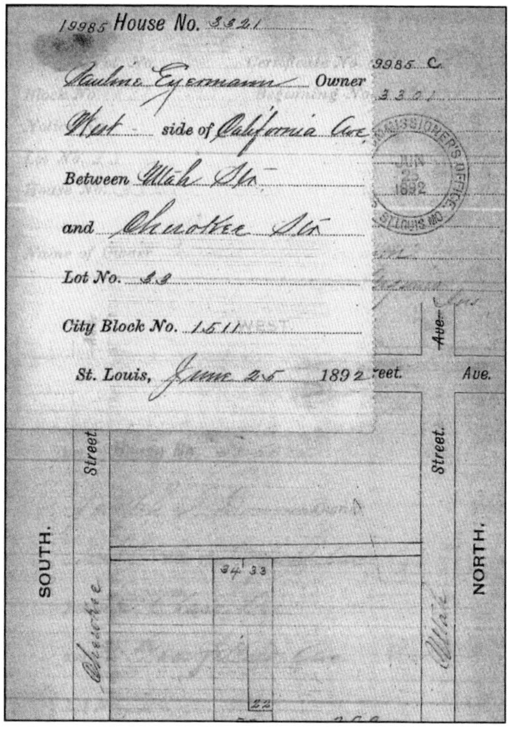

19985 House No. 3321

Pauline Eyermann Owner

West side of California Ave

Between Utah Str.

and Cherokee Str.

Lot No. 33

City Block No. 1511

St. Louis, June 25 1892

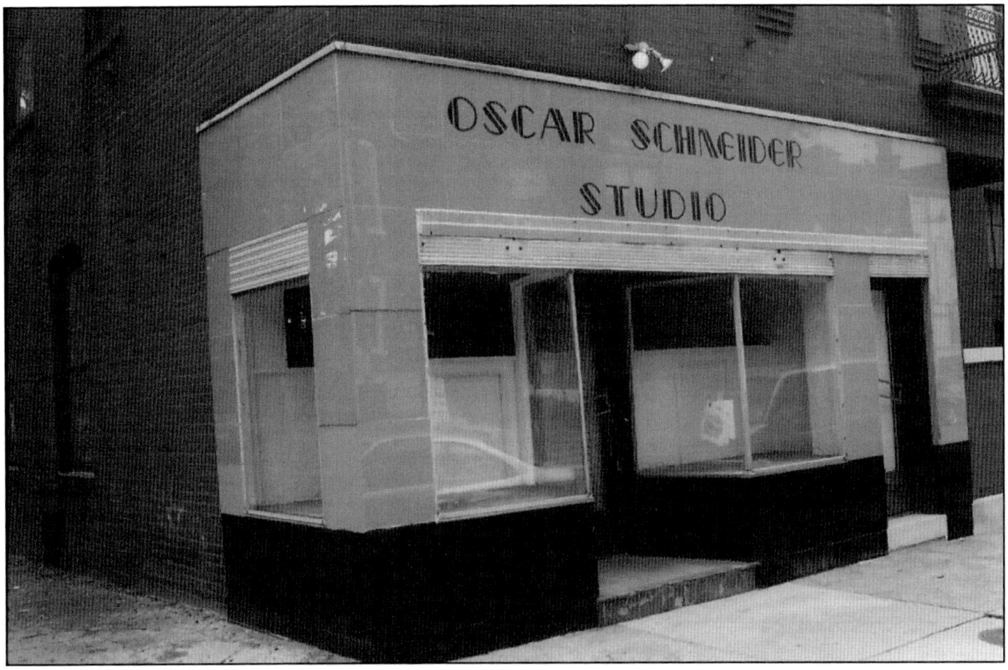

Site C10: Schneider Photography Studio, 3314 California. Before Mr. Schneider moved his studio to this address, he was listed at 3414A California in 1913 and 1914. The studio remained at this location at least until 1980. In 1952, Mr. Schneider shared the address with Raymond Davenport, a dentist. In the early years, Oscar Schneider and his wife, Bertha, were also listed here as residents.

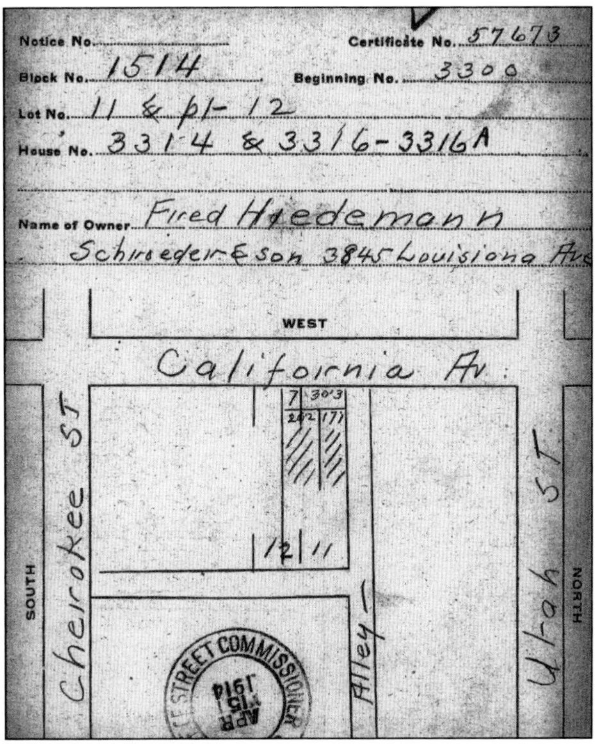

Notice No.
Certificate No. 57673
Block No. 1514
Beginning No. 3300
Lot No. 11 & pt 12
House No. 3314 & 3316-3316A
Name of Owner Fred Hiedemann
Schroeder & Son 3845 Louisiana Av
WEST
California Av.
SOUTH
Cherokee St
NORTH
Utah St
Alley
STREET COMMISSIONER
APR 15 1914

Street Commissioner's Office Building Permit. The permit lists 3314, 3316, and 3316A California. Who were the residents of 3316? In 1920, F. G. and Mary Weiss lived at 3316, and L. E. and Emma Tussner lived in 3316A. In 1925 and 1930, Helen and August Meyer were the new residents of 3316, and Arthur and Lillie Edel were in 3316A. By 1935, the Edels had moved into 3316, and 3316A was occupied by Harold and Elizabeth Woodley.

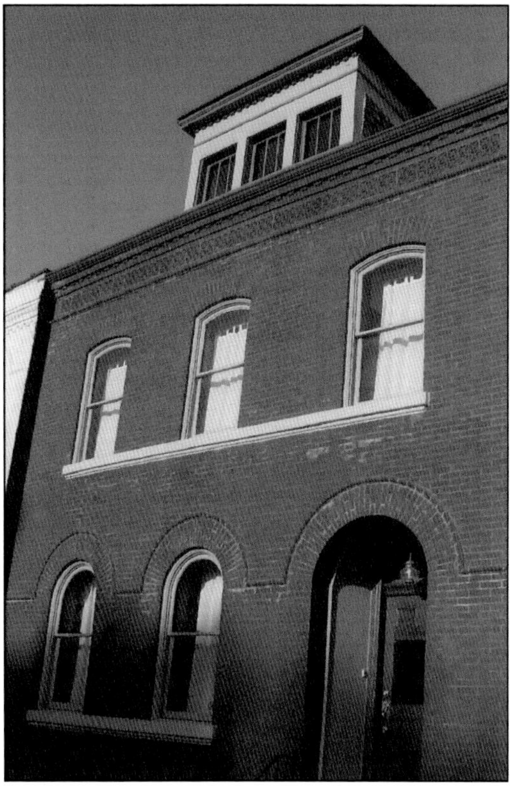

Site C11: Dr. Adam Fuhrmann's Rental Property, 3227 California. In the 1890s, Dr. Fuhrmann owned this house and the one next door at 3221 California. He and his family resided at 3221 and this house they rented out. In 1900, Charles Sommer, his wife Minnie, and their children lived here. Mr. Sommer was born in Germany and came to America in 1858; he was a school principal. Their son Carl was a traveling salesman. In 2004, Beachfront Properties bought these two houses for rehabilitation.

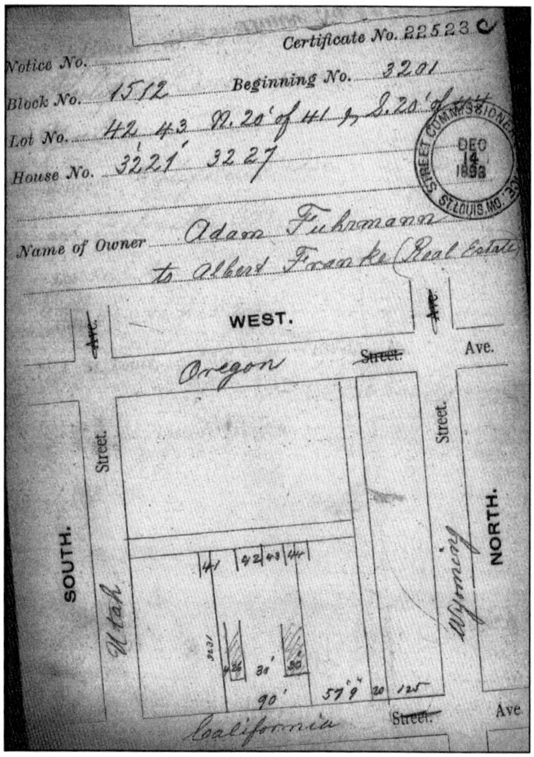

1893 Building Permit for 3221 and 3227 California. This building permit is from the Street Commissioner's Office. The other permit was issued in 1892 for a one-brick dwelling at the cost of $3,400. Dr. Adam Fuhrmann built the two houses, but got only one permit, so it is unclear which home was built for $3,400. It is quite common for building permits to be missing, or for only one permit to be issued for several houses.

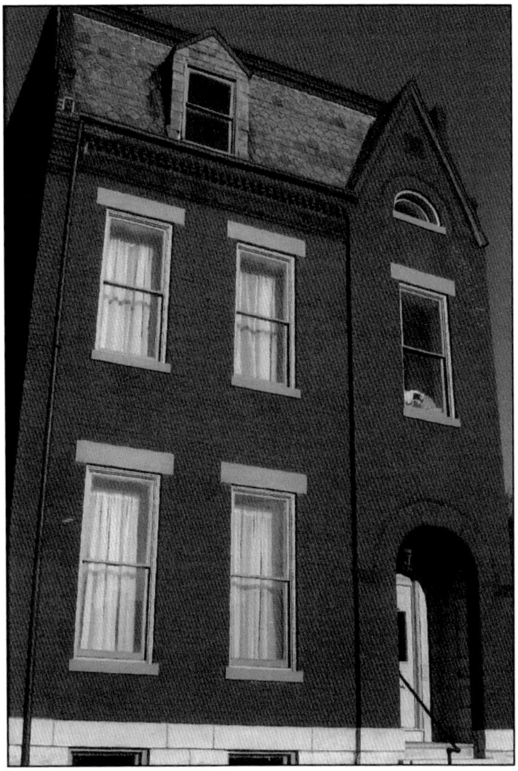

Fuhrmann Residence, 3221 California. Adam Fuhrmann was a physician, born in Missouri to German immigrant parents in 1854. In 1900, he and his wife, Emma, had been married for 21 years. Mrs. Fuhrmann gave birth to eight children, but only six were living. Richard, the oldest, was in college; Jesse was a grocery salesman; and Carrie, Frank, and Bessie were in school.

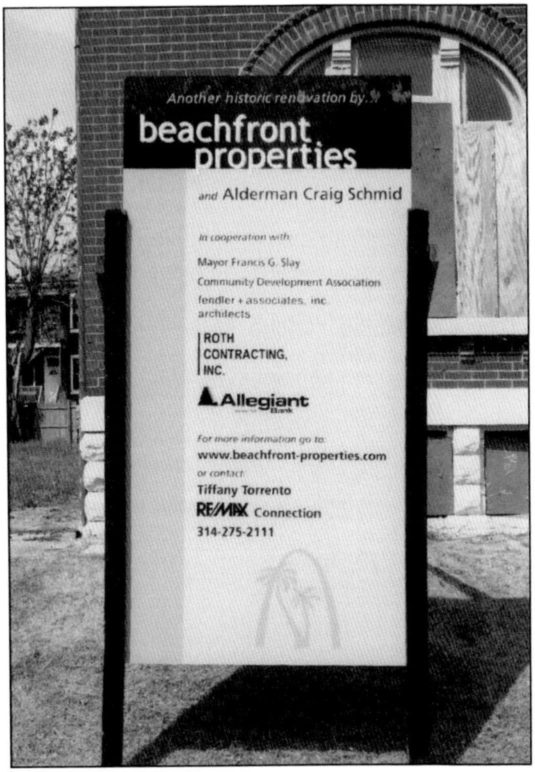

Beachfront Properties. Neal Josehart started the company with one property in 2001. Today Beachfront has projects throughout the city with concentration in Benton Park West and Benton Park. Josehart works exclusively with Paul Fendler of Fendler & Associates Architects. The company updates the living space in historic homes for modern-day living. Other properties in the neighborhood rehabilitated by Beachfront are at 2818 Wyoming, and 3248 and 3250 California.

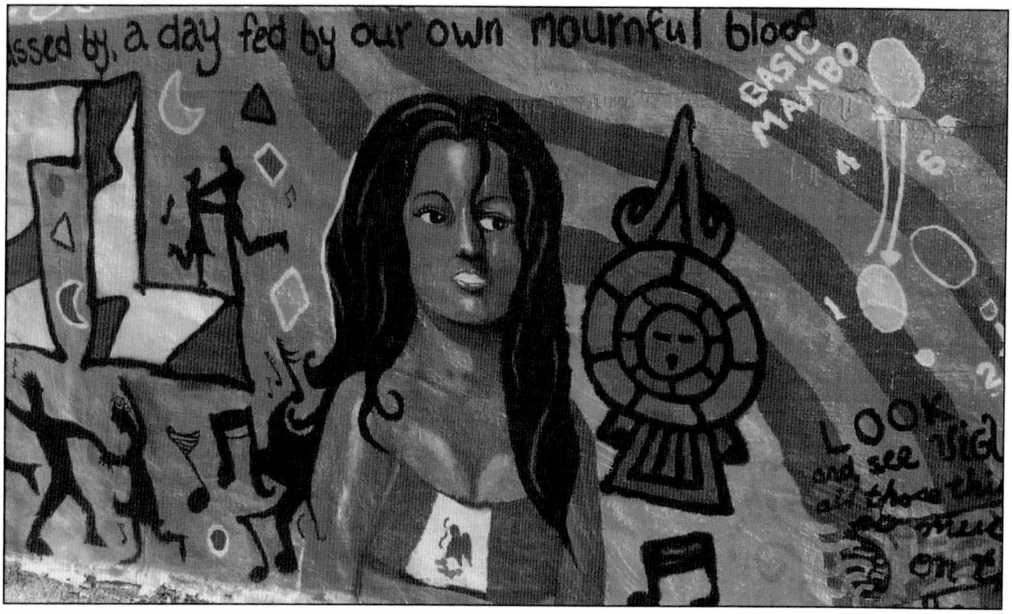

Site C12: Wall Mural, 3333 Iowa. The Casa Loma Ballroom donated the wall space for this project. Students from the Immigrant Youth Group of the Southside Catholic Family Services Hispanic Center and members of the community painted the mural. This after-school program provides tutors and mentors from Washington University to help underprivileged Hispanic students. It is coordinated by a nonprofit organization and Washington University Spanish Department's Volunteer Program for Students of Spanish.

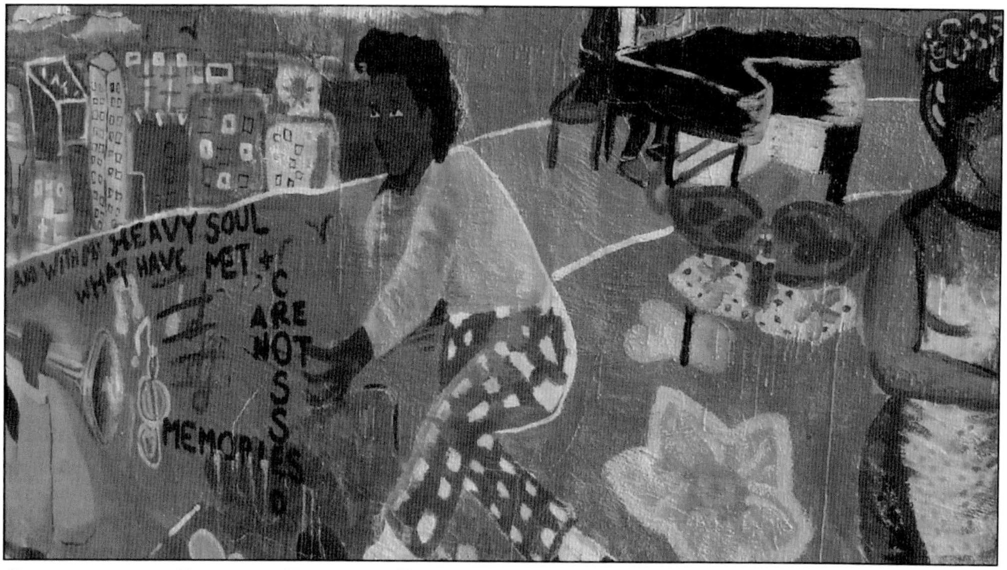

Celebration of Cultural Diversity, Painted 2002. Washington University Professor Virginia Braxs spearheaded this project. Other coordinators were local artists Sarah Paulsen and Eric Repise. The Cherokee Business District and the Cherokee community also supported the project. Materials were donated by ICI Paint–based in Puerto Rico; Home Depot; and private donors. Mayor Slay unveiled the MAP (Mural Art Project) during the Cinco de Mayo Celebrations on Cherokee Street.

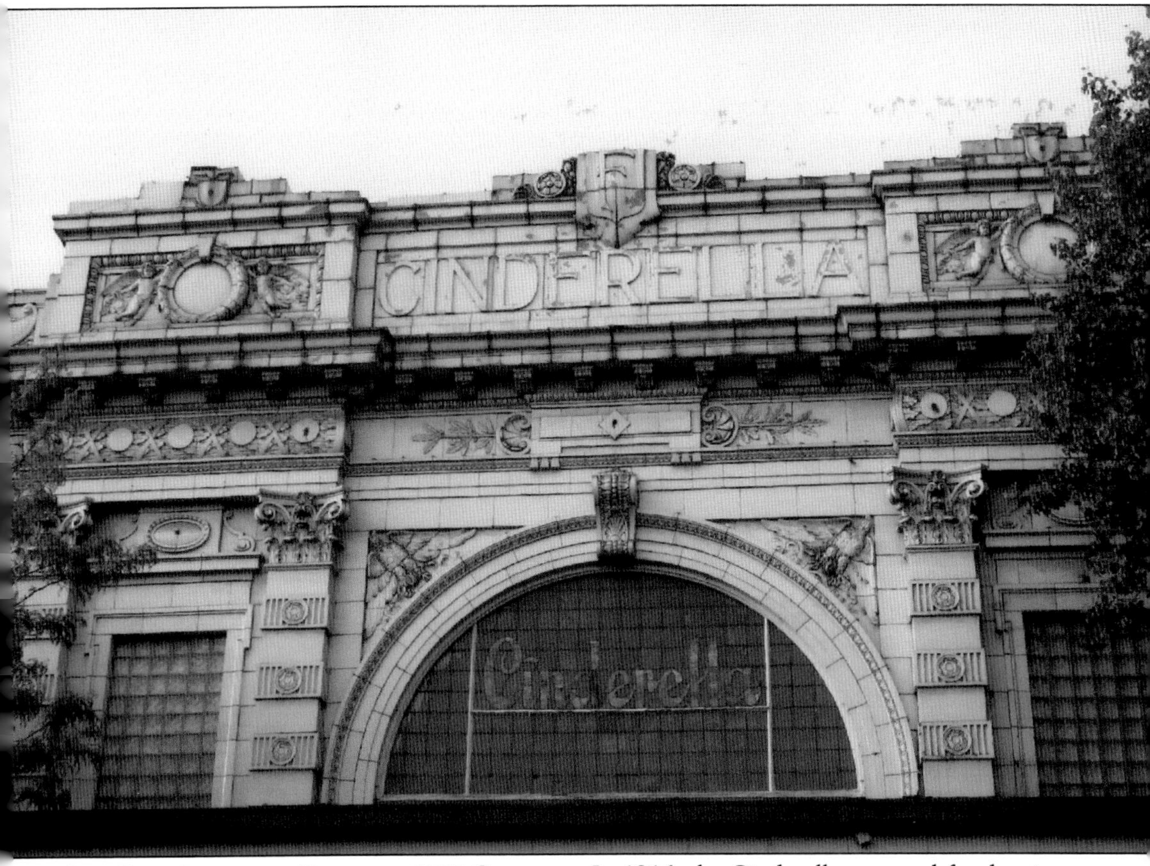

SITE C13: CINDERELLA BUILDING, 2737 CHEROKEE. In 1916, the Cinderella was used for dancing and skating. In 1918, there were several Cinderella businesses listed on Cherokee Street: the Cinderella Candy Company at 2703, the Cinderella Summer Theatre at 2727, and the Cinderella Theatre at 2735. By 1923, the Cinderella's businesses had changed again, and there were the Cinderella Restaurant at 2726 Cherokee and the Cinderella Air Dome at 2727. The back of theater was demolished in 1962, leaving the front facade of the building for shop and office space. Cherokee Street has plenty of theater history, and the Wehrenberg Theatres are still in operation today. Fred Wehrenberg was a former blacksmith who opened a saloon, grocery ,and butcher shop at the corner of Cherokee and South Jefferson. During the 1904 World's Fair in St. Louis, he was intrigued by one of the exhibits at the fair, a film clip. In 1906, he turned the bakery space into the Cherokee Theatre, setting up 99 kitchen chairs and a piano. Business took off, and the saloon became the concession stand. It went so well that Wehrenberg opened his second theater, St. Louis's first Airdome. He fenced in a vacant lot and set up chairs and benches with a projector at one end and a screen at the opposite end to show the movies. In the winter, a tent and potbelly stoves were set up to keep the customers warm.

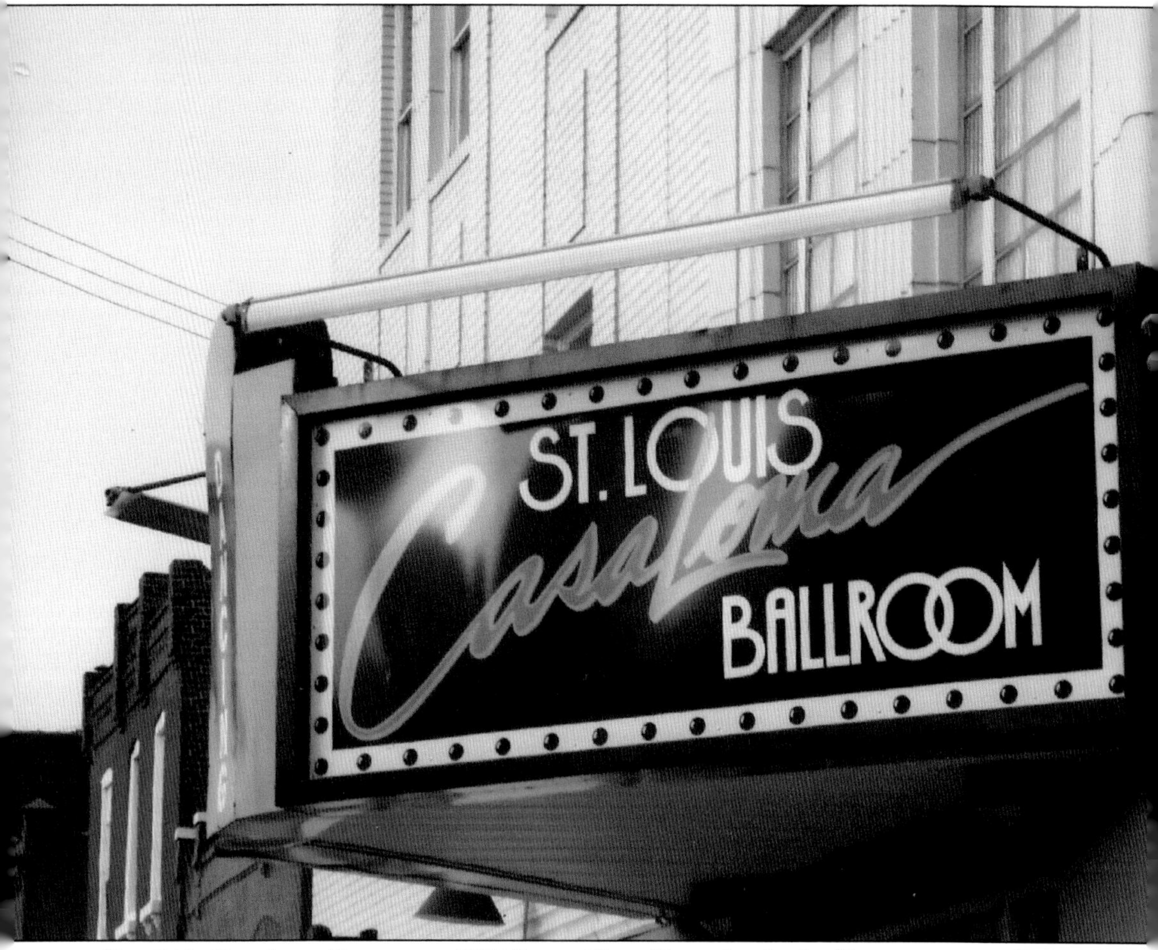

Site C14: Casa Loma Ballroom, 3354 Iowa. The address for this building was originally listed as 3342–3354 Iowa and 2715–2725 Cherokee. On April 4, 1926, H. & E. Freund was granted a building permit for a two-story brick store and hall costing $62,300. After the Freund brothers, the next owners were Art Kawell and H. J. Burian. In 1967, Ellen and Norman Reichert bought the ballroom from Art Kawell. The ballroom, known as the Cinderella Dance Academy, the Cinderella Dance Palace, the Showboat, and finally the Casa Loma Ballroom, is still in full swing. The Brannons bought the ballroom in 1990 and schedule events throughout the year. The ballroom is available for wedding receptions, parties, business meetings, special events, and of course, dancing.

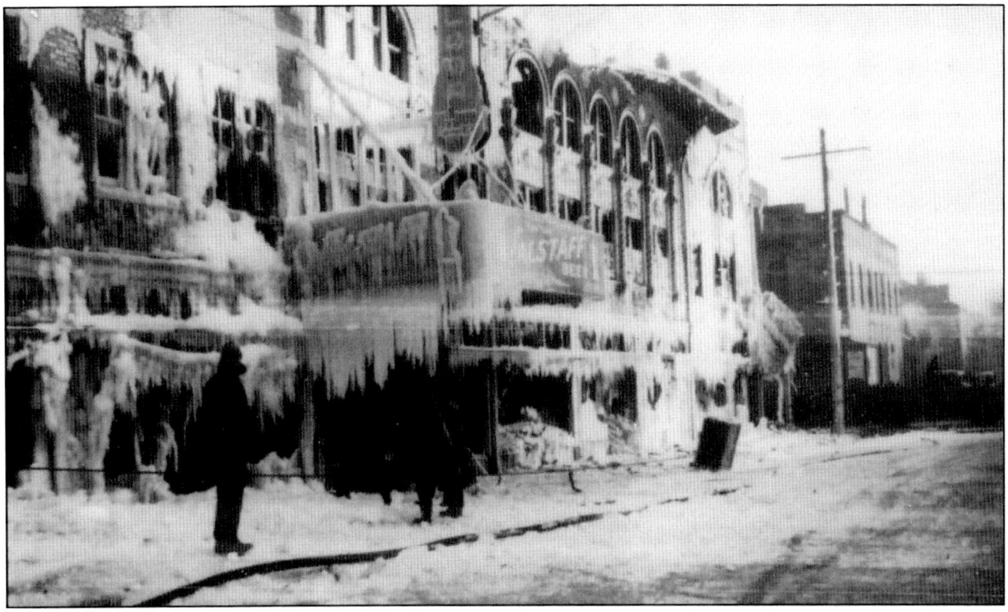

MORNING AFTER THE FIRE. The ballroom is a south St. Louis Landmark, dating back to the mid-1930s. On January 19, 1940, a fire broke out, but within a year, the ballroom was reopened. It featured big names like Tommy and Jimmy Dorsey, Frank Sinatra, Benny Goodman, the Mills Brothers, Tony Bennett, and Nat King Cole. The wooden dance floor measured 5,000 square feet. It brought in 2,000 people during its heyday when admission was 35¢ a head.

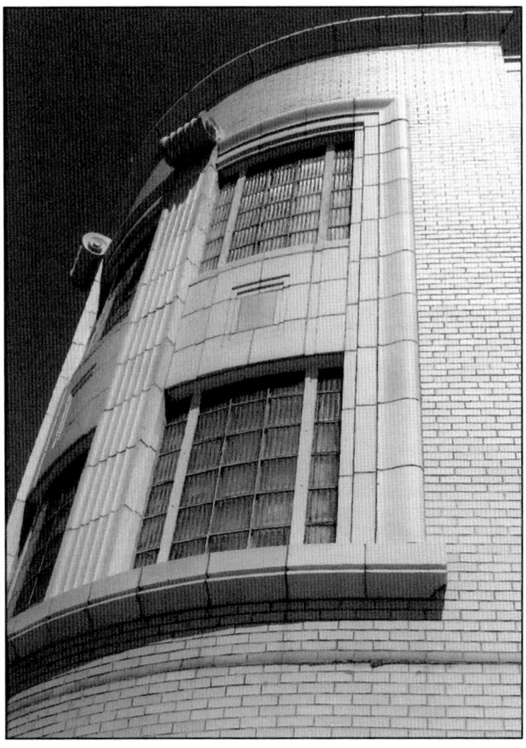

A PLACE TO REMEMBER. The dance floor was cushioned so dancers could waltz and dance the foxtrot without getting tired. One story claims that Tennessee Williams crafted the Paradise Dance Hall in his play *The Glass Menagerie* on the Casa Loma Ballroom. Tennessee Williams came to St. Louis with his family in 1918, later attending Washington University. He was inducted into the St. Louis Hall of Fame, located at 6500 Delmar, in 1989.

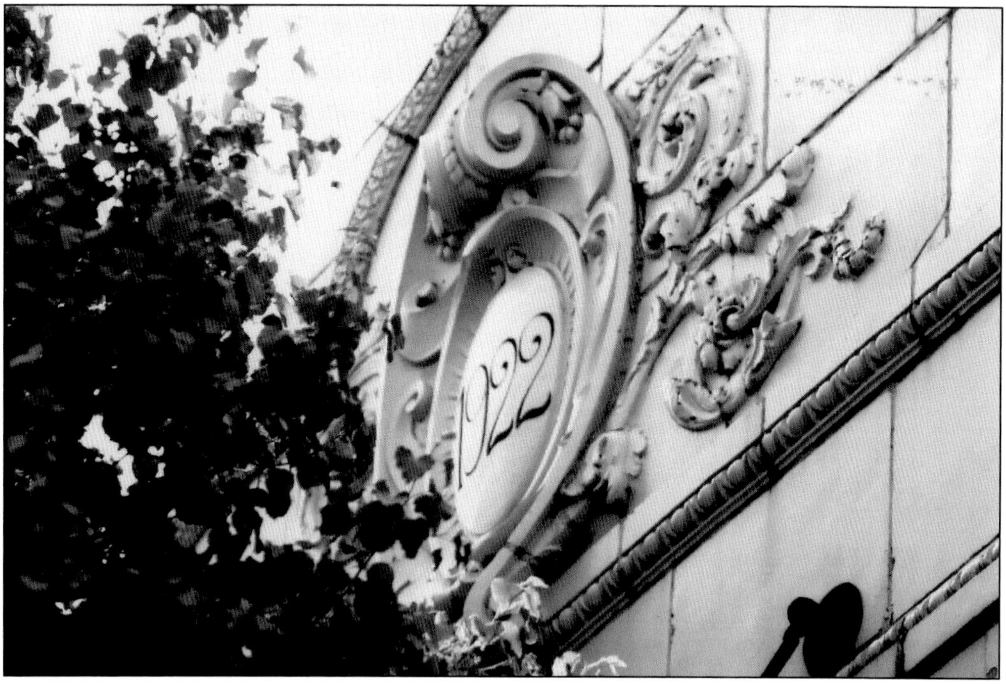

SITE C15: FORMER CHEROKEE BREWERY SITE, 2720 CHEROKEE. The brewery was established in 1867. Starting out as Herold & Loebs Brewing Company, it later became the Cherokee Brewery, covering the entire block. The company brewed lager beer, ale, and porter. In the early days, it employed 40–50 hands and used 10–12 wagons and 40 horses daily to deliver its product. In 1922, the building got a face lift when it became Smith's Furniture.

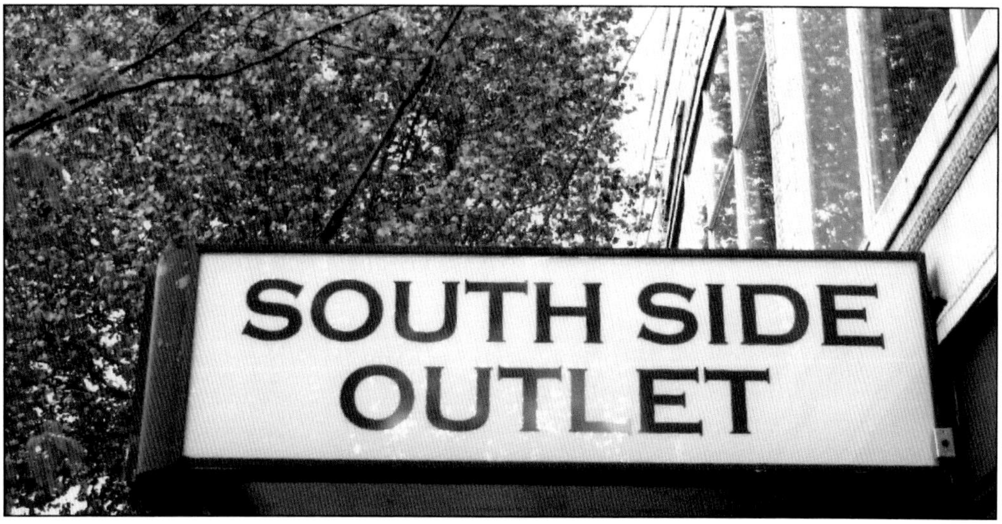

SOUTH SIDE OUTLET. In 2002, the South Side Outlet opened as part of the Cherokee Place business incubator, a project sponsored by SSDN to help revitalize Cherokee Street. The business incubator provides retail and office space below market rates and helps owners develop business plans and provides basic business training. The goal is for tenants to move into a larger space on Cherokee Street within five years. Pam Jacobsen manages, and is an owner of, the South Side Outlet.

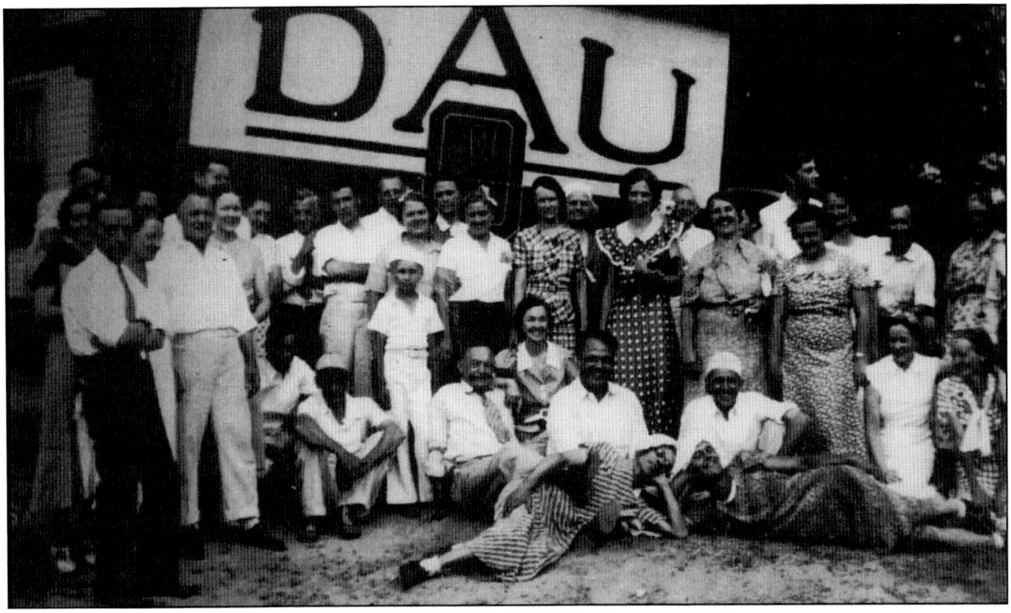

Dau Furniture Company Employee Picnic. Smith's Furniture Company opened at 2720 Cherokee in the early 1920s, where it remained until 1932. Dau, the house furnisher who had been at 2649 Cherokee, was at this address from 1937 to 1980. The Dau family has been in the furniture business in the St. Louis area since 1894. The original store was located at 1214 Cass. They also had branches at 2730 North Grand, 5950 Easton, and 3409 South Jefferson.

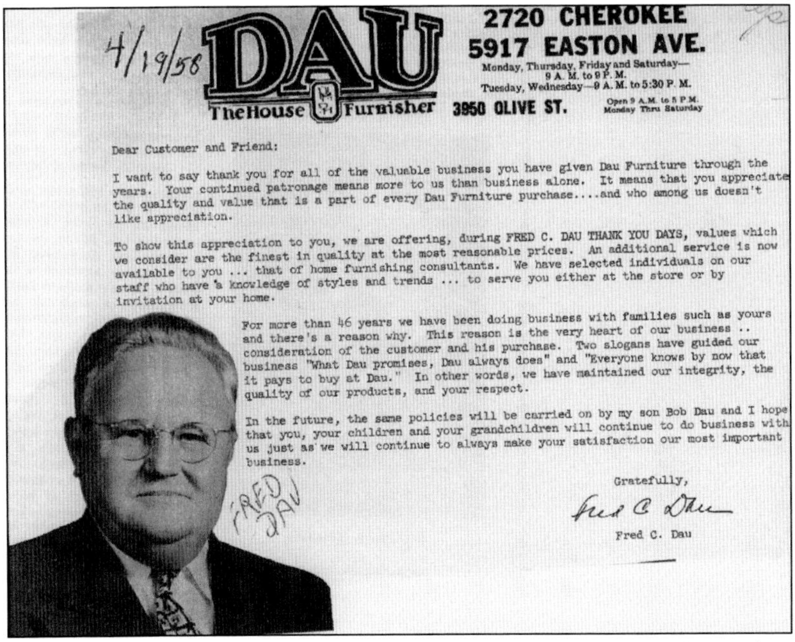

4/19/58

DAU The House Furnisher

2720 CHEROKEE
5917 EASTON AVE.
Monday, Thursday, Friday and Saturday— 9 A. M. to 9 P. M.
Tuesday, Wednesday—9 A. M. to 5:30 P. M.
3950 OLIVE ST.
Open 9 A.M. to 5 P.M. Monday Thru Saturday

Dear Customer and Friend:

I want to say thank you for all of the valuable business you have given Dau Furniture through the years. Your continued patronage means more to us than business alone. It means that you appreciate the quality and value that is a part of every Dau Furniture purchase....and who among us doesn't like appreciation.

To show this appreciation to you, we are offering, during FRED C. DAU THANK YOU DAYS, values which we consider are the finest in quality at the most reasonable prices. An additional service is now available to you ... that of home furnishing consultants. We have selected individuals on our staff who have a knowledge of styles and trends ... to serve you either at the store or by invitation at your home.

For more than 46 years we have been doing business with families such as yours and there's a reason why. This reason is the very heart of our business .. consideration of the customer and his purchase. Two slogans have guided our business "What Dau promises, Dau always does" and "Everyone knows by now that it pays to buy at Dau." In other words, we have maintained our integrity, the quality of our products, and your respect.

In the future, the same policies will be carried on by my son Bob Dau and I hope that you, your children and your grandchildren will continue to do business with us just as we will continue to always make your satisfaction our most important business.

Gratefully,

Fred C. Dau

Fred C. Dau

FRED DAU

1950s Dau Furniture Company Letterhead. This company was founded by Ferdinand Dau, a cabinet maker. Mr. Dau was born in Germany and came to America in 1868. Fred C. Dau went to work for his father in 1916 and was put in charge of the Cherokee branch store in 1920. He was a business leader who helped make Cherokee Street the place for South Siders to shop. Today the store is located in Ellisville. Ferdinand's great-grandson Paul Dau is president.

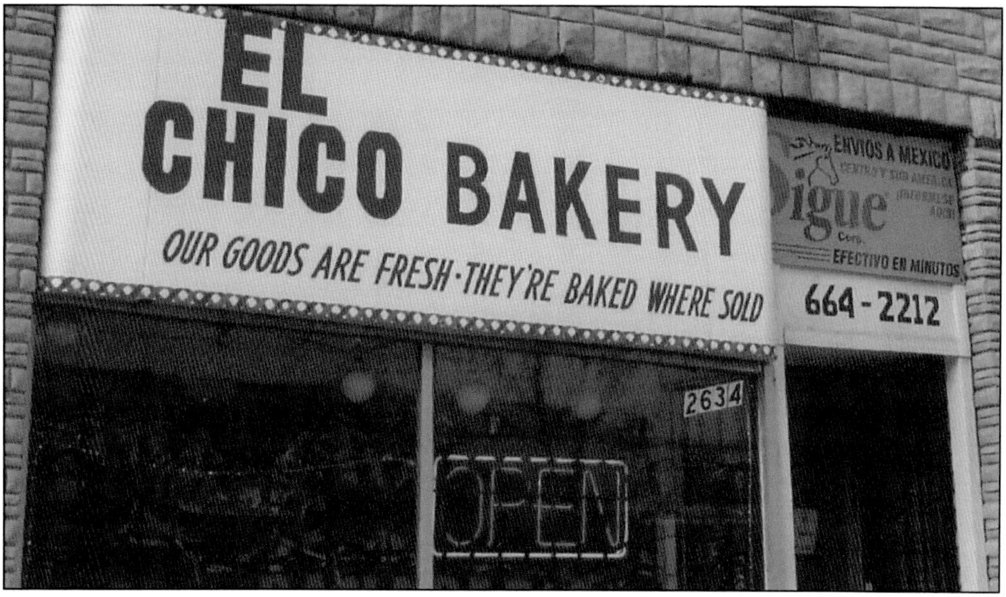

SITE C16: FORMER FROEHLICH BAKERY, 2634 CHEROKEE. In 1912, Henry Froehlich had 2632 and 2634 built by G. Kappler for $8,000. We know there was a frame structure at 2632 before 1912, because two days before the permit was issued to build the current building, there was a permit to wreck a structure on the site. Mr. Froehlich was already on the block; in 1883, he had a one-story frame store built at 2646 for $150.

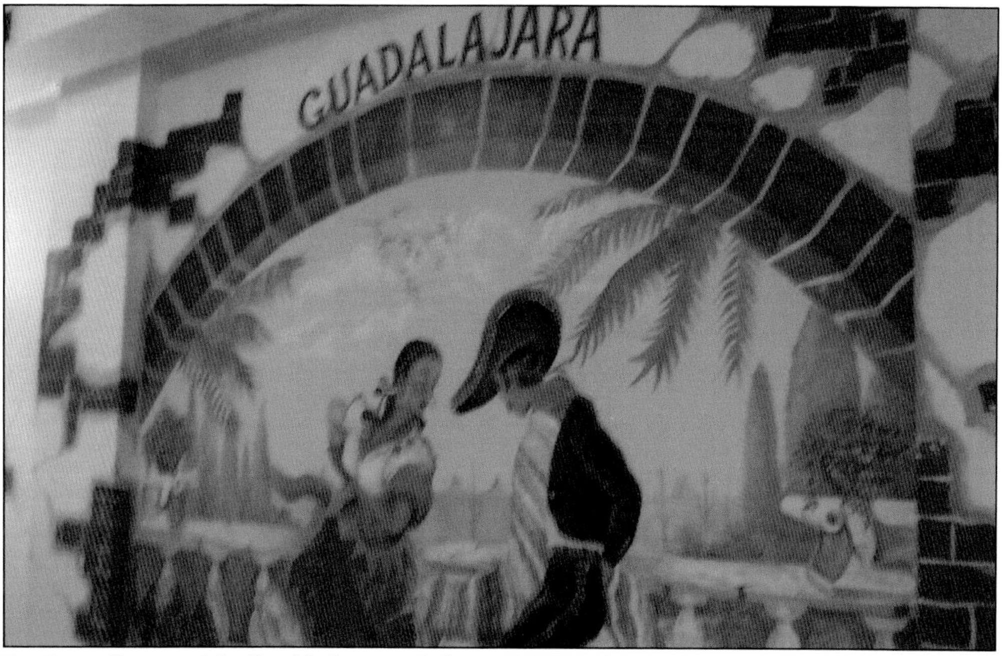

EL CHICO BAKERY. Mr. Froehlich was a baker at 2634 and rented 2632 to other businesses. By 1922, the bakery had changed hands and Emil Weinbrecht was granted a permit to repair a bakery oven for $250. The Riveras bought the building in 1999 for their bakery and began by renting out 2632 to another business while they ran the bakery from 2634. This mural is on a wall in 2632, which is currently a sitting area for the bakery.

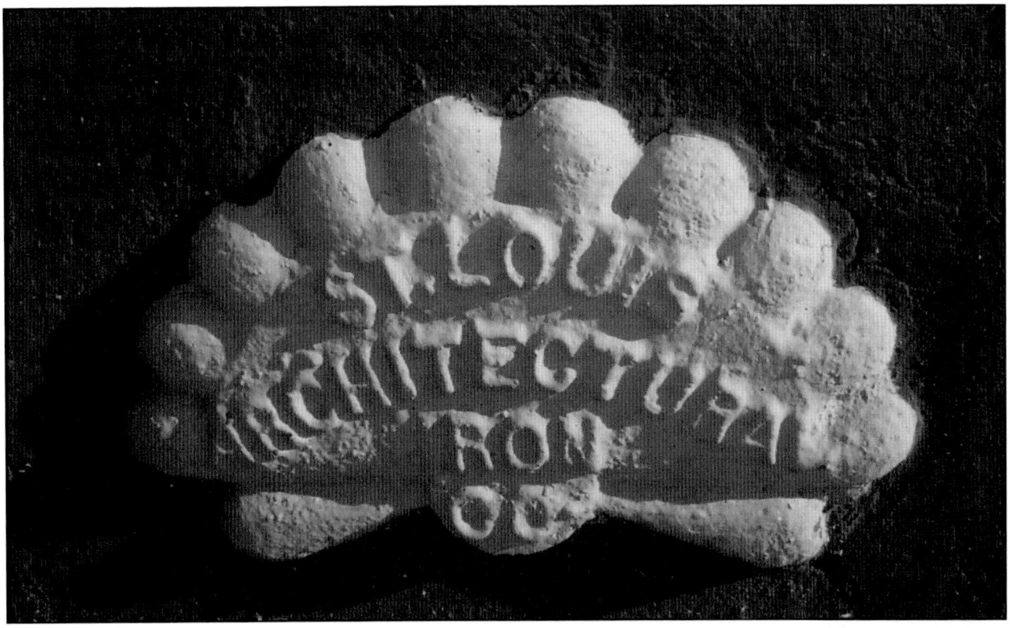

SITE C17: STOREFRONTS, 2617 AND 2619 CHEROKEE. These storefronts were manufactured by St. Louis Architectural Iron Company for the Muellers in 1892. Fred Mueller came from Germany in 1867 and was a wagon manufacturer. His wife, Henrietta, was born in Missouri, and in 1900, had been married to Fred for 19 years. They had three sons; the oldest, Fred, was a candy salesman; Alfred was a messenger; and Henry was in school. Their business and residence were at 2617.

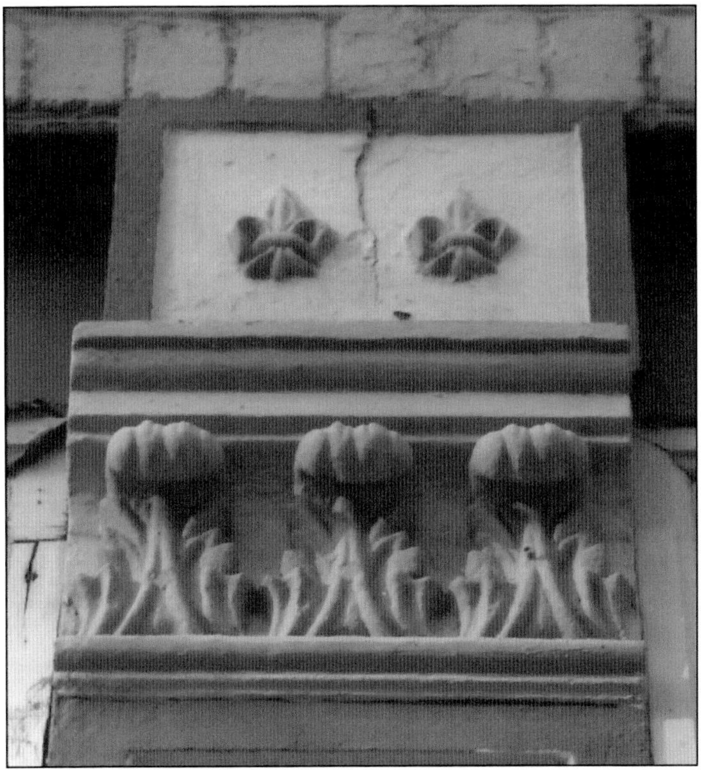

EVA REINER AND NEIGHBORS, 2619 CHEROKEE. Eva Reiner, a widow, rented this space from the Muellers. Born in 1840, she came to America from Germany in 1860. Next door to the widow at 2621 was the Buol family. Paul Buol was one of the brothers who owned Buol Brothers Livery and Undertaking. The family had a servant and took in boarders. The boarders all worked for the livery as machinist for the buggies, watchmen, hostlers, and drivers.

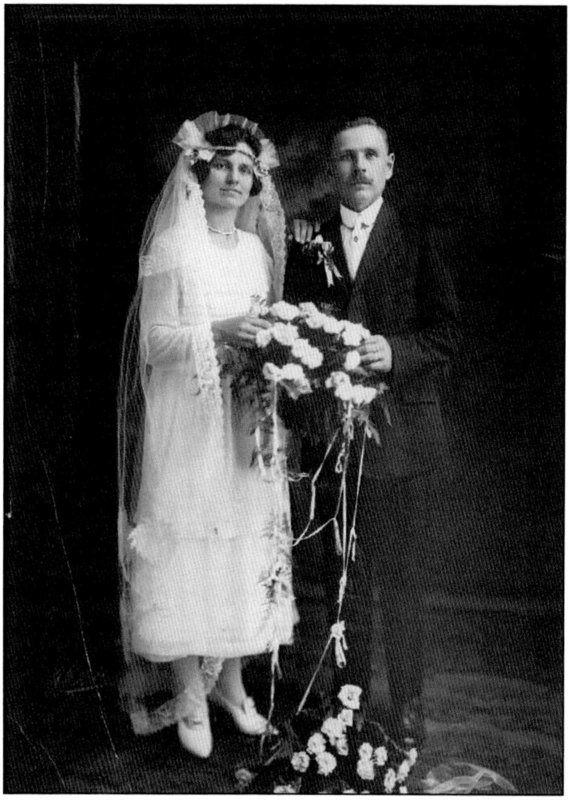

Site C18: First Generation Moskus Family, 3311 and 3323 South Jefferson. Both Anna and John were born in Lithuania, she in 1898 and he in 1888. Anna immigrated to the United States in 1913, while John came in 1914. They married in 1919. The house at 3311 was built in 1922 by E. Clarke for $6,500. John Moskus was employed by the streetcar line, working his way up from janitor to machinist. The couple had one son named Frank.

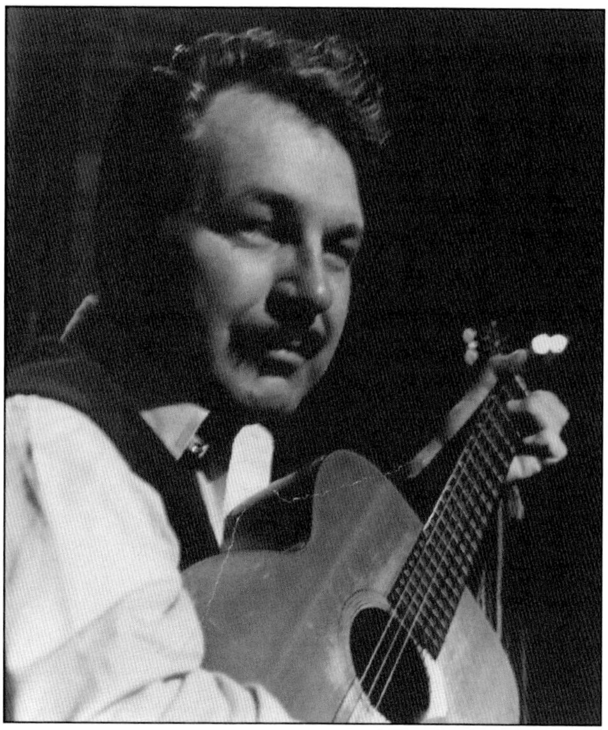

Frank V. Moskus. Frank was a bar owner, entertainer, and artist. In the early 1960s, he owned the St. Louis Yacht Harbor Club, located on the *Becky Thatcher* river boat. Later he owned the Gaslight Bar at Gaslight Square. His paintings decorated the walls of his bars. He sponsored the Soulard Mardi Gras art show in the early 1990s where they featured some of his work. From 1989 to 1997, he played with his own band. He passed away in 1998.

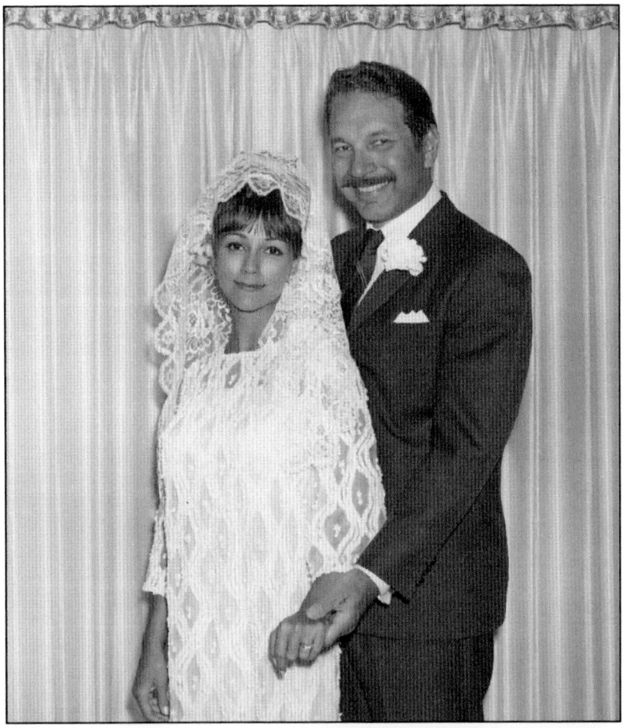

SECOND GENERATION MOSKUS FAMILY. From 1969 to 1984, Frank and his wife, Jan, were the owners of the In Exile Bar in south St. Louis. They were also well-known entertainers who gave "a number of show-business beginners their first chances to perform." Jan was a dancer and singer-songwriter, and Frank was a musician who played piano, drums, and guitar. They had one son, Joe, who lives at 3311 with his wife, Penny.

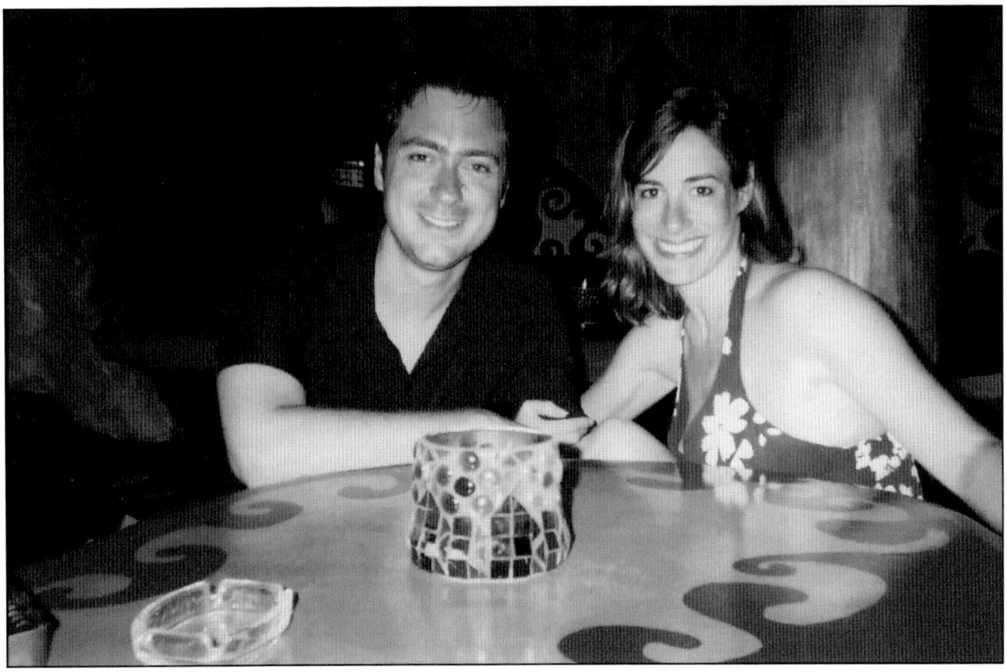

THIRD GENERATION MOSKUS FAMILY. Penny and Joe have restored the old family home and enjoy living in the same neighborhood the Moskus family has been calling home since the early 1920s. Penny is in film production and is a professional belly dancer, while Joe is a radio personality. There are many families in south St. Louis who are third and fourth generation residents in these historic neighborhoods.

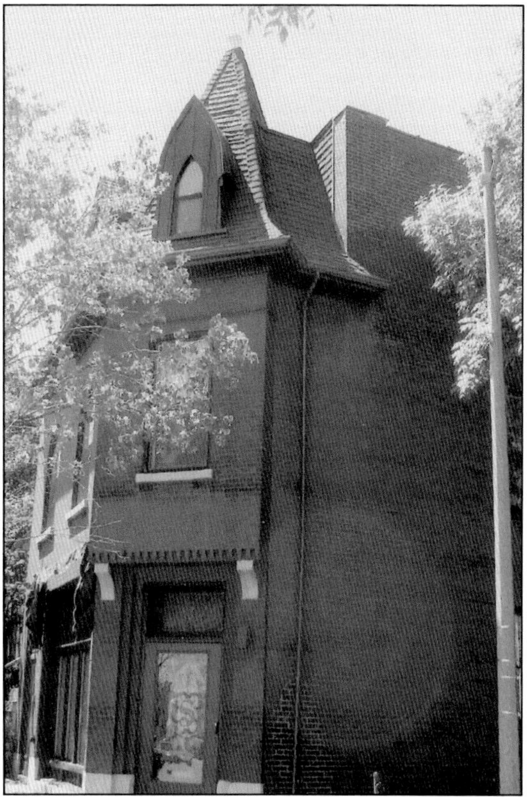

FORMER SCHNEIDT PHOTOGRAPHY STUDIO, 3301 SOUTH JEFFERSON. In 1903, Gustav Schneidt was granted a permit to build brick flats at a cost of $5,000. The builder was Frank Schroeder. In 1918, this address was listed as Gustav Schneidt, photographer. The Schneidt family owned the building until 1981, when Robert Shay bought the building and became the second owner since 1903. Mr. Shay owns Shay Productions and purchased the building for his studio and business offices.

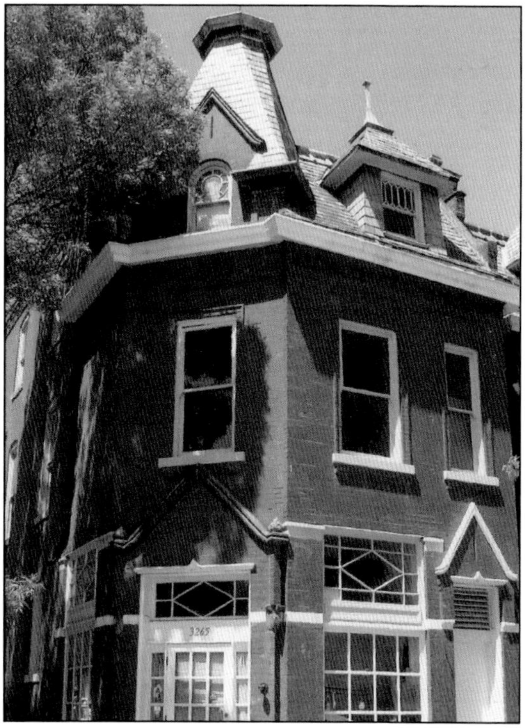

FROM GROCERY TO BOARDING HOUSE, 3263 AND 3265 SOUTH JEFFERSON. In 1911, Albert Richard resided at 3263 and added to the store and dwelling. In 1918, William Swaby had a grocery at 3265 and Alphonse Richard lived at 3263. The Waelters served soft drinks at 3200 in 1925, during Prohibition. In 1935, Mrs. Dintelmann had a confectionery here, and in the 1940s through the 1960s, the building was a delicatessen. Later it became the Jefferson Avenue Boarding House.

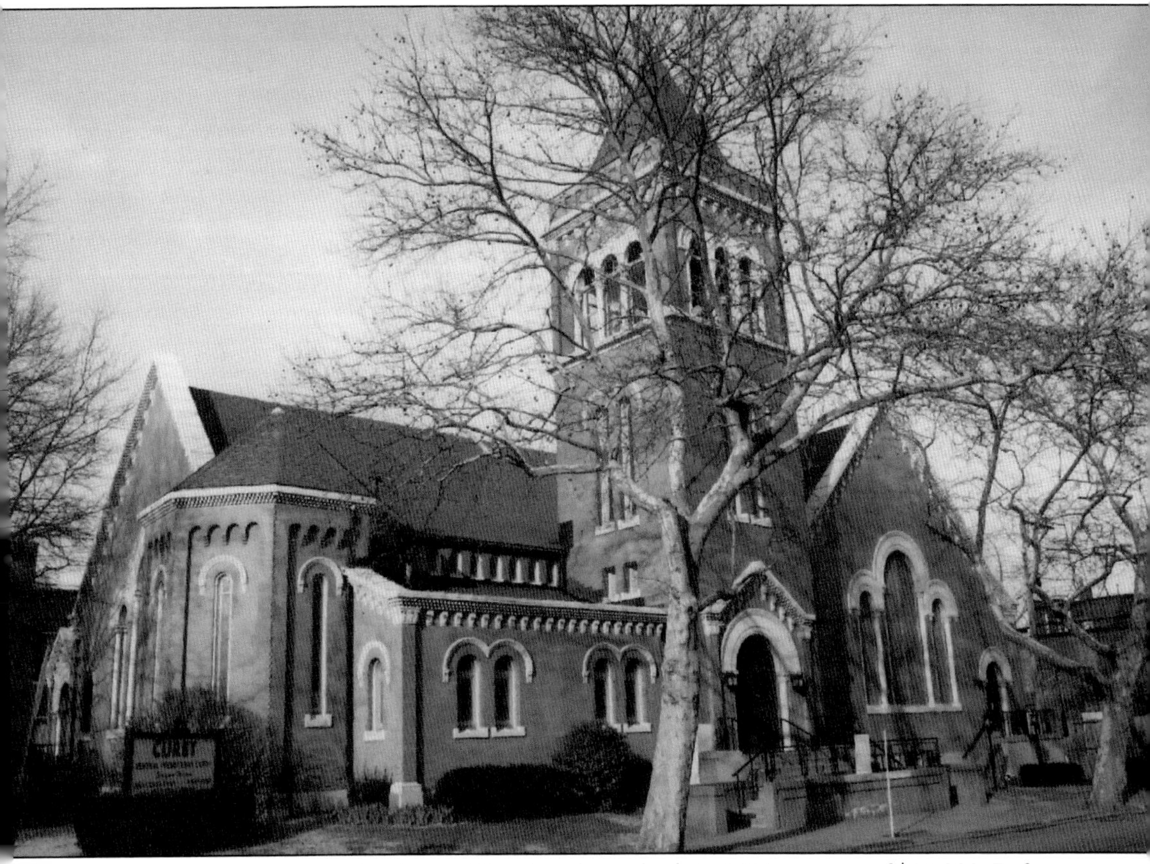

SITE C19: CURBY CHURCH, 2621 UTAH. The church was built in 1898 at a cost of $17,000. Before becoming Curby Memorial Presbyterian Church, the congregation organized in 1873 in rooms at 3500 South Broadway and was known as Westminster Presbyterian Church. The original church at Eighteenth and Pestalozzi was a frame structure built in the late 1870s. Colonel J. L. Curby proposed building a new church and donated $10,000 for the building of the present structure. It was named in memory of Colonel Curby's only daughter, Joseph Anna (Joey) Curby. When it was dedicated in 1898, the congregation had 170 members and a Sunday school consisting of 278 students and teachers. In 1899, Curby Church took on the responsibility of Gravois School Mission. The school was located around Arsenal and Gravois and was a Sunday school mission. As in most urban churches, membership is down and the church has less than 100 members. The congregation is lead by Reverend Gordon Senechal.

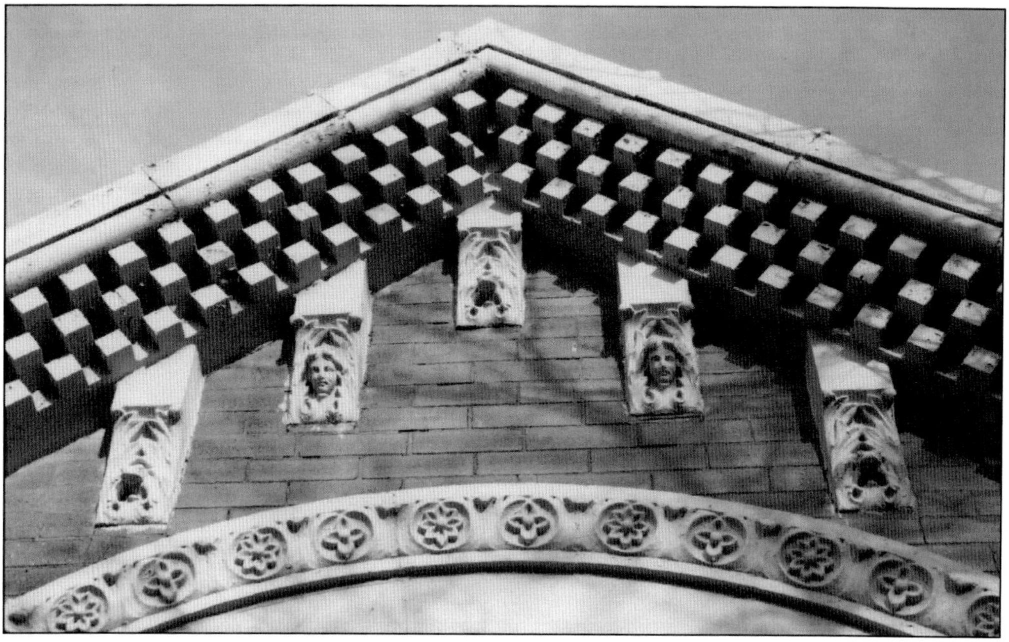

Architectural Brick Design. Weber & Groves were responsible for the architectural brick designs. The firm was founded by Alfred Grable, and when August Weber became a partner in 1884, the name became Grable & Weber. In 1894, Albert B. Groves joined the firm and the name changed to Grable, Weber & Groves. After Mr. Grable retired, the name became Weber & Groves. Mr. Groves was a graduate of Cornell University and traveled throughout Europe, taking an architectural course at the École de Beaux Arts in Paris.

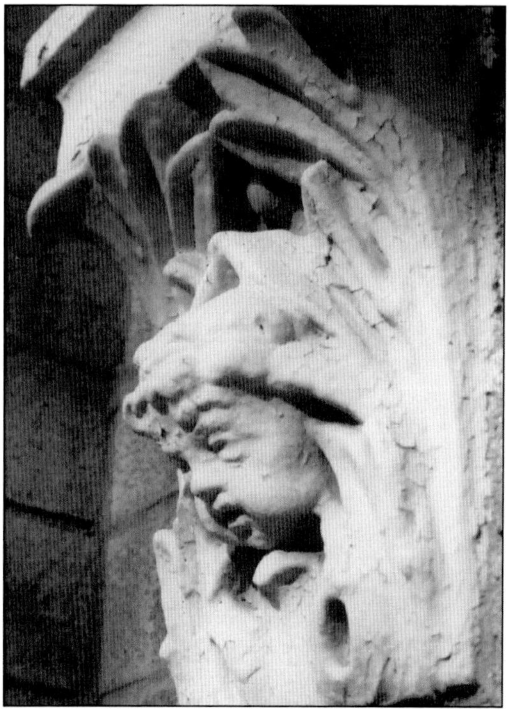

Community Meeting Place. The Ladies Aid Society, later organized as a Women's Association, was a quilting group in the early days that supported the church and met here. In 1924, Boy Scout Troop No. 163 was chartered and sponsored by the church. In the 1960s, the Joint Neighborhood Ministry Committee joined with Epiphany UCC to begin a neighborhood ministry. Today the church still serves the community. The Benton Park West Neighborhood Association has hosted special events in the church hall.

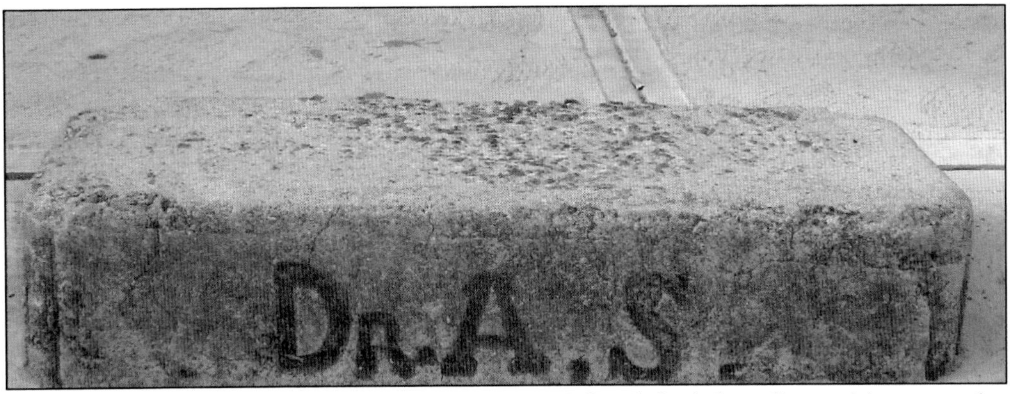

SITE C20: CARRIAGE STONE, 2614 UTAH. Dr. August Schmidt built his office and home on this corner at a time when horses and carriages were the means of transportation. Usually, carriage stones have a last name, initials only, or are completely blank. This one is a real treasure because it has "Dr. A. S." inscribed, and the old stone hitching post is at the same site. Dr. Schmidt came from Germany in 1888. He was married and had six children.

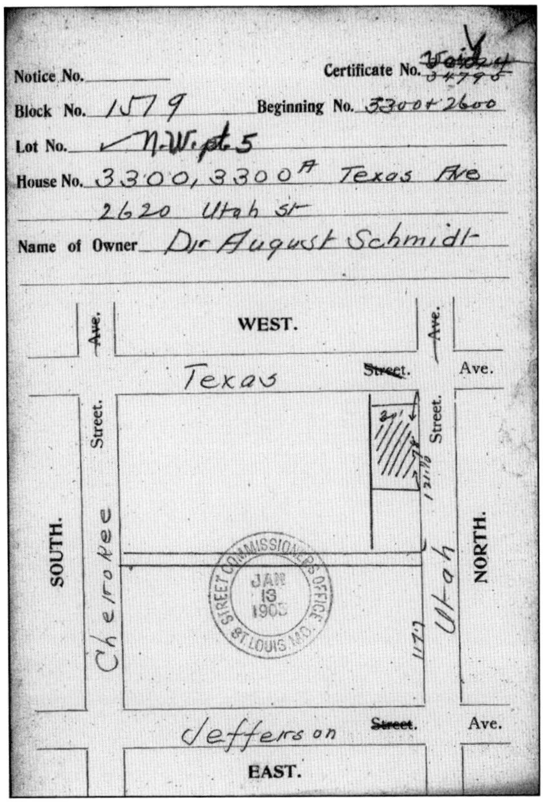

Notice No. ______ Certificate No. 34795

Block No. 1579 Beginning No. 3300+2600

Lot No. N.W. pt. 5

House No. 3300, 3300A Texas Ave
2620 Utah St

Name of Owner Dr August Schmidt

WEST.

Texas ~~Street.~~ Ave.

SOUTH. Cherokee Street. Utah Street. NORTH.

STREET COMMISSIONER'S OFFICE JAN 13 1905 ST. LOUIS, MO.

Jefferson ~~Street.~~ Ave.

EAST.

DR. SCHMIDT'S OFFICE AND HOME BUILDING PERMIT. This building permit for an office and flats was issued to Dr. August Schmidt on January 13, 1905. The architect was H. W. Kehr and construction costs were $6,300. On the same day, the doctor got a permit to build a one-story frame shed for $150. By 1906, Dr. Schmidt was already listed as a physician with his office on Utah and his residence at 3300 Texas.

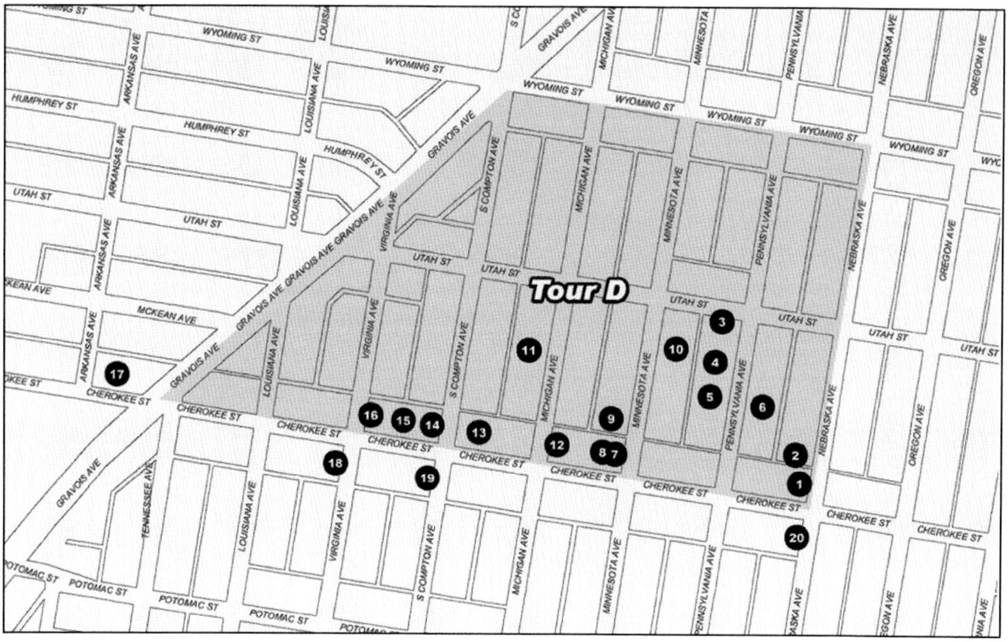
Tour D
WYOMING ST
HUMPHREY ST
UTAH ST
MCKEAN AVE
CHEROKEE ST
POTOMAC ST
GRAVOIS AVE
ARKANSAS AVE
LOUISIANA AVE
VIRGINIA AVE
S COMPTON AVE
MICHIGAN AVE
MINNESOTA AVE
PENNSYLVANIA AVE
NEBRASKA AVE
OREGON AVE
TENNESSEE AVE
1
2
3
4
5
6
7
8
9
10
11
12
13
14
15
16
17
18
19
20

MAP OF TOUR D.

Four

Tour D

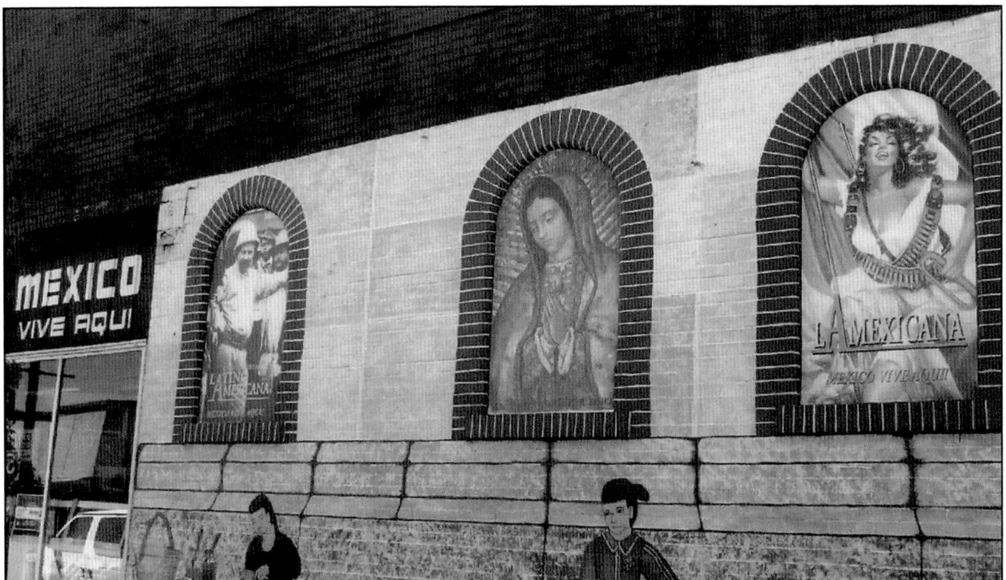

The Changing Face of Cherokee Street Business. In the early days, Cherokee Street was lined with butcher shops, bakeries, confectioneries, drug stores, clothing stores, tailors, beer gardens, saloons, and undertakers. Kretschmar Sausage Manufacturing Company was located at the southeast corner of Cherokee and Ohio Avenue. The company was founded in 1881 by Ernest Kretschmar and started out producing cured meats and sausages. In 1918, the Ely-Walker Company had a textile plant at Cherokee and Texas Streets. In the 1920s, you could find restaurants, real estate and insurance agents, photographers, cleaners, and barber and beauty shops. Later came the stores that sold jewelry, shoes, flowers, and the chain stores like Woolworth, Walgreens, Kroger, and J. C. Penney. It was also a place to be entertained, as there were several movie theaters, and people came from around the city in streetcars and later buses. Where signs read in English and German in the late 1800s and early 1900s, today signs are displayed in English and Spanish along this street that is still lined with storefronts.

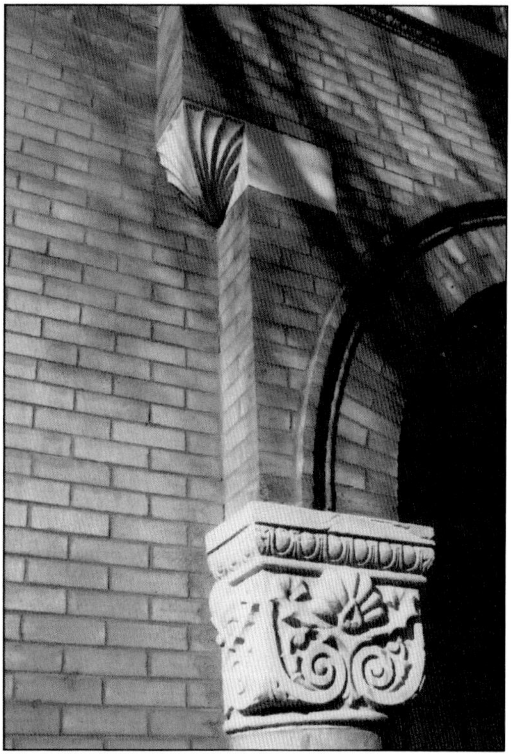

SITE D1: CORNER STOREFRONT, 2901 CHEROKEE. This corner structure was built in 1901. When the building permit was issued to owner Jacob Graul, the addresses listed were 2901, 2903, and 2905 Cherokee. The builder was Victor Architectural and Building Company owned by Edward H. A. Volkmann and Charles F. Hall. Around 1910, when the publication *Southwest Saint Louis: Its Mercantile Interests and Prominent Citizens* was published, the company had 22 buildings under construction, many in the Tower Grove Park area.

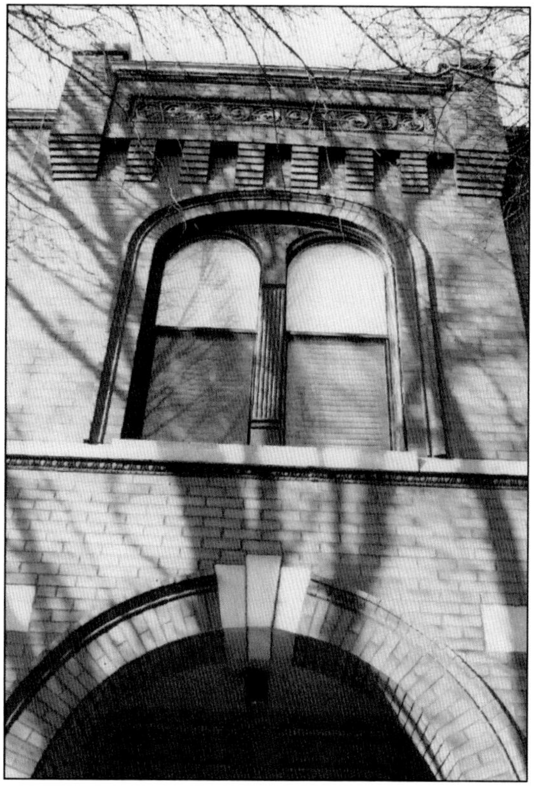

FRANCISCAN CONNECTION, 2903 CHEROKEE. In 1991, the storefront at 2903 opened its doors to help the poor in south St. Louis. Friars Gratian Nosal and Tom Shaughnessy were asked to minister and respond to the growing needs of the neighborhood. Friars from the Sacred Heart Province have kept the center open and aid each family walking through the doors. Most of the families request assistance with utility expenses. The friars have helped more than 4,000 families in need.

SITE D2: WETTA UNITS, 3341 AND 3343 NEBRASKA. Basil Wetta was a machinist and resided at 2812 Wyoming in 1906. He had come from Germany in 1893. By 1907, he was a clerk at Hamilton Brown & Company and had moved his family to 3343A Nebraska. By 1910, he had worked his way up to foreman. In 1915, Basil Jr. enlisted in the Army as a musician corporal. He listed his address as 3343A Nebraska and Grant School as alma mater.

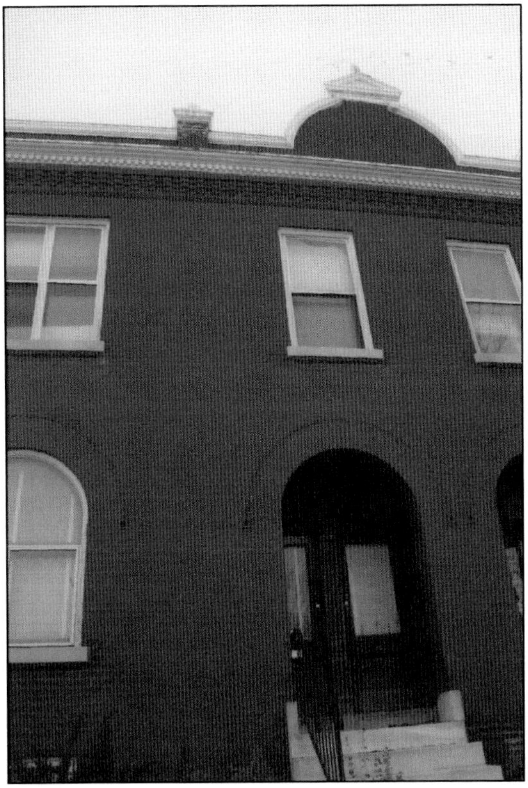

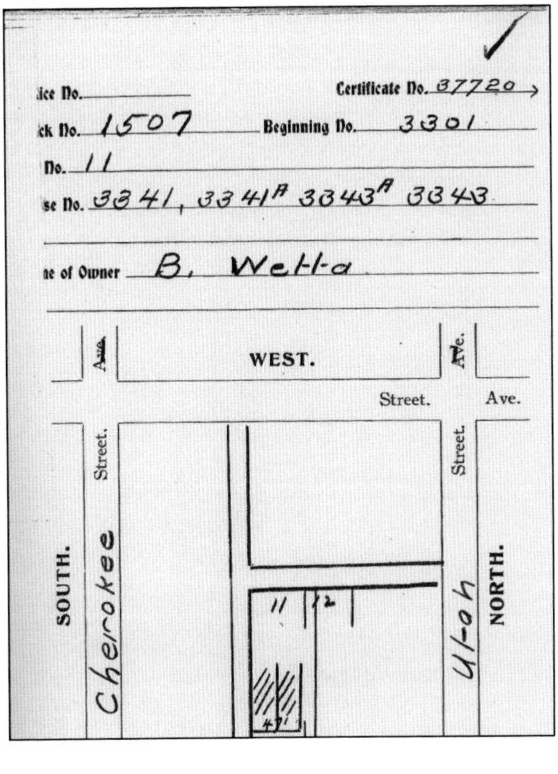

ice No.

Certificate No. 37720

ck No. 1507 Beginning No. 3301

No. 11

se No. 3341, 3341A 3343A 3343

ne of Owner B. Wetta

FOUR FAMILY UNITS BUILDING PERMIT. These double flats were built in 1906 for Basil Wetta by C. F. Hall for $8,000. Charles F. Hall was a partner in Victor Architectural and Building Company. In 1919, the Wetta family lived in 3343A. Jacob Olsen, a saddler, and his family lived in 3343. Steamboat engineer Robert Peterson and his family resided at 3341, and saloon bartender Adam Hoerner and his family lived in 3341A.

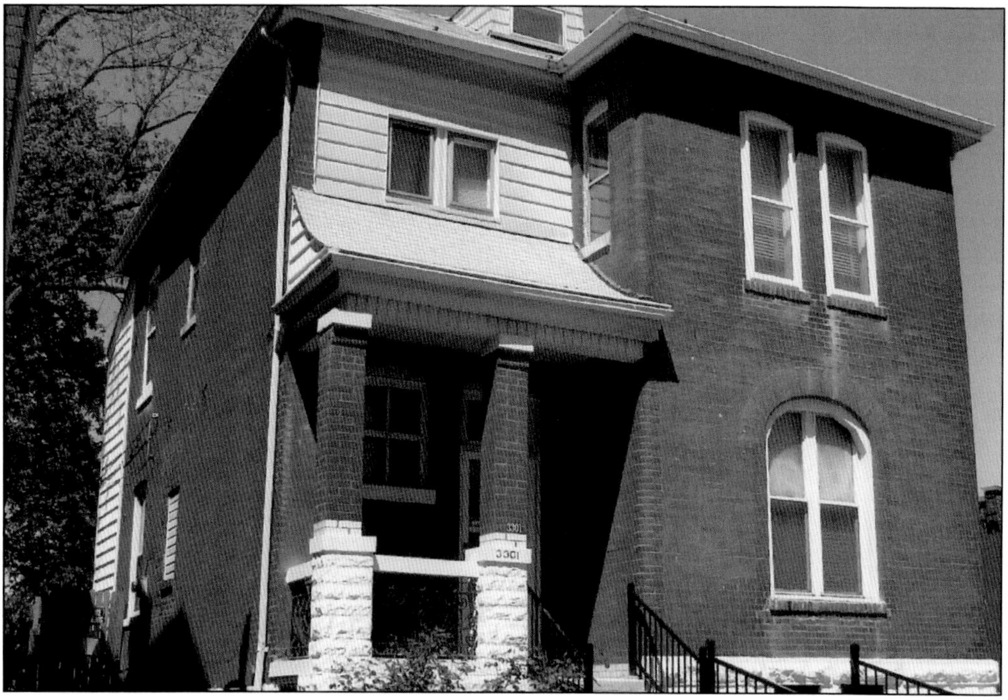

SITE D3: TAILOR'S HOUSE, 3301 PENNSYLVANIA. John Hamtil, a tailor, and his family were the residents of this house in 1905. Previously, they had lived at 2104 South Eleventh. Mr. Hamtil and his wife, Anna, both immigrated from Germany in 1888. In 1910, they had been married 13 years and had 6 children. Mr. Hamtil was listed as a cutter in clothing and the owner of 3301 Pennsylvania in the 1910 census.

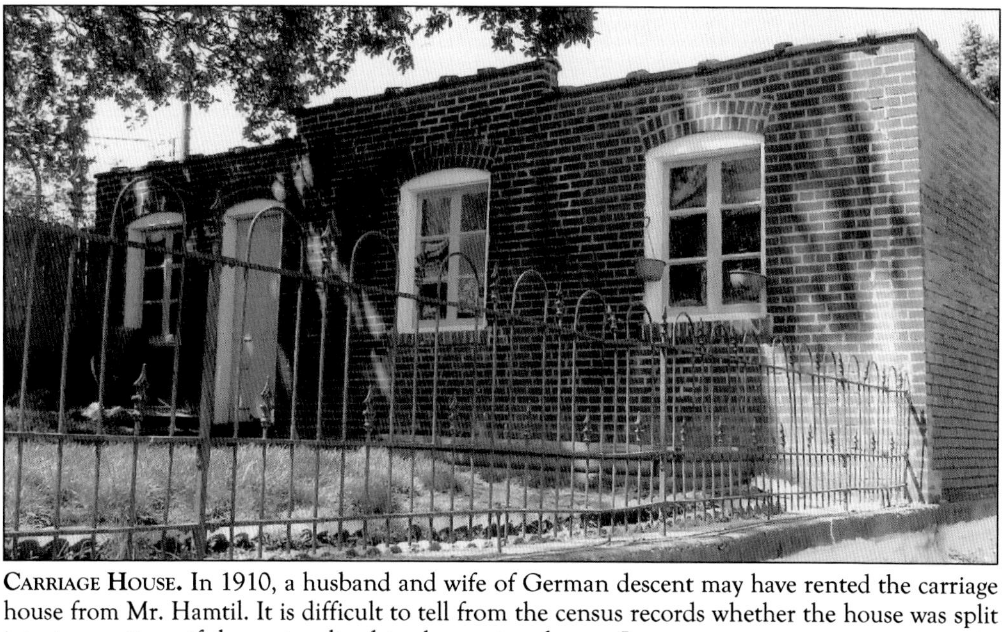

CARRIAGE HOUSE. In 1910, a husband and wife of German descent may have rented the carriage house from Mr. Hamtil. It is difficult to tell from the census records whether the house was split into two units or if the renters lived in the carriage house. It was common to rent out space in carriage houses. Sometimes carriage houses were sold separately from the main house.

Site D4: Pomegranate Masonic Temple, 3311 Pennsylvania. In 1940, the following chapters met here: Chapter No. 397 OES, Lodge No. 95 AF & AM, Poinsetta Chapter No. 472 OES, Algabil Chapter No. 409 OES, Harmony Chapter Order of DeMolay Tower Grove, Chapter No. 445 OES, Mt. Olive Shrine No. 15 WS of J., Job's Daughters Bethel No. 14, Betsy Ross Conclave No. 14 Order of True Kindred, Spring of Acacia Conclave No. 10 Order of True Kindred, and Alagabil Lodge No. 544 AF & AM.

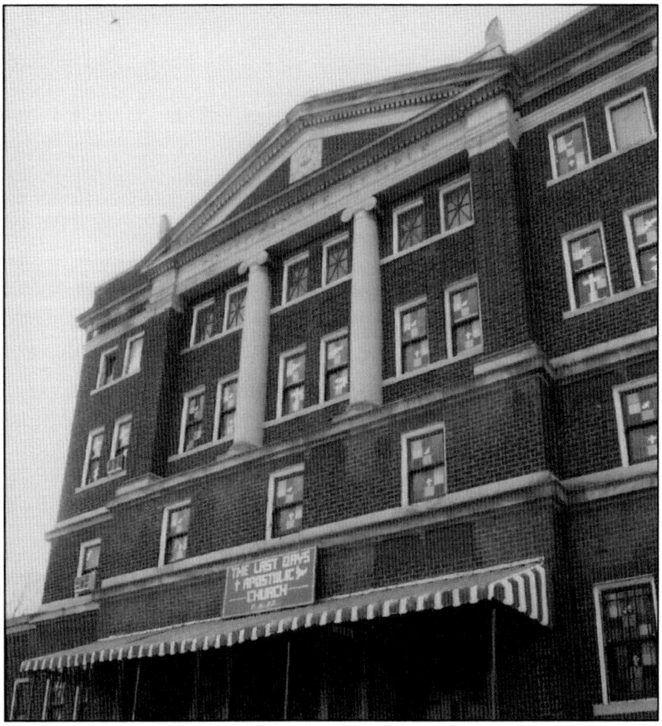

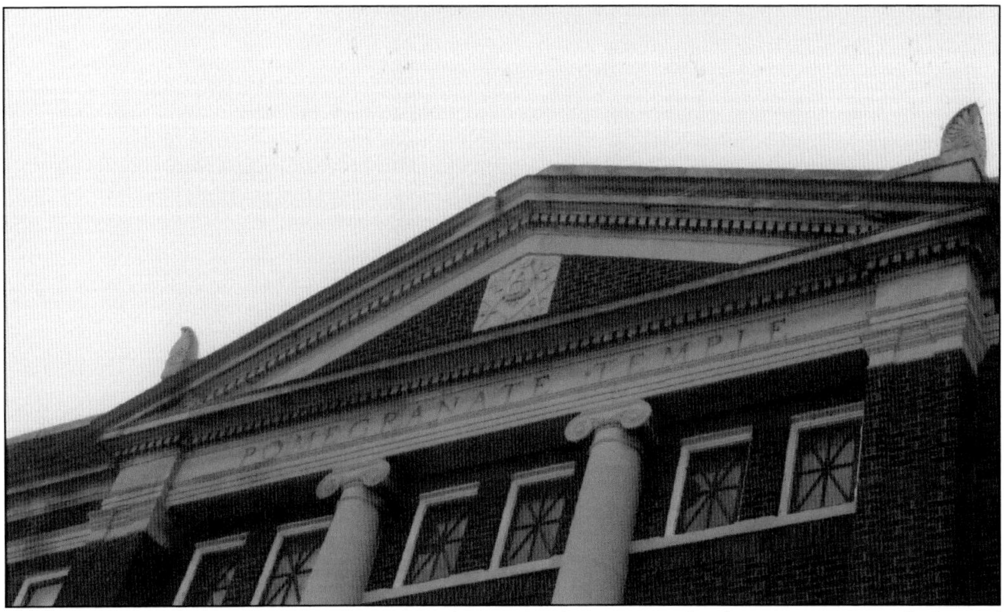

Last Days Apostolic Church. The temple was built in 1927 for $25,000. It actively hosted organizations for more than 50 years, and in 1980, the following groups were listed: Abagil Lodge No. 514, Chapter No. 14 (Job's Daughters), Loyal Chapter No. 511, Venus Chapter No. 153, Pomegranate Chapter No. 397, St. Louis Harmony DeMolay, Tower Grove Chapter No. 445, Mount Olive Shrine No. 15, Queen Elizabeth Amaranta No. 11. In the late 1990s, it became the home of the Last Days Apostolic Church.

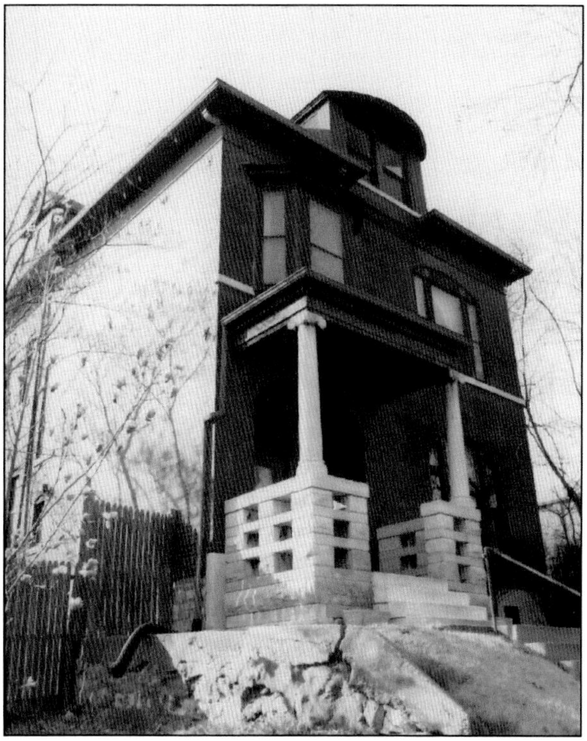

SITE D5: WILLIAM PAPE HOUSE, 3329 PENNSYLVANIA. In 1889, Mr. Pape purchased this lot for $720, and in 1896, he built the house for $5,000. He already lived in the area at 3307 Pennsylvania. William C. Pape was the general superintendent of city parks, with an office was on the third floor of city hall. His son, Frederick W. Pape, was a florist, and he too resided at 3307 and then 3329. William Pape died in 1899.

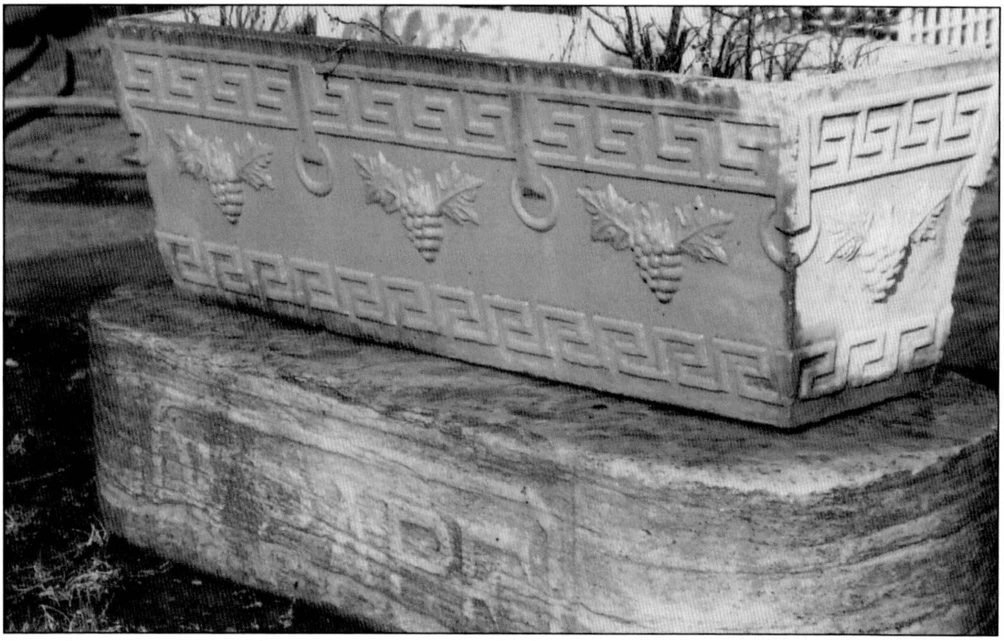

PAPE CARRIAGE STONE. This carriage stone is in the backyard. After William Pape died, he left the house to his wife, Anna, and their six children. Frederick W. Pape went on to be an assistant city forester with an office at 330 Municipal Courts Building; his sister Anna took over for him at the flower shop at 3307 Pennsylvania, which became Pape & Bergstermann. The Pape family lived in the house until the mid-1940s.

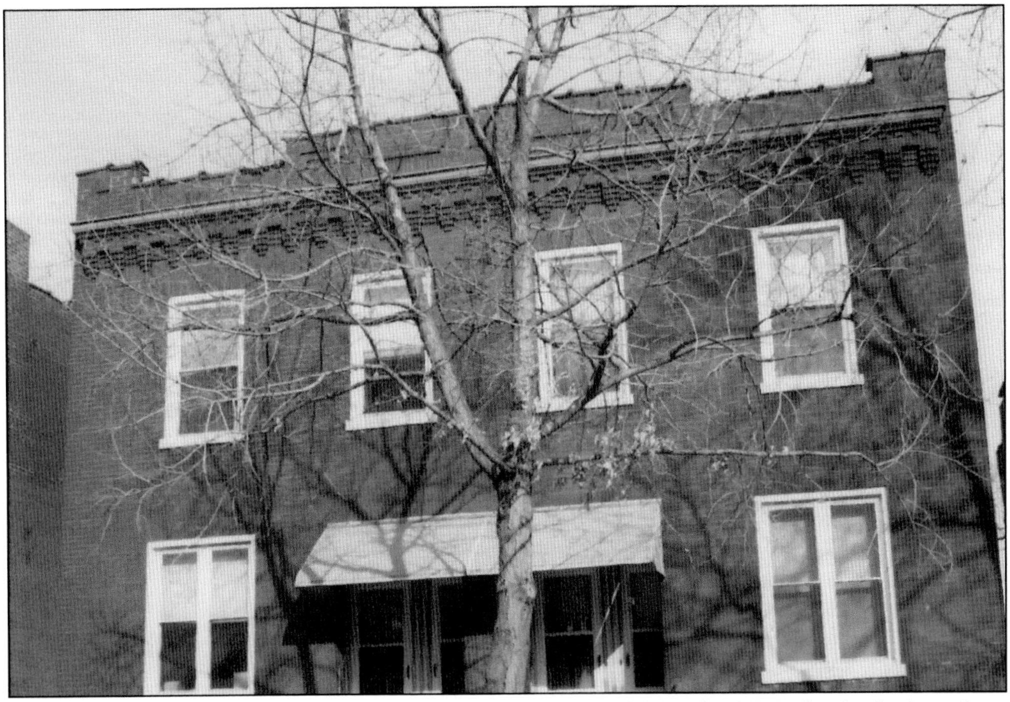

SITE D6: LUKAS FLATS, 3326 AND 3328 PENNSYLVANIA. In 1906, John M. Lukas built these four-family flats for $7,000. Mr. Lukas was a partner with Joseph Kadlec in John M. Lukas & Company; they were tailors. The builder was Frank J. Leibinger of Leibinger & Son, which had offices at 2011 Allen. Mr. Leibinger was born in Germany in 1857 and came to America in 1882. He had been a millwright and a soldier in Germany.

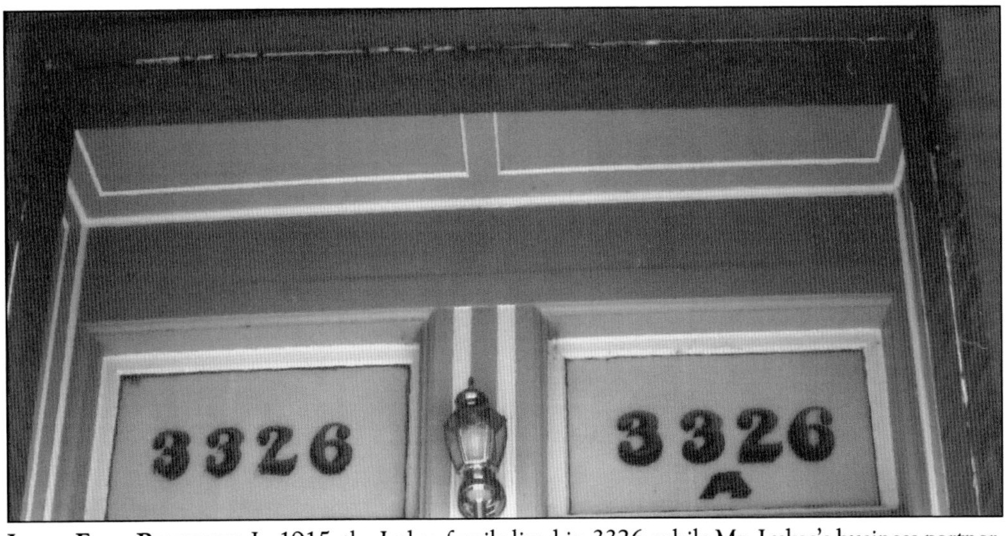

LUKAS FLATS RESIDENTS. In 1915, the Lukas family lived in 3326, while Mr. Lukas's business partner, Mr. Kadlec, was close by at 3322. Engineer Edward A. Conley lived in 3328, and a paper hanger named Frank Vanecek lived next door in 3328A. In 1918, Mrs. Emma Stroh, a widow, resided at 3326A. The Lukas family owned the flats until 1955, and a member of the family always lived in 3326. The current owners are Marlene and Bruce Levine, who live at 3326.

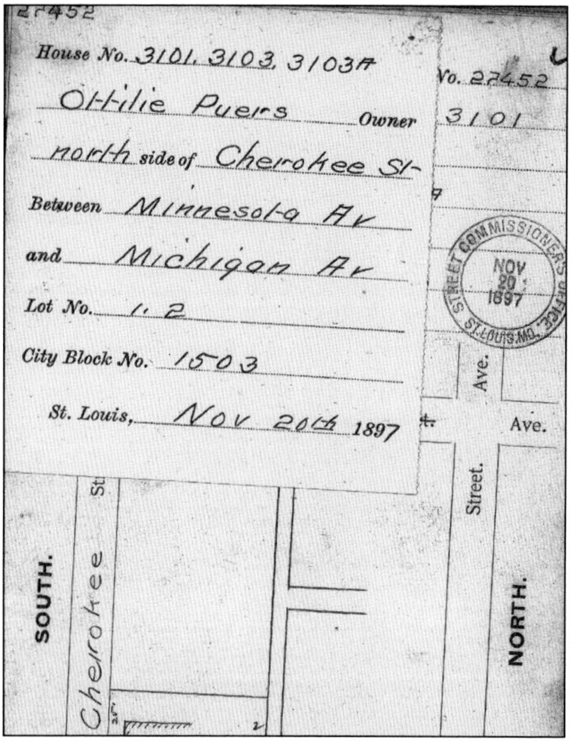
House No. 3101, 3103, 3103A

Ottilie Puers Owner

north side of Cherokee St

Between Minnesota Av

and Michigan Av

Lot No. 1, 2

City Block No. 1503

St. Louis, Nov 20th 1897

No. 27452

3101

STREET COMMISSIONER'S OFFICE NOV 20 1897 ST. LOUIS, MO.

Ave.

Ave.

Street.

SOUTH.

Cherokee St

NORTH.

SITE D7: BUILDING PERMIT FOR 3101 AND 3103 CHEROKEE. In 1897, a permit was issued to Ottilie Puers to build a store and dwelling for $5,000. By 1899, Casper Puers, a salesman for Columbia Preserving Company, resided at 3103A. In 1918, Delbert Kuhn had a confectionery at 3101, and the Cherokee Rug company was at 3103. By 1925, there was a bakery in 3101 and a butcher shop at 3103; they were both still there in 1935.

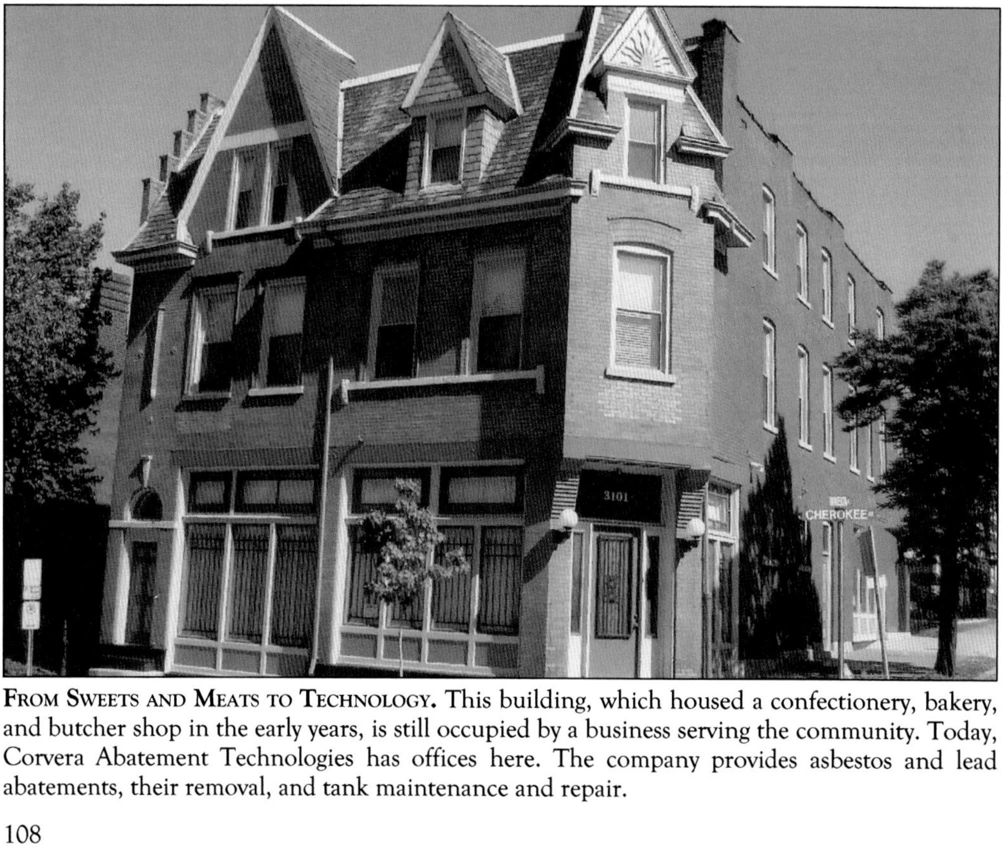

FROM SWEETS AND MEATS TO TECHNOLOGY. This building, which housed a confectionery, bakery, and butcher shop in the early years, is still occupied by a business serving the community. Today, Corvera Abatement Technologies has offices here. The company provides asbestos and lead abatements, their removal, and tank maintenance and repair.

SITE D8: GLOBE IRON AND FOUNDRY FENCES, 3105, 3107, AND 3109 CHEROKEE. The fence and gates were manufactured here in St. Louis by the Globe Iron & Foundry Company, which operated from 1891 to 1903. According to the building permit, the structure at 3109 was built in 1893. The 1900 census lists two families residing in 3109 and 3107. Emil Zeis owned the foundry, located at 901 Victor; his residence was at 2339 South Twelfth.

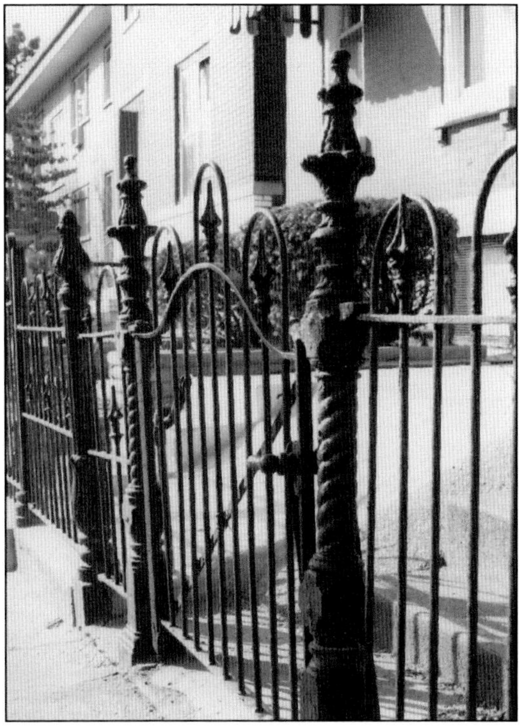

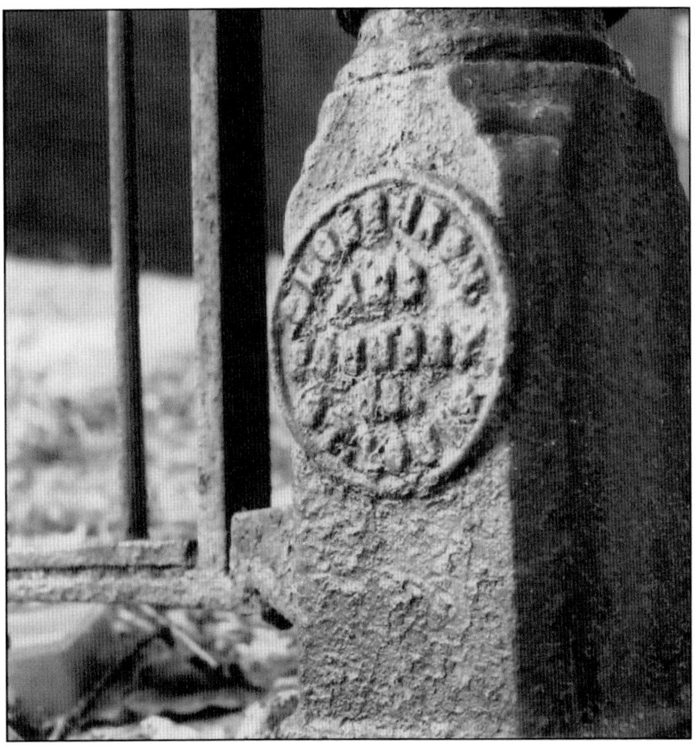

CENTURY-OLD EMBLEM. There are many iron fences still standing from the late 1800s along Cherokee Street, but few have the company's emblem stamped on the posts. There are many examples of Globe Iron works throughout south St. Louis. Most are in the form of iron storefronts. Some of the most elaborate storefronts are in the Soulard neighborhood, as that is where Mr. Zeis' business and residence were located.

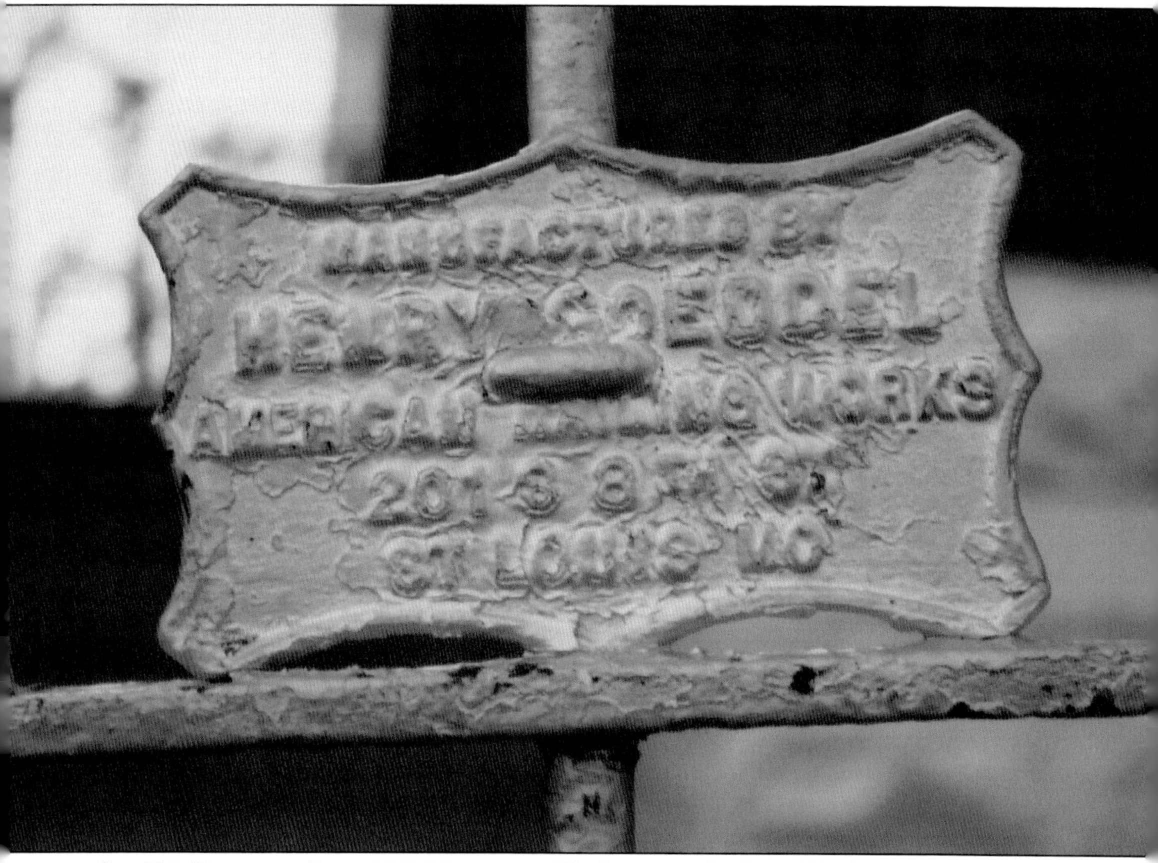

Site D9: Fence and Gate, 3343 Minnesota. The house was built in 1891 by Henry Hiemenz, who was in real estate. In 1900, fresco artist Henry Doellner lived in this house with his wife, Laura, and their daughter, Laura. The fence and gate were crafted by Henry Goeddel American Railing Works, and little of their work can be found locally. Goeddel was a small company which operated from the late 1800s to the early 1900s, and was not listed among the other iron works companies in the city directory. However, Goeddel family members are listed as iron workers. Julius Goeddel was a rail maker in 1892 and resided at 1559 South Broadway. In 1894 and 1896, his occupation was listed in iron. In the 1900 census, Henry Goeddel was listed as a laborer; he was 27 at the time, married to Louisa, and had one son, Arthur. Adam Goeddel was listed as an iron painter, and Conrad Goeddel was listed in the city directory as working in iron. In the 1910 census, Conrad was a finisher in iron works. There are many iron wrought fences and railings in the neighborhood, but only a few identify the names of their manufacturers.

SITE D10: HENRY EIDMANN HOUSE, 3312 MINNESOTA. Mr. Eidmann was a carpenter. In 1900, the house was home to three different families. Jacob Auggler was a stationery engineer who had come from Switzerland in 1883; his wife, Christina, migrated from Germany in 1883. Jacob Yost was a wood turner who came from Germany with his wife, Julia, in 1893. Peter Wollscheidt was a sign painter. He and his wife also migrated from Germany.

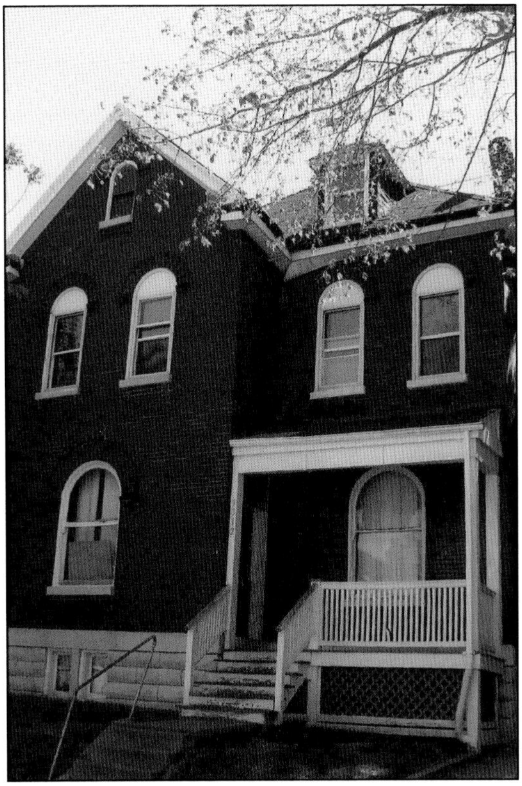

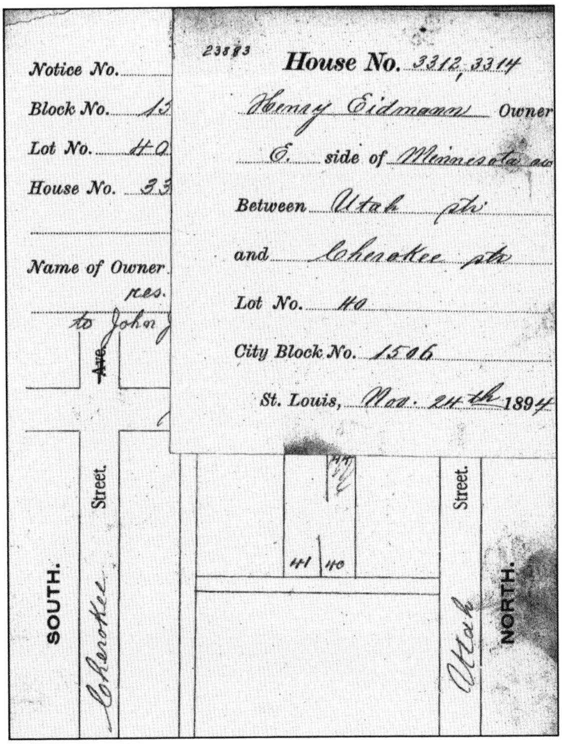

STREET COMMISSIONER'S OFFICE BUILDING PERMIT. This house cost $3,500 to build. Henry Eidmann was a resident of the block before 1894, and there were building permits issued to him in 1890 for a shed and in 1891 for a one story frame kitchen for his home at 3318 Minnesota. By 1900, Mr. Eidmann no longer resided at 3318, and the new owner was Henry Froske. Mr. Froske was a German saddler who came to America in 1856.

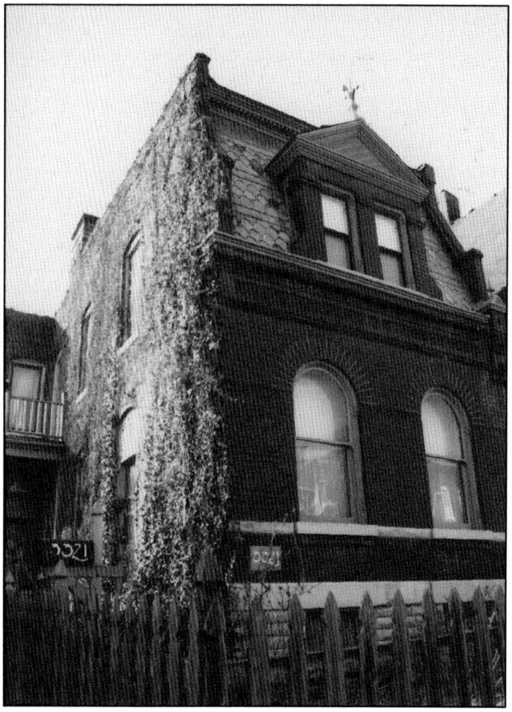

Site D11: George F. Davis House, 3321 Michigan. Mr. Davis built this house in 1894, and by 1900, John J. Hurley was the new owner. Born in Ireland in 1852, Mr. Hurley came to America in 1853. He and his wife had been married 24 years and had 4 living children, 3 of them still at home. James worked in upholstery, Walter was a boiler maker, and Mary was a dress maker.

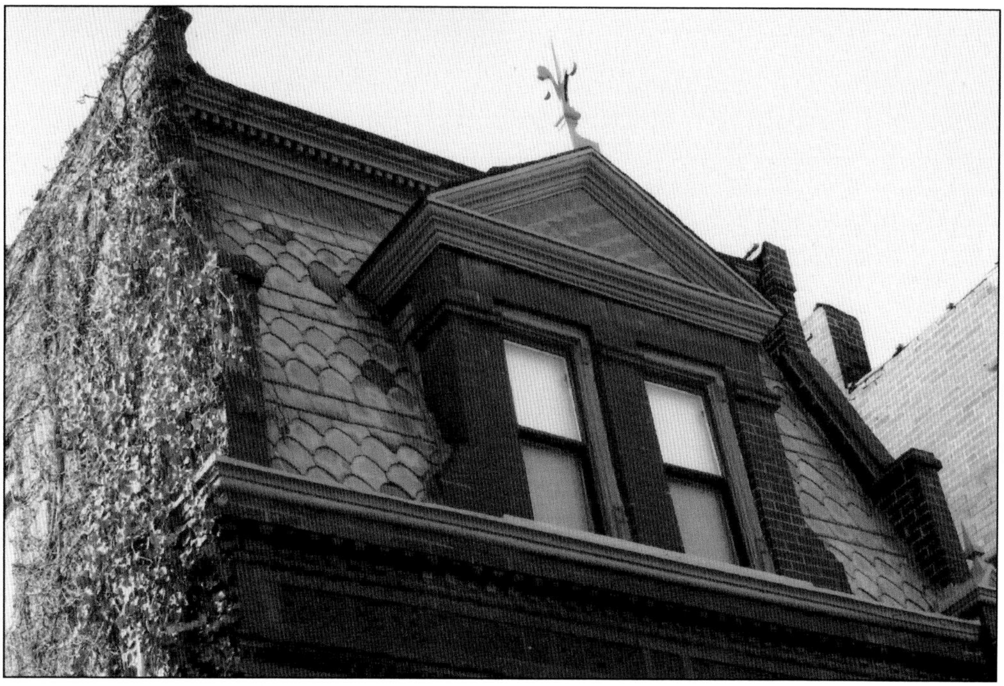

Simple Mansard Roof. The second floor has plenty of details, a simple mansard roof, and a gable dormer. Right under the roof line and across the roof top, tooth-like dentils provide decoration, followed by the decorative brick across the front. There are many different brick and panel designs throughout the neighborhood: floral, basket weaves, stars, egg and dart, leaf carving, and face silhouettes. Even the smallest houses have decorative brick details to enhance their front facades.

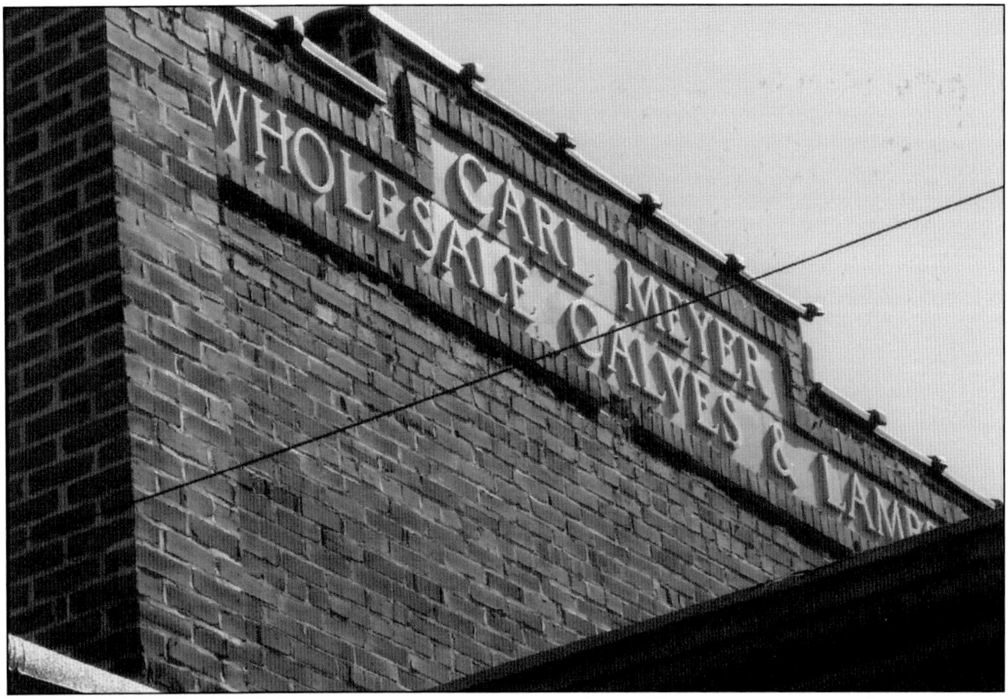

SITE D12: APARTMENT, 3125 CHEROKEE. In 1900, Louis Schlake, his wife, Bertha, and their children—Louis, Ella, Bertha, and Arthur—lived in this apartment rented from Carl Meyer. Bertha kept house and Louis was a laborer in iron works. The building directly behind the Schlake's apartment was used as part of Mr. Meyer's business, and in 1918, 3125A was listed as Mr. Meyer's butcher shop; 3125–3127 was Carl Meyer Wholesale Calves & Lambs.

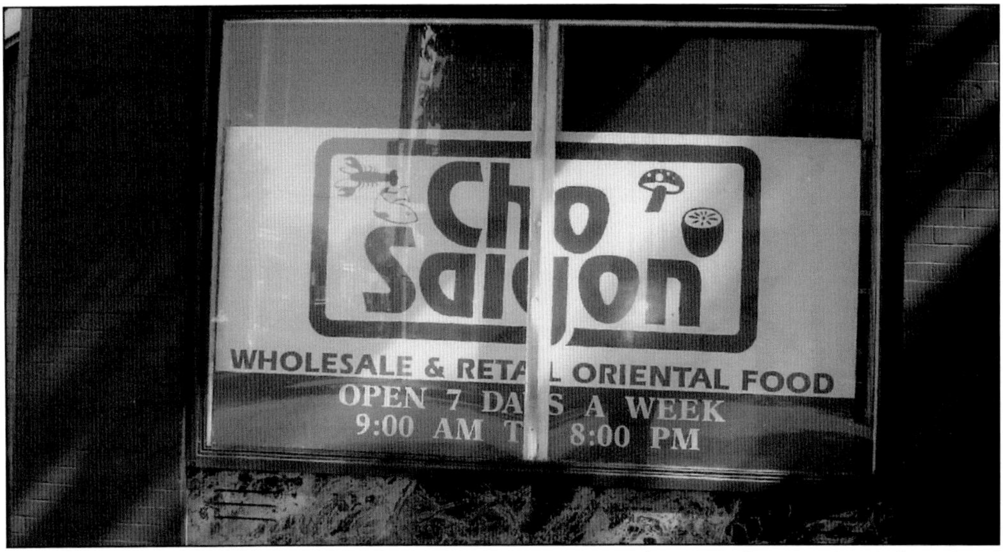

FROM BUTCHER SHOP TO ORIENTAL FOOD, 3127 CHEROKEE. The two adjoining brick flats, 3125 and 3127, were built for Carl Meyer in 1895 for $3,700. Mr. Meyer was born in Germany in 1864, and came to the United States in 1886. His wife, Salina, was born in Switzerland in 1863 and came to America in 1884. Today, the old butcher shop has Asian owners who sell oriental foods and spices.

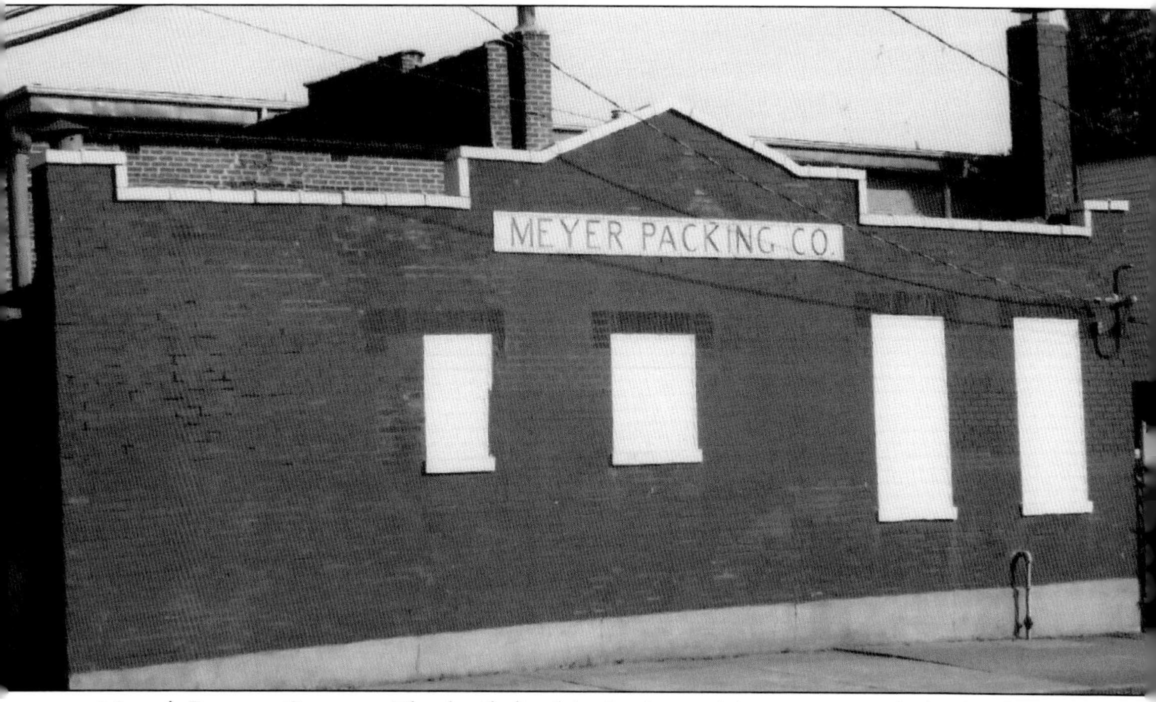

MEYER'S PACKING COMPANY. The family lived in the front of the property with the butcher shop downstairs and the packing plant in the back of the property. In 1922, Mr. Meyer had a one-story addition, a garage, and a cooler built for $3,000. In 1924, he was issued a permit to alter the frame slaughterhouse for $600, and in 1929, he had a one-story brick wall built in the ice plant. While Mr. Meyer ran his business from this location, he also rented 3127 to the Kroger Grocery and Baking Company in the late 1910s and 1920s. Today the building serves as the warehouse for Cho Saigon Wholesale & Retail Oriental Food.

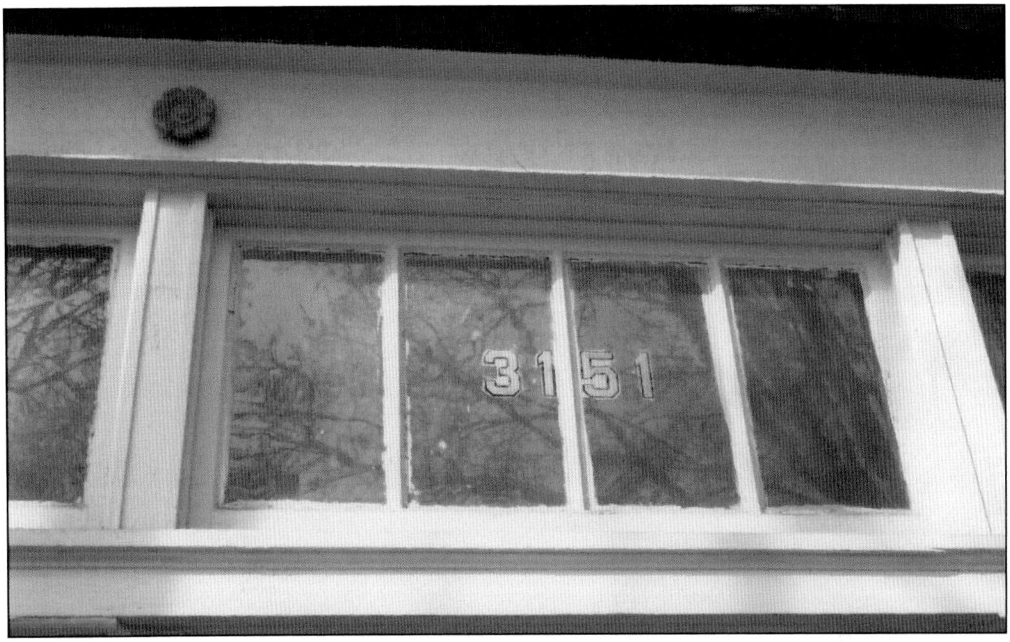

SITE D13: FORT GONDO COMPOUND FOR THE ARTS, 3151 CHEROKEE. Galen Gondolfi is doing exactly what business men were doing a century ago: they set up their shops and lived in apartments over their businesses or owned houses just down the street. They invested in several buildings along Cherokee and were involved in their community. Their neighbors could depend on them and they were often called to serve. In 2004, Galen was the president of the Benton Park West Neighborhood Association.

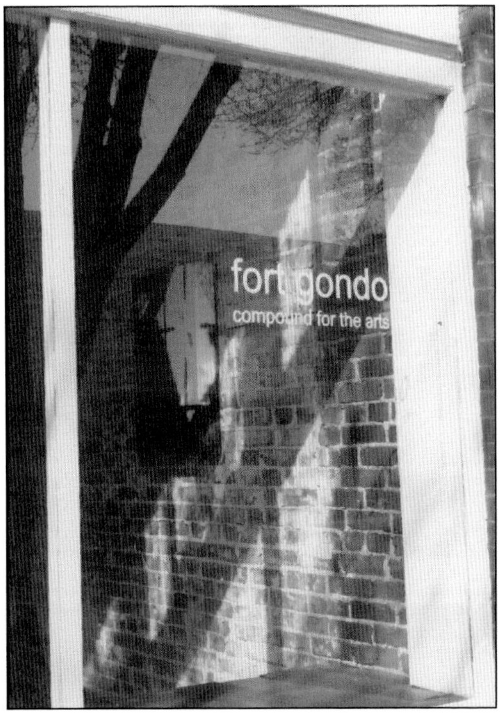

FROM BUTCHER SHOP TO HIP URBAN PERFORMANCE CENTER. The two-story brick store and tenements were built in 1911 for $4,000 for F. M. Nagel. The architect/builder was William Dagenhardt. The first occupant was John Goelz, a butcher, followed by Bruno Weber, a grocer. Gaskill Supports occupied the building from the 1940s to the 1970s. They supplied custom-made surgical supports and elastic stockings.

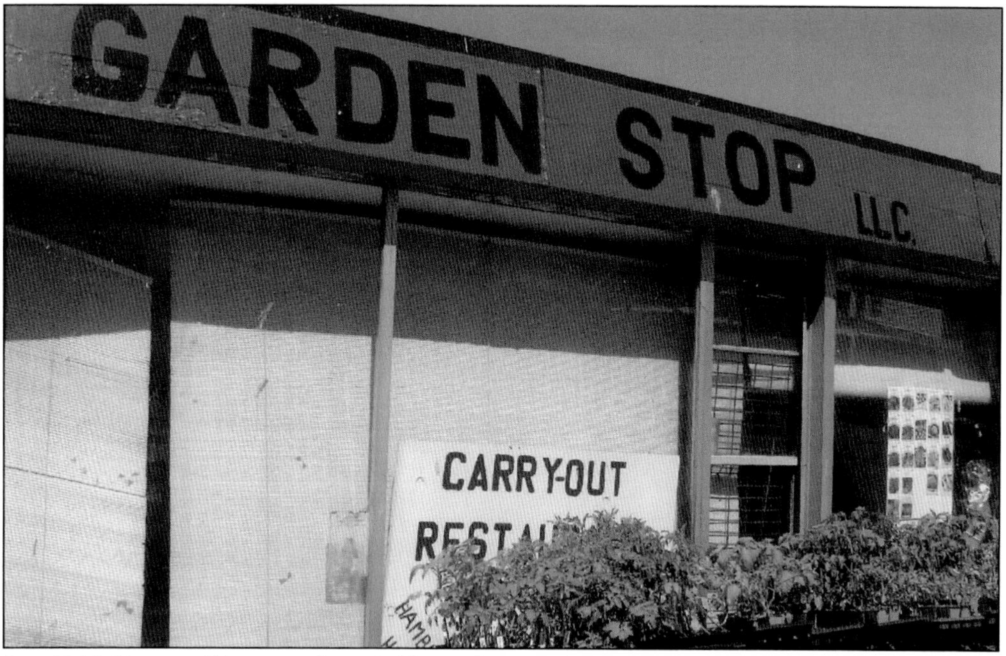

Site D14: Former Home of Allen's Drive In and Carry Out, 3201 Cherokee. In 1963, a pavilion for an outdoor restaurant was built by Jesse F. Allen at a cost of $15,000. Before this location became a restaurant, there was a frame stable on the corner built in 1891 for $125 for Mrs. Shaefer. In 1904, there was a brick dwelling here, along with the stable. The Liebig family owned the property before Mr. Allen.

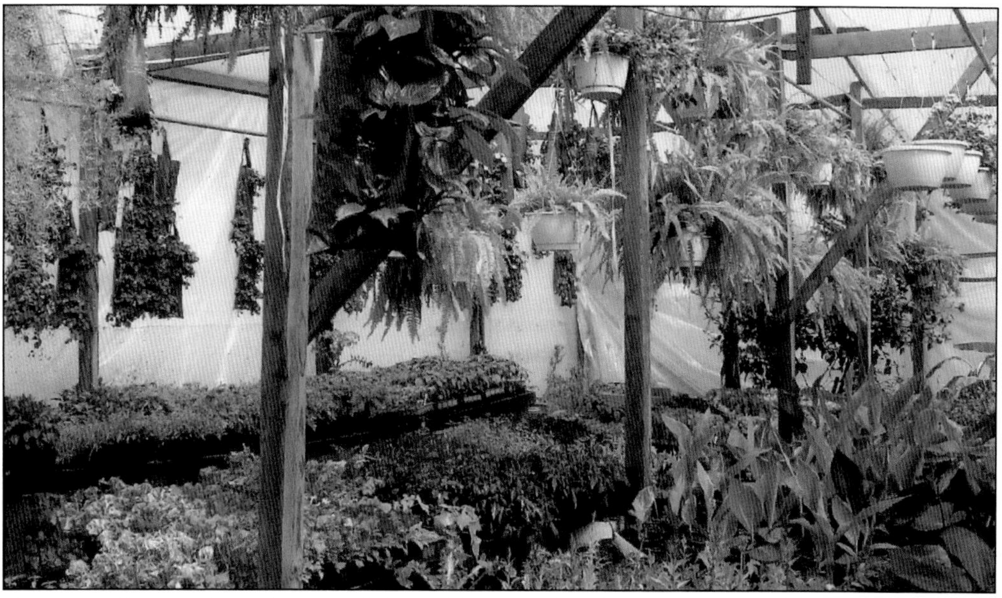

Southside Garden Stop, Inc. Mr. Allen sold watermelons here before he sold hamburgers in the 1960s. Christmas trees have also been sold at this location for almost 50 years; in 1957 and 1959, Mr. Allen was granted a permit to sell them. The current owner is Joe Waeltermann, whose family has been in business in south St. Louis for more than 100 years. He is kin to the Groebl family, featured in Tour A, Site No. 5.

SITE D15: OLD AUTO PARTS STORE, 3211–3215 CHEROKEE. This storefront was built in 1924 for $5,000. The addresses were separate businesses until the 1960s. In 1925, the Ladewig family had a variety store at 3211, and 3215 was Carter's Auto Supplies. In 1935, Clayton Cleaning & Dying Company and Heggar-Schmidt Art Glass were listed at this location. By 1946, auto parts were being sold at 3213 and 3215, and Otto Walther had an electrical repair shop at 3211.

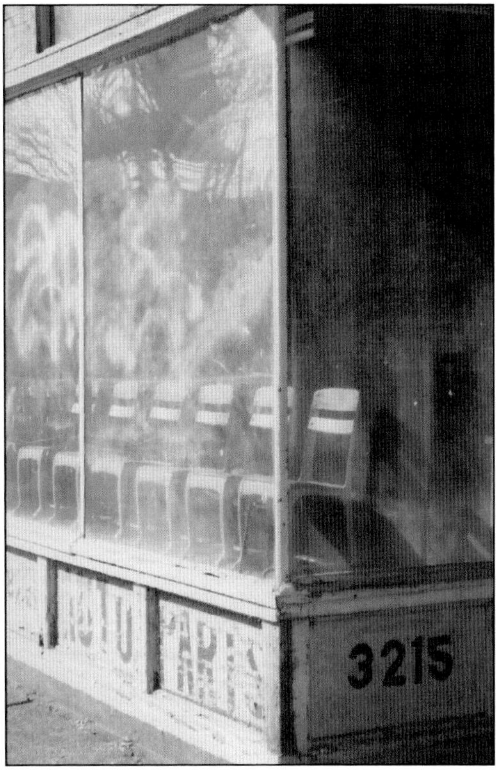

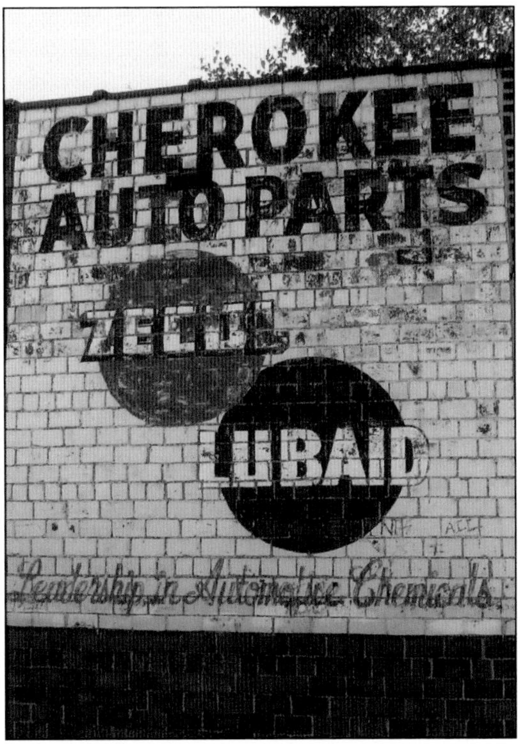

VINTAGE SIGN. By 1965, the Cherokee Auto Parts Company, Inc. had taken over all three addresses. This advertisement on the side of the building is the largest vintage sign; in front of the building still hangs one which reads "Cherokee Auto Parts, Walker Mufflers & Pipes." On the front doors are more vintage signs. The most colorful one advertises Anco Rain Master Windshield Wiper Service Blades.

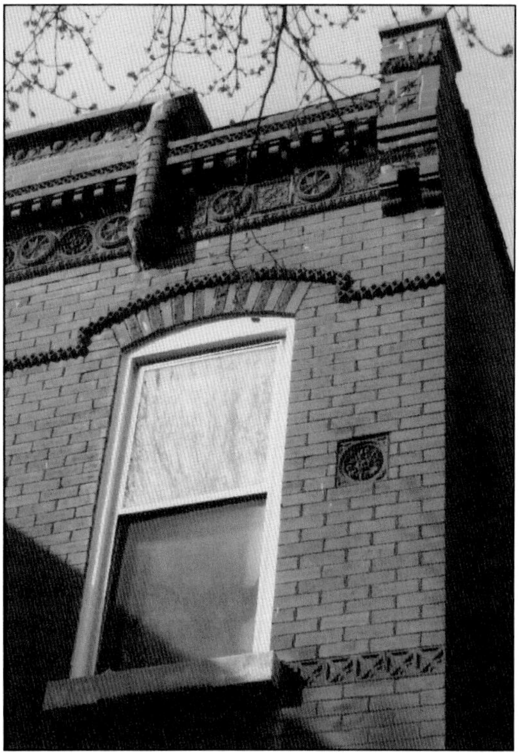

SITE D16: FORMER BRICKLAYER'S HOME, 3225 CHEROKEE. This townhouse is typical of homes built to display the owner's craft. August Viermann was a bricklayer. The German immigrants were skilled craftsmen who brought their traits with them. The decorative bricks show many different motifs. Mr. Viermann came to this country in 1880; his wife, Sophia, came in 1876. In 1900, five of their nine children were still living, and Frieda, August, Edwin, and Walter were still at home.

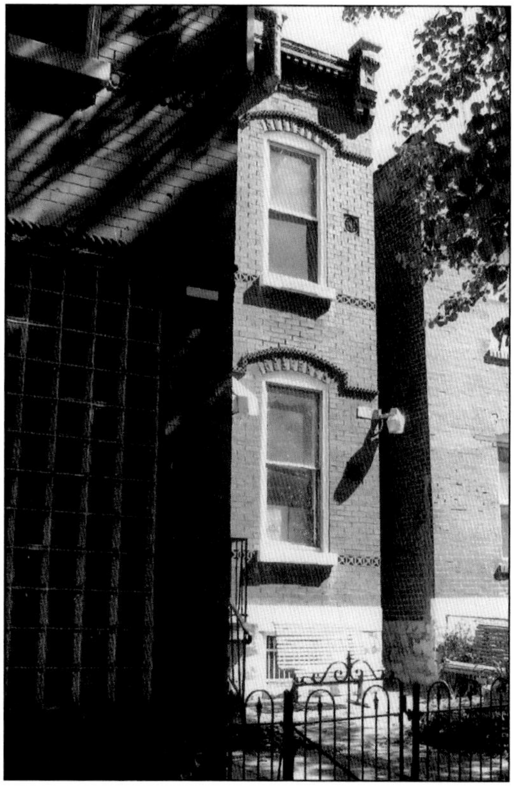

APARTMENT, 3225 CHEROKEE. In the second unit lived a Belgian couple who rented from Mr. Viermann. Built in 1893 for $1,800, this townhouse/apartment has housed plumbing contractors, salesmen, and many other working people from the neighborhood; it is still an apartment today. The owners, Galen Gondolfi and Dave Early, live in the neighborhood on Cherokee Street and are owners of other local properties. They take an active role in the revitalization of their community.

RADIO CHEROKEE, 3227 CHEROKEE. This addition to 3225 was completed in 1898 by August Viermann for $1,400. In 1900, August Aufderheide, a church janitor who had come from Germany in 1870, rented the store and dwelling for his family. His wife, Sophia, had her dry goods store downstairs. By 1918, it was a saloon. The old tavern which sold soft drinks during Prohibition is currently a coffee house and music club, owned by Galen Gondolfi and Dave Early.

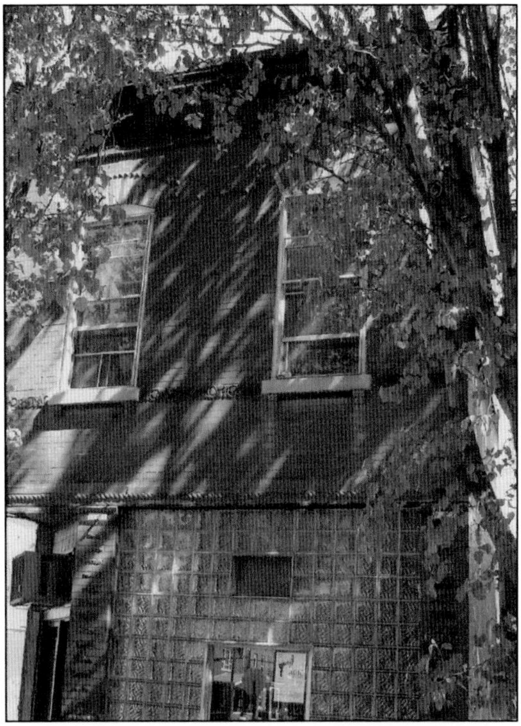

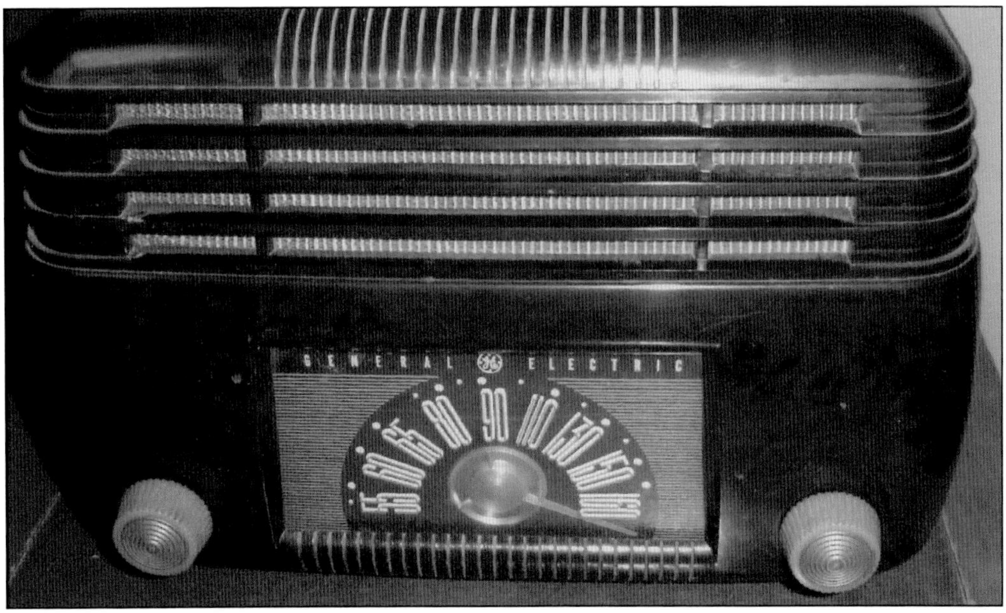

RADIO HISTORY. Radio Cherokee is home to different models of vintage radios. In 1898, when this structure was built, the first radio had already been constructed in 1896. Guglielmo Marconi opened the first radio factory in 1899 in England. His initial radio link was between Britain and France. In 1901, he established a link with the United States. These links were only signals transmitted by wireless telegraph. In 1921, radio as we know it today came through as voice over air.

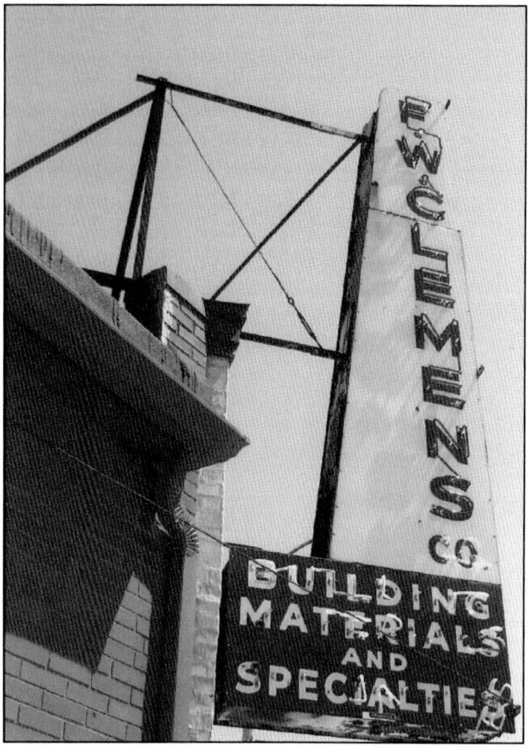

Site D17: F. W. Clemens Company, 3357 Gravois. Today this company sells building materials, but it started out as F. W. Clemens Feed Company in 1878. The founder and president, Frederick W. Clemens, was born in Germany in 1855. He started out as a grocery clerk when he arrived in St. Louis at age 16. Mr. Clemens was also vice-president, and then president, of the Farmers' and Merchants' Trust Company and a member of the Tower Grove Turnverein.

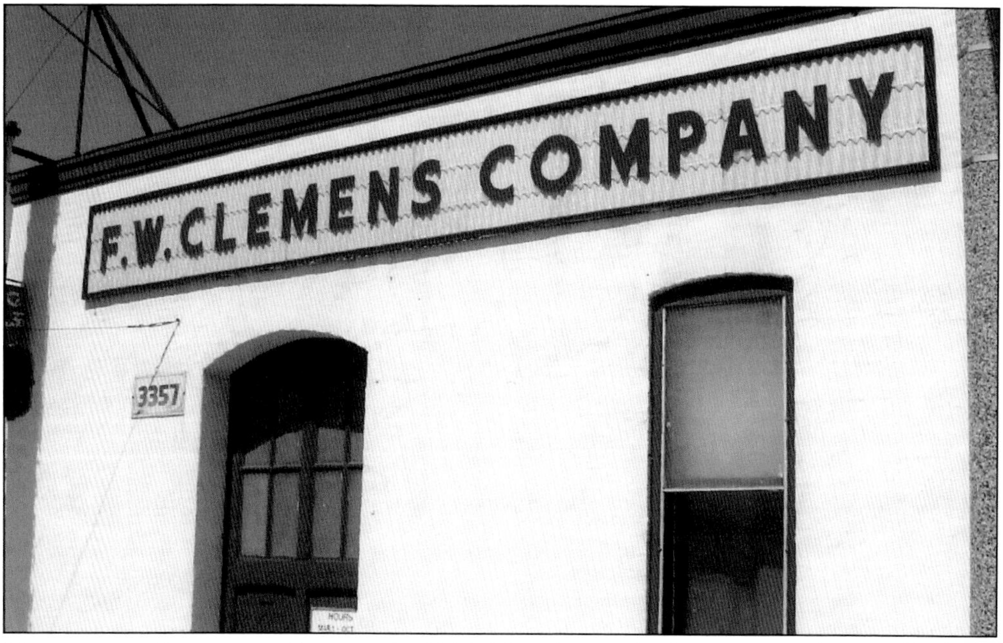

More than a Century of Clemens. In 1884, Mr. Clemens had a one-story frame stable built, and in 1918, he altered a frame warehouse. Mr. Clemens died in 1925 at age 69. He had married Gertrude Sutter in 1878. In 1959, Frank G. Afton was president of Clemens when the business expanded to include a warehouse at 2607 Texas. F. W. Clemens was already dealing with building materials. Hank Caby, current owner, bought the Clemens Company in 1983.

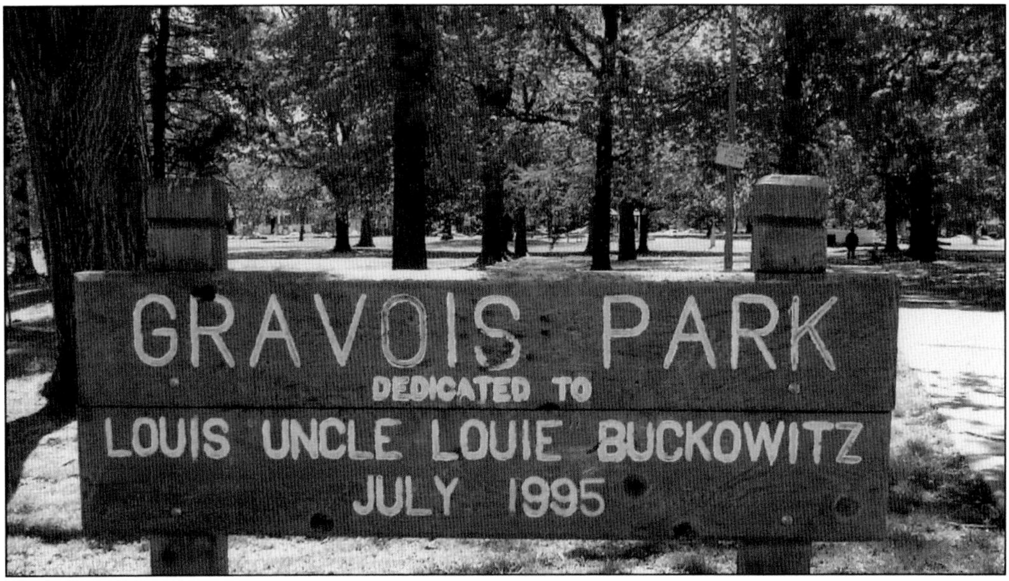

Site D18: Gravois Park from 3300 Cherokee. In the 1910 census, there was an entry for the location of Gravois Park. John A. Johnson and his family were listed as residents at this address. Mr. Johnson came from Sweden in 1893 and was listed as the park keeper. His wife was also Swedish and came to America in 1885. In 1910, they had been married for 11 years and had four children, ages two to nine.

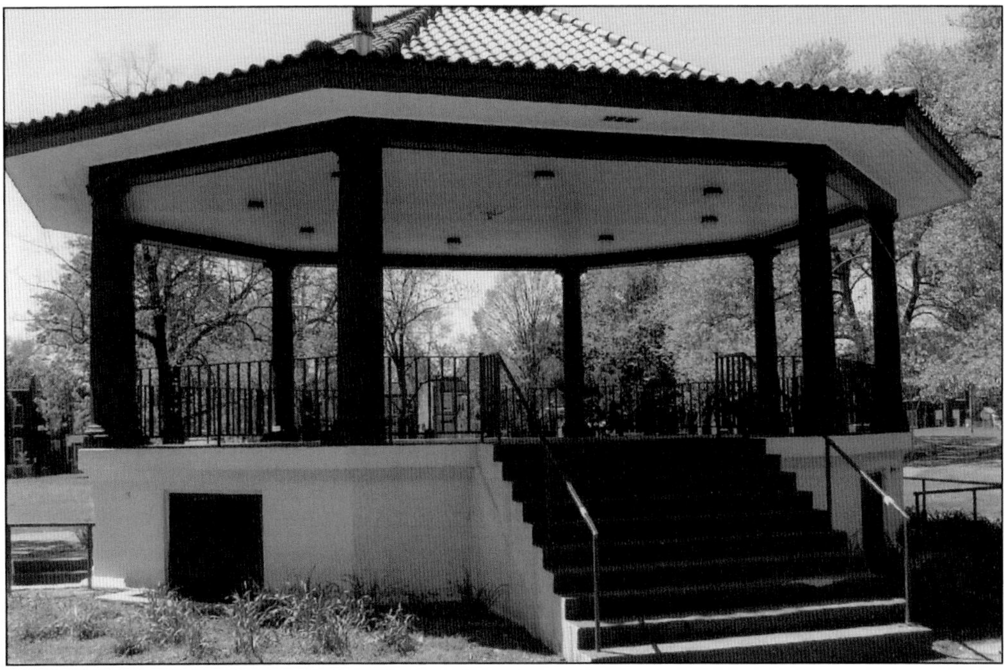

Gravois Park Bandstand. Before the bandstand was built, there was another structure in the park, which shows up on a plate in the *1875 St. Louis Pictorial*. The pictorial states that the park encompassed about eight acres and that improvements were in process with more planned. Gravois Park is in the Gravois Park Neighborhood, which was originally part of the Marquette-Cherokee Neighborhood.

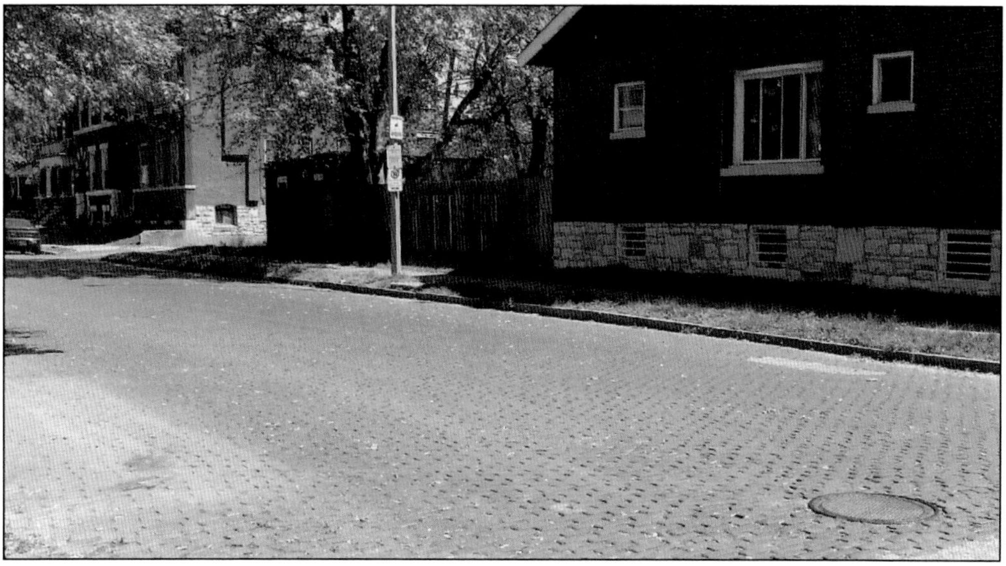

BRICK STREET. According to William Stage in the June 1986 *St. Louis Magazine* "St. Louis ranks with Philadelphia, Boston, and Manhattan as one of the most 'brickified' cities in the country, if not the world." The most common pavers in the city were "Hydraulic" and "Laclede." The treasures on this street are the filler pavers stamped "Albion, Ill." In 1877, bricks were made in this neighborhood at the Gravois Brick Company, located at the southwest corner of Arsenal and South Jefferson.

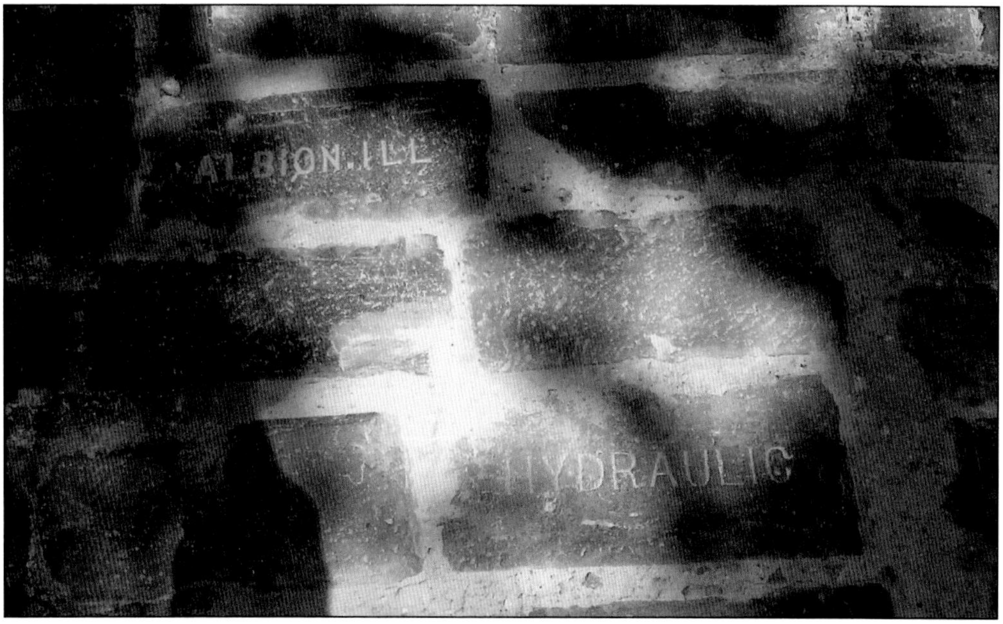

HYDRAULIC PRESS BRICK COMPANY. Near the park, visitors can find brick pavers with the Hydraulic name stamped on them. The company was incorporated in 1868 by E. C. Sterling, who introduced St. Louis to the hydraulic press brick machine. Mr. Sterling's company owned several clay fields in the city and at one time operated 22 brick factories and 13 branches in St. Louis and around the country; 85 agents represented them in the United States and Canada.

Site D19: Storefront by St. Louis Architectural Iron, 3200 Cherokee. The original storefront included 3200 and 3202, built in 1906 for $8,000. The owner was Emil West Blaha, and Theo Welge Jr. was the architect. Mr. and Mrs. Blaha both came to the United States from Bohemia, Emil in 1880 and Pauline in 1885. Mr. Blaha operated his grocery store on this corner. Today the building houses a church thrift store.

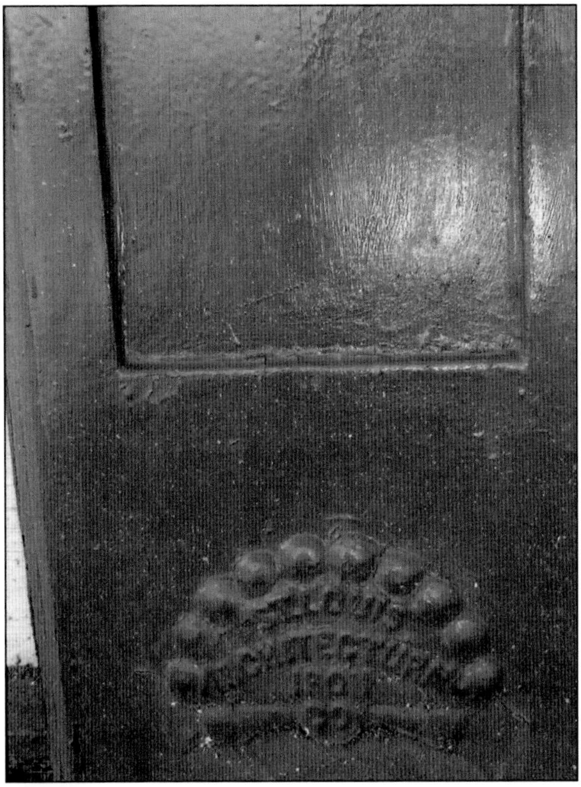

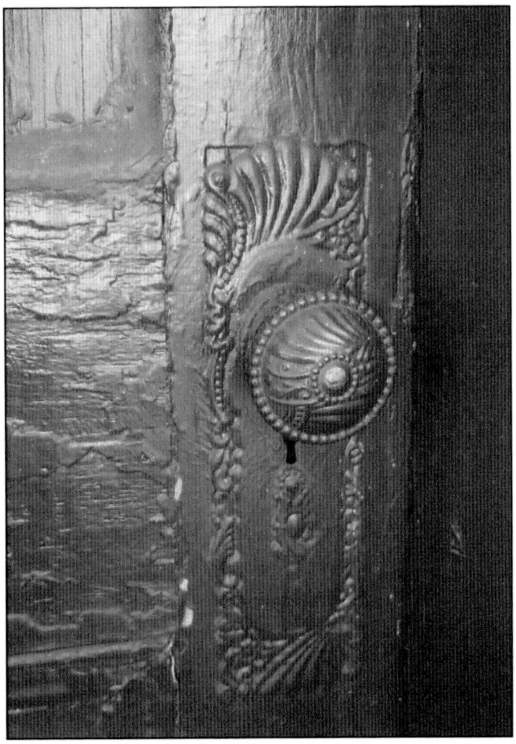

A Century of Business, 3200 and 3202 Cherokee. Imagine how many people this antique door knob has greeted in almost 100 years. This location has housed a grocery, a shoe store, a confectionery, a photograph company, an electrical repair shop, and a radio store. Today one can shop for vintage jewelry and clothing, almost-antique furniture, or matching pieces to mother's old china set.

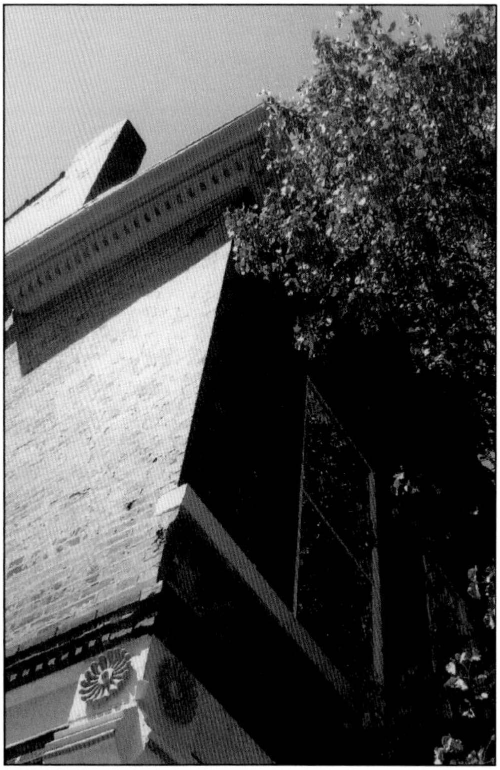

SITE D20: GROCERY STOREFRONT, 2900 CHEROKEE. There was a grocery store here for many years before Charles Hager opened up a restaurant on this corner in 1935. By 1946, Edward Ettling had his bicycle repair shop here, and in 1955, ABC Radio and Electric Company was the new occupant. This storefront with unique architectural details is in desperate need of a total renovation.

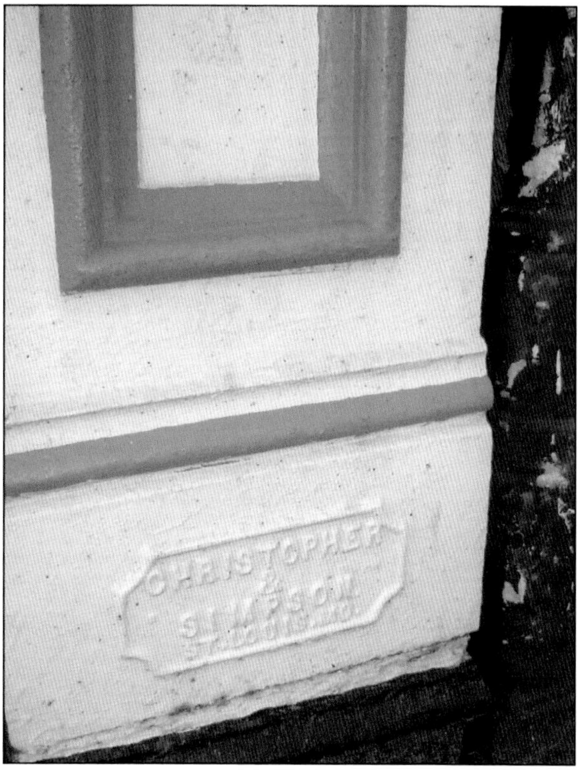

CHRISTOPHER & SIMPSON ARCHITECTURAL IRON AND FOUNDRY COMPANY. The company was founded in 1873 and incorporated in 1882. In 1891, Jacob Christopher was president, vice-president was William A. Rutter, and William S. Simpson was secretary/treasurer. Mr. Christopher and Mr. Simpson were brothers-in-law. The company manufactured iron works for many major buildings in St. Louis; one of their projects was Anheuser-Busch's Stock House No. 3. Their offices were on Park Avenue from Eighth to Ninth. The foundry was demolished in 1952.

Select Bibliography

Books

Amsler, Kevin. *Final Resting Place.* Virginia Publishing Company, 1997.

Hannon, Robert E., ed. *St. Louis: Its Neighborhoods & Neighbors, Landmarks and Milestones.* St. Louis Regional Commerce & Growth Associations, 1986.

History of St. Louis Neighborhoods

History of the Archdiocese. Western Watchman Publishing Company, 1924.

Hyde, William and Conrad Halderman, eds. *Hyde & Conard Encyclopedia of the History of St. Louis, Volumes II & III.* Conrad & Company, 1899.

J. M. Elstner & Company. *The Industries of St. Louis,* 1885.

McAlester, Virginia and Lee. *A Field Guide to American Houses.* Alfred A. Knopf, 1984.

Missouri Historical Society. *Where We Live: A Guide to St. Louis Communities.* St. Louis: Missouri Historical Society Press, 1995.

Pen & Sunlight Sketches of St. Louis. Chicago: Phoenix Publishing Company, 1898.

Schild, James J. *House of God.* The Auto Review, 1995.

St. Louis: Queen City of the West. St Louis: The Mercantile Advancement Company, 1898–1899.

Story, C. C., ed. *Men of Affairs in St. Louis.* Press Club of St. Louis, 1915.

Winter, William C. *The Civil War in St. Louis: A Guided Tour.* St. Louis: Missouri Historical Society Press, 1994.

Newspapers

"St. Louis Deaths." *St. Louis Post-Dispatch,* December 6, 1998.

Young, Julie. "Concrete Evidence." *Richmond Time-Dispatch,* March 6, 2004.

Magazines, Journals, Periodicals, and Scrapbooks

The History of South Side Day Nursery. South Side Day Nursery, 2002.

Missouri Historical Society. *Library Biography Scrapbook.*

——, *Mercantile & Manufacturing Scrapbook,* Vol. 2.

Moore, Bob. "Yes Vote by St. Louis School Board Meets a Strong No by Parents and Teachers," *St. Louis Front Page,* July 16, 2003.

Nevin, Lucile, ed. *Dau Family Album,* October 28, 1999.

"Obituaries." *St. Louis Post-Dispatch,* June 30, 1939.

Southwest Saint Louis: Its Mercantile Interests and Prominent Citizens, c. 1910.

St. Louis Genealogical Society Quarterly, Fall 1922.

Miscellaneous Sources

Hinderberger, Major Philip R. USMCR (RET), *The Western Turner Rifle Story*, 2001.
Missouri Historical Society. *Hardcastle Scrapbook.*
Missouri Historical Society. Necrology, Volumes 20, 13
Missouri Historical Society Library. Vertical Files.
St. Louis City Directories, various years.

Websites

www.explorestlouis.com
www.broadleafcigars.com/history.htm
www.asbj.com
www.stlouis.missouri.org
www.beachfront-properties.com
www.wehrenberg.com
www.confessingchurches.homestead
www.thefriars.org
www.stlcin.missouri.org/assessor/
www.riverfronttimes.com/issues
www.radiocherokee.net
www.didyouknow.cd/music/radiohistory.htm
www.stlouiswalkoffame.org/inductees/tenesseewilliams.html
www.catholicforum.com/churches/
www.thecommonspace.org/

Photo and Image Credits

Maps courtesy of the City of St. Louis Planning and Urban Design Agency: 2, 8, 36, 68, 100
Jo Ann Vatcha, Community Development Administration of the City of St. Louis
William R. Bailey, GIS Specialist/Graphic Designer
Tony Meyers, Manager, GIS Mapping Section, Planning and Urban Agency
Ron Untener: 10, 11, 12, 13, 15B, 16, 21A, 24B, 26A, 28B, 29, 30A, 31A, 32A, 39, 41, 44, 45A, 46A, 51B, 52B, 53B, 57B, 59A, 60A, 61, 62, 63A, 64, 69, 70, 71A, 73, 75, 76A, 77B, 78, 82A, 83A, 85B, 87, 88, 90, 92A, 93, 97, 98, 102, 103A, 105, 106, 107, 109, 110, 112, 114, 115, 117A, 118A
Edna Campos Gravenhorst: 14A, 15A, 17, 18A, 20, 21B, 22, 24A, 23, 27, 28A, 31B, 33, 40A, 42A, 43, 50, 51A, 52A, 55, 56A, 60A, 64, 65, 66A, 72, 74, 77A, 79, 84A, 85A, 86, 89B, 92B, 96, 99A, 101, 104, 108B, 111A, 113, 116, 117B, 118B, 119, 120, 121, 122, 123, 124
Nick Ballta: 14B, 25, 26B, 30B, 32B, 45B, 76B, 82B, 83B, 84B, 99B, 103B, 108A, 111B
St. Louis: Missouri Historical Society: 9, 38, 47
Jim Paradoski: 57A, 58, 59B
City Hall: 40B, 46B, 63B
Bill Hart: 37
SSDN: 34, 35
Jan Beekman & Henrietta Kupferer: 80, 81
Penny and Joe Moskus: 94, 95
Alfredo Ciolek and John Hargis: 89A
James West: 49
Five Star Senior Center: 53A
Paul Dau: 91

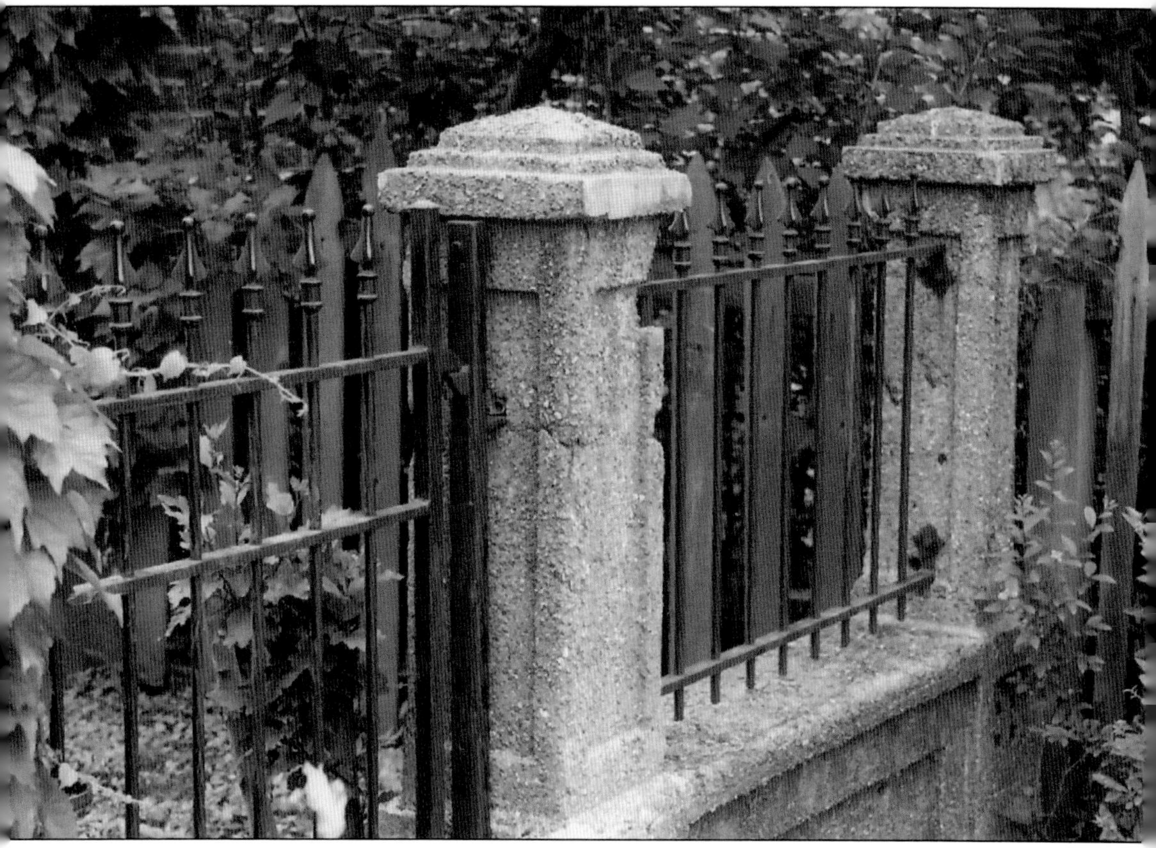

A WORD FROM THE AUTHOR. My great-grandmother gave me an appreciation for history, and after a long life of 103 years, she passed along this wisdom to me: if you don't know your history, then how will you know where you've been? How will you know where you are? How will you know where you are going? And most importantly, how will you know who you are? History gives us a sense of place, and our community gives us a sense of belonging.

Edna Campos Gravenhorst